VIŚVAKARMĀ

Examples of Indian Architecture, Sculpture, Painting, Handicraft

ANANDA K. COOMARASWAMY

One Hundred Examples of Indian Sculpture

MANOHAR
2025

First published 1914

Reprinted, 2025

ISBN 978-93-6080-071-0 (hardbound)

ISBN 978-93-6080-404-6 (ebook)

Published by
Ajay Kumar Jain *for*
Manohar Publishers & Distributors
4753/23 Ansari Road, Daryaganj
New Delhi 110 002

Printed and bound in India

"Viśvakarmā, Lord of the arts, master of a thousand handicrafts, carpenter of the gods and builder of their palaces divine, fashioner of every jewel, first of craftsmen, by whose art men live, and whom, a great and deathless god, they continually worship."

Mahābhārata.

PREFACE.

"Not in bread alone doth man live, but in every word that proceedeth from the mouth of God."

NOW that the admiration of Greek Sculpture of the "classical" period and especially that of Phidias which obsessed the cultured persons of the nineteenth century has somewhat subsided, it is perhaps possible to clear our minds of cant and to ask with some hope of a reasonable answer what Art really is and why so many laborious men have, in the course of the historical period, engaged in it.

For that the art of Phidias and his kind is specious and, for all its dexterity and dignity, inferior to that of its archaic predecessors is a conclusion the truth of which is now demonstrable.

The fact is that owing to misconceptions as to the very nature of art, the world has been led astray by the blatant technical accomplishment of the Periclean age and has been led to suppose that the zenith of any art period has been reached when, as in the time of Phidias, elegance, dignity, a certain æsthetic completeness—in a word material beauty, are the predominant characteristics of the work done.

This is the more easily understood in as much as a commercial age like our own is essentially an irreligious age, and any art which has a prophetic or visionary or mystical basis, as opposed to one having purely sympathetic qualities, is of too discomforting a kind to find acceptance with the modern connoisseurs.

It is true a great quantity of tears has been spilt over the art of Mediæval Europe. But that such tears are largely of the crocodile order is evident from the phenomenon called "The Gothic Revival." Nobody with the least understanding of the nature of Gothic would have supposed it for a moment possible that in the nineteenth century such buildings and such works as the middle ages produced could be done again. At its best the idea was the most absurdly romantic and sentimental.

However—this by the way. The connoisseur is essentially the man seeking beauty for its own sake and, for him, the art of Greece seemed all that could be desired. The idealism which he saw in it sufficed for such spiritual needs as he could lay claim to and the appreciation of art became a veritable snobbery.

Primitive art, on the other hand, relies for its power on none of these things. It is indeed desirable that what is at present called Classic should be called Decadent, and what is now called Primitive should be called Classic. For, if by 'Classical period' we wish to denote the highest or best period, it is obvious that our current nomenclature is all wrong. The zenith of Greek art was reached long before the time of Phidias. By his time men had long since been seduced and deflowered by their own prowess and it was left for the modern world to praise them in their shame.

All primitive art, so called, is a combination of the Real and Realism. I do not think this has been noticed. Such Realism as that which in these days goes by the name is merely the more or less complete imitation of appearances and appearances are, by definition, not realities. No, the nineteenth century 'realist' is no such thing. For the true realism you must go to the works of men who did not merely make copies of what things looked like, but who made images, so far as that was possible, of what things actually were to them. Realism I shall define, then, as the imaging of the essential quality of things.

But behind the 'thing' whose essential quality is to be discovered and proclaimed there are its cause and causes—there are God and Gods. The primitive or archaic arts therefore (I say 'therefore' because it needs a "primitive" type of mind to be unsophisticated enough to imagine God and Gods—to disregard mere beauty) are the works of men seeking the Real and using for the expression of such reality as they can come at—Realism.

The failure of the modern realist to achieve even an illusion of reality is apparent if one should look with untired eyes on such a piece of work as the Strangford Apollo in the British Museum.* Here is indeed no mere imitation of appearances. But realism of the most arresting kind there certainly is. In it is proclaimed with passionate emphasis more of reality than could be shown in innumerable photographs of models—indeed it may be said that in it *all* models are resumed.

Opposed to such things are the arts of later Greece and of Rome, of the European "Renaissance" (though how any one could be born again in a manner more vain-glorious it is difficult to imagine) and of our own time. But the nineteenth century obsession of admiration of decadent Greece now shows, thank God, some signs of deliquescence. The turmoil of Victorian commercialism has been too much to sleep through—discontent is widespread—all values are being revalued and it is coming to be seen that even for persons so learned and cunning as ourselves there are God and Gods—that there can be no lasting satisfaction in the tasting of the sugar and pepper of appearances—that a hard clear vision of what things are is better than an elegant and "gentlemanly" avoidance of the subject.

* The real thing or at least the full-size plaster cast of it must be seen—no photograph can convey its extraordinary vivacity and perfection and significance.

The nineteenth century, for all its boasted hard-headedness, was soft-hearted and loose-thinking. It shirked realities. It counted its coppers and pored over its protoplasmic pedigree, but for that essential quality of things and for the reality behind the universe it cared for the most part little enough.

We have only to consider the works of sculpture which our modern world has produced to see in what a small degree our artists, who are, in spite of themselves, in their works, the material reflection of the heart and mind of their time—how little they have cared either for reality or realism. They neither gave expression to any sense of God or Gods (indeed the modern world is not encumbered with such) nor had they any passionate understanding or appreciation of that quality in the substance of things which moves the desiring hearts of men. The change which is now taking place in the attitude of artists towards their work is some evidence of the truth of these contentions.

The awakening of interest in the work of so-called "archaic" periods—in early Gothic and Byzantine and Chinese sculptures and, particularly, as regards this book, in Hindu and Buddhist art is not merely the result of a fashion for the quaint and barbaric (though, undoubtedly, among collectors, there is a good deal of that sort of stupidity). It is a genuine reaction against the irreligious gentility and banality of modern European art. And among the sculptures of India and Ceylon are to be found perhaps the best examples for us of really great work—the "best" examples as showing more clearly than others the particular qualities of appreciation and understanding which are, as I claim, the only reasonable excuse and motive for the artist's existence—"more clearly" and "for us" because the work of China is too remote and too scarce, the work of "archaic" Greece is too much confused in our minds with that of the Athens of the Parthenon, the work of the early Gothic sculptors is too full of associations and of a certain splendid asceticism foreign to our mood, and also because in India—"a British possession"—our irreligious commercialism and mechanical good-government and the remains of the former religious civilization confront one another so closely that the contrast is, more than elsewhere, conspicuous.

I am not unmindful of the fact that much of their thought and, consequently, much of their work must be for ever alien to us. We cannot wish it otherwise. But to European artists and at this particular time it is more than ever desirable that the particular lessons which these works can teach should be learned.

And this is more particularly so, in that the reaction, like all reactions, may, for lack of sobriety and the fear of God, end in a running amok among aesthetics. The essays in spiritism with which the Post-Impressionist movements have already made us familiar, if catalogued and locked away, make very proper companions for all the essays in representation against which they are the inevitable and too obvious reaction. There are works having no significance but their utility, and there are works having no significance but their form. The former are works of pure craftsmanship—the latter of pure art. But the greater part of work, as the greater part of life lies in a combination of the two extremes, and it should be the business of the artist who is also a craftsman—naturally and properly the fate of most—as it is that of the religious who is not a hermit, to endow utilities with Godliness. Pure art—that is the making of things having in them nothing but "significant form"—is the art of the museum or the mantleshelf just as the unalloyed contemplation of God is the business of the hermit in the desert or of the child at his prayers. In Heaven, we may suppose, it is not so. Heaven might indeed be defined as the achievement of unalloyed contemplation of God in surroundings having no significences but those of form. But "here below" we have a different game to play and it is in such playing that the consideration o fthese Indian sculptures may be of assistance.

First, then, there is in all Indian art a recognition of the fundamental principle that art has not for its raison d'être the satisfaction of man's desire for material beauty in his surroundings. Such satisfaction is but by the way—though attained all the more inevitably in that it was not sought either as a means or as an end. It was, as it must always be, an accident. Beauty, like happiness, is the accompaniment of health and of virtue. In spite of appearances, in spite of the professors of the academies, in spite of the exuberant out-pourings of social-reformers of certain well-known schools, beauty and happiness are actually unattainable if sought directly or even desired. In all Indian art there is a recognition of the fact that art is primarily prophecy—that it is a translation into material form of the inspiration man receives from God.

As there is God, so all work is God's—both His and for Him. The whole business of art is entirely without importance except in so far as it is conceived of and conducted as the material expression of religion. Indian art like that of mediæval Europe or early Greece is essentially a religious art and as such is a true image of Indian civilization just as was the art of thirteenth century England and that of Greece in the sixth century before Christ.

I do not know what Craft organizations existed in Early Greece, but it is beyond question that the Craft Gilds in the Europe of the Middle Ages, as those in India up to quite recent times, were founded in the inspiration of traditional and dogmatic religion and under the direct supervision of religious authority.* The spiritual and emotional consequence of such inspiration and supervision is plain enough in what are called the 'fine' arts. But it is also apparent in the 'crafts'. There is a spirit, a freedom, an innocence and exuberance, a subordination of individual personality and an absence of the display of ambition and of the advertisement of originality which betray very clearly the fact that life in such times and in such places was informed with something very different from the commercial atheism of our England of to-day.

* These Gilds were destroyed in England at the time of the Protestant Reformation and their religious organization was actually made an excuse for their destruction!

And the aesthetic consequence of the prevailing atmosphere of dogmatic religion is no less apparent. Authority is the basis of dogmatic religion as it was that of the mediæval craft organizations and of such organizations elsewhere. And authority likewise is the basis—the visible basis—of the work done under such conditions. There is little or no pandering to the individual fancy whether that of buyer or workman. They spoke as men having authority. They did their work in such and such a way because it was the right way—the prescribed way and they gave to it a sublimity, a monumental calm in which eternity itself is echoed.

How then was there room for that freedom—that innocence and exuberance? There was all the more room. It is not merely that you may get tired of "too much liberty," but also that too much liberty is a weight, a positive hindrance. Do we not often say that so-and-so has got "off the rails"? Do we not thereby imply our instinctive recognition of the fact that there must be rails on which to run? Truly Freedom is only found within bounds and Rule is the removal of fetters.

It is not appropriate that artists should be, as they often are at this present time, too conscious of the theoretical bases of their work. Such bases as we can divine must be very largely of our own invention or discovery and must be more or less obscured and besmirched by our own idiosyncrasies. But it is possible, I think, in the light of such works as this book illustrates and as discovered in them, to ennumerate some elementary technical and spiritual rules of life and work.

They believed in God and devoted all their work to Him. They did not carve, paint or draw anything of which they could not imagine the significance or give it such. They avoided the model but carved that which they loved and as they loved it. They were clear, clean and hard about everything from the beginning to the end.

The making of mere representations of what was before them—mere records of things seen or remembered was not their business. They were artists and an artist's business is not copying. For there is no real reason why artists, as artists, should make anything *like* anything. In a work of art representation is accidental. The substance of a work of art is its spiritual quality. An artist is a herald and all good art is heraldic. An artist is a maker of *things* and not of pictures of things.

And when we see them it is not for beauty that we should desire them. Surely they have borne our griefs.

E.G.

LIST OF PLATES.

BUDDHAS AND BODHISATTVAS.

I. BUDDHA: seated in *dhyāna mudrā*.

Crystalline limestone; colossal: about the fourth century A.D., near Jetavanārāma Dāgaba, Anurādhapura, Ceylon.
(Coomaraswamy, 'Arts and Crafts of India and Ceylon,' fig. 2).

II. BUDDHA: standing, with glory.

Clad in a *saṅghāṭi* which covers both shoulders. A girdle is indicated round the waist, supporting the under-garment seen at the ankles. The left hand holds the hem of the upper garment; the missing right hand was formerly raised in *abhaya mudrā*. The *ushṇīsha* protuberance of the skull is clearly indicated: the hair is designed in little curls, turned to the right. Remains of kneeling figures are at the base of the statue probably represent the donors. The inscription of two lines in Gupta character of the fifth century reads, translated:
"This is the pious gift of the Buddhist monk Yaśadinna. Whatsoever merit in this gift, let it be for the attainment of supreme knowledge by his parents, teachers and preceptors, and all sentient beings."
Sandstone; height 7ft. 2½in.; fifth century A.D. (Gupta).
From the Jamālpur Mound, Mathurā; now in the Museum at Mathurā.
('Catalogue of the Archæological Museum at Mathurā,' 1910, pp. 49, 50 and Pl. IX).

III. BUDDHA: seated, with glory and two flying siddhas.

Clothing as in Plate II. The hands are in *dharmacakra mudrā*.

Below the throne, a number of persons are reverencing the Wheel of the Law. Fifth century (Gupta).
White sandstone; height 5¼ feet.
Excavated at Sārnāth; now in the Museum at Sārnāth.
(Vincent Smith, 'History of Fine Art in India and Ceylon,' Plate XXXVIII: Coomaraswamy, 'Selected Examples of Indian Art,' Pl. XXII and p. 13).

IV. PRAJNĀPĀRAMITĀ: seated on a lotus throne.

The hands in *dharma-cakra mudrā*. Over the left arm rises a lotus blossom supporting a book, the 'Transcendent Wisdom' of which she is the personification. Elaborate dress and jewellery. The *ūrṇā* distinctly indicated on the forehead.
Trachyte; middle of the fourteenth century A.D.
From Malang in Java; now in the Ethnographische Reichs museum, Leiden.
(Coomaraswamy, 'Selected Examples of Indian Art,' Pl. XVI, and p. 10; Juynboll, 'Kat. des Ethn Reichsmuseums,' 1909, p. 33—Cat. No. 1587.)

V. PRAJNĀPĀRAMITĀ:

The same figure in front view.

VI. USHṆĪSHA-VIJAYA (Tārā): head and upper part of torso.

Eight-armed and four-faced.
Shale; height of the fragment, 19in.; Twelfth century A.D. (Pālā).
Sārnāth; now in the museum at Sārnāth.
(Coomaraswamy, 'Selected Examples of Indian Art,' Pl. XVIII and p. 11.)

VII. BUDDHA: head and torso.

Smiling, with half-closed eyes. *Ushṇīsha* clearly shown. Remains of glory broken away.

Sandstone; height 22in.; thirteenth to fourteenth century A.D. (Khmer).
Cambodia; now in the collection of M. Victor Goloubew.
('Eleven Plates,' Pls. IX, X; 'Collection Victor Goloubew,' Musée Cernuschi, Pl. IV).

VIII. BUDDHA: head.

Smiling, with half-closed eyes. *Ushṇīsha* strongly developed, and the figure of a Dhyāni Buddha in front of it.
Sandstone; thirteenth to fourteenth century A.D. (Khmer).
Cambodia; in the Trocadero, Paris.

IX. BUDDHA: standing.

The outer robe (*saṅghāṭi*) covering the left shoulder, and supported by the left hand; the under robe seen at the ankles. Indication of the girdle below the upper robe. The *ushṇīsha* clearly developed, the hair in curls. The eye-sockets excavated for insertion of separate eyes of some precious material, now missing. The right arm is also lost.
Crystalline limestone: above life size; third to fourth century A.D. ('Gupta').
At the Ruanveli Dāgaba, Anurādhapura, Ceylon.

X. BODHISATTVA, perhaps MAITREYA: standing figure in royal costume.

The two arms broken away.
Crystalline limestone: above life size; third to fourth century A.D. ('Gupta').
At the Ruanvẹli Dāgaba, Anurādhapura, Ceylon.

XI. AVALOKITEŚVARA: standing figure, in royal costume.

Right hand in *varā mudrā*; left hand originally holding the stem of a rose lotus, of which the flower and leaf touch the left shoulder; *trivaṅka* stance.

Copper gilt, jewelled; height 12⅛in.; about tenth century A.D.
Nepal; collection of Dr. A. K. Coomaraswamy.
('Eleven Plates,' Pl. XI.)

XII. AVALOKITEŚVARA: back view of No. XI.

XIII. AVALOKITEŚVARA: seated figure.

The right hand in *vitarka mudrā;* a Dhyāni Buddha in the head dress.
Bronze; height 3⅝in.; eighth century A.D.
Ceylon; collection of Dr. A. K. Coomaraswamy.
(Coomaraswamy, J.R.A.S., 1909, p. 288, 'Mahāyāna Buddhist Images from Ceylon and Java').

XIV. AVALOKITEŚVARA: back view of No. XIII.

XV. BUDDHA: standing figure.

The *ushṇīsha* surmounted by a flame, in the late Sinhalese style.
The figure otherwise resembles No. IX in type, but is less felt.
Gneiss; colossal; perhaps thirteenth century A.D.
Awkana, Ceylon.
(Vincent Smith, 'A History of Fine Art in India and Ceylon,' fig. 180; Bell, 'Ann. Rep. Arch. Sur. Ceylon,' 1895, pp. 6, 12).

XVI. MANJUŚRĪ: seated figure.

The right hand holds aloft the sword of wisdom, the left holds a book. Above, four smaller replicas (modes) of the same Bodhisattva. The eyes half closed. An inscription at the back states that the figure was made for the Aryan king Ādityavarma in the year 1343 A.D.
Trap rock; height 42in.; fourteenth century A.D.
Java: now in the Kgl. Museum fur Volkerkunde, Berlin.
(Friederich, Zeit. d. Deutsch. Morgenl. Ges., Bd.

XVIII, 1864, pp. 494-505; Grünwedel, 'Buddhist Art in India,' p. 199).

XVII. BODHISATTVA: torso, in royal costume.

Red sandstone; height 34¾in.; fourth to fifth century A.D. (Gupta).
From Sānchī; now in the Indian section, Victoria and Albert Museum, London.
('Eleven Plates,' Pls. I and II).

XVIII. BUDDHA: seated figure, with undecorated glory.

The hands in *dharma-cakra mudrā*. The robe covering both shoulders. The *ushṇīsha* and *ūrṇā* clearly developed; the hair waved. Below the seat, a small Buddha figure with four worshippers.
Slate; height 36in.; about second century A.D.
From Gandhāra; now in the British Museum.
(Burgess, Journal of Indian Art, vol. VIII, pl. 9 and p. 33).

XIX. TĀRĀ: seated figure, on *padmāsana*.

Eight armed, with various attributes, including the rose lotus and the *vajra*.
Brass gilt and jewelled; about fifteenth century A.D.
Nepal; Calcutta School of Art.
Collection of Dr. A. K. Coomaraswamy.
(Now first published).

XX. BUDDHA: seated figure.

The robe without folds, covering both shoulders. The hands in *vitarka mukrā*. The *ushṇīsha* prominent, the hair in curls.
Copper gilt; height 3½in.; probably ninth century A.D.
Nepal; collection of Dr. A. K. Coomaraswamy
(Now first published).

XXI. BUDDHA: seated figure, wearing a *dhotī*, on *siṅhāsana*.

The hands webbed, in accordance with one of the traditions of the Buddha's physical peculiarities. The right hand raised in *abhaya mudrā*. The *ushṇīsha* inconspicuous, the hair quite smooth. Below, two seated figures, and the Wheel of the Law. Dedicatory inscription of 448-9 A.D.
Sandstone; fifth century A.D. (Gupta).
From Mānkuwār, near Allahābād.
(Bloch, J.A.S.B., vol. lxvi, pt. i, p. 283; Vincent Smith, 'History of Fine Art in India and Ceylon,' fig. 120).

XXII. BUDDHA: seated figure, on *siṅhāsana*.

The robe covering left shoulder only. The hands in *vitarka mudrā*. Details of eyes, *ūrṇā*, and ornament are inlaid with silver and copper. The *ushṇīsha* prominent, the hair curly. Dedicatory inscription in script of the sixth century.
Brass, with inlays of silver and copper; height 11¾in.; sixth century A.D. (late Gupta).
From Fathpur, district Kāngrā: now in the Lahore Museum.
(Vogel, 'Ann. Rep. Arch. Surv. India', 1904-5, pp. 107-9).

XXIII. ŚRĪPADA (feet of Buddha): with worshipping figures.

Limestone; second century A.D.
Amarāvatī.
(Burgess, 'Buddhist Stupas of Amarāvatī and Jaggayyapeta,' Pl. XLIX fig. 3).

XXIV. BUDDHA: two standing figures.

Marble; height 6ft. 4in.; third to fourth century A.D.
Amarāvatī.
(Vincent Smith, 'History of Fine Art in India and Ceylon,' fig. 108).

XXV. ELEVATION OF THE BOWL RELIC.

The translation of Buddha's *pātra* or begging-bowl

to the Tusita heavens, by the Devas, who occupy the lower two-thirds of the composition, and apsarasas who occupy the remainder.
Marble; second to third century A.D.
Amarāvatī; now in the British Museum.
(Burgess, 'Buddhist Stūpas of Amarāvatī and Jaggayyapeta,' Pl. XVII, fig. 1, and p. 45).

BRĀHMANICAL DIVINITIES

XXVI. YAKSHA, perhaps KUVERA: standing figure.

Clad in a *dhotī*, with girdles and jewellery.
The fragmentary inscription in Maurya Brāhmī indicates that the image was "made by Bhadpugarin . . . Gomitaka, the pupil of Kunika."
Sandstone; height 8ft. 8in.; second century B.C.
Parkham, 14 miles south of Mathurā; now in the Mathurā Museum.
(Vogel, 'Catalogue of the Archæological Museum at Mathurā,' p. 83 and Pl. XII).

XXVII. Left, ŚIVA (BHAIRAVA).

Four-armed, with necklace of skulls and skull in head-dress. The door-jamb of a ruined temple.
Śirpur, C.P. Eighth to ninth century A.D.
(Arch. Sur. Western India, Progress Rep. for year ending 30th June, 1904).

Right, SŪRYA (?)

Detached sculpture, temple of Rāma.
Śirpur, C.P. Eighth to ninth century A.D.
(Arch. Sur. Western India, Progress Rep. for year ending 30th June, 1904).

XXVIII. ŚIVA (GAṄGĀDHARA); standing figure, four-armed.

Deer and axe symbols missing from two upper hands. Cobras and skull (?) in headdress. No earring on proper right, a woman's earring on the proper left. A half-dancing pose.
Copper; about twelfth century.
In a Śaiva temple in Tanjore.
(Coomaraswamy, 'Selected Examples of Indian Art,' P . XXVII).

XXIX. ŚIVA; standing figure, four-armed.

The feet crossed in half dance. Hands with symbols, axe and deer. Headdress with skull, and earrings different on the two sides, the proper right a man's, the proper left a woman's. As in XXVIII, the arms dichotomise at the elbow.
Copper; height 26⅝in.; tenth to thirteenth century A.D.
Polonnāruva, Ceylon; now in the Colombo Museum.
(Coomaraswamy, 'Bronzes from Ceylon, chiefly in the Colombo Museum,' 1914, Pl.V, 8; Bell, 'Arch. Sur. Ceylon Ann. Rep.' 1908 (1913), Pl. XIX).

XXX. ŚIVA (NAṬARĀJA): dancing figure, four-armed.

The encircling *tiruvāsi* is broken away. Skull, moon, cobras and *Cassia* leaves in the headdress, no earring on proper right, a woman's earring on the left; upper right hand with drum *(ḍamaruka* or *uḍukkai)*, upper left with flame. Right foot trampling a dwarf, the left raised in the *nadānta* dance.
Copper; height about 4ft; twelfth to sixteenth century.
In the Madras Museum. (Frequently published: for the significance, see *Siddhānta Dīpika*, vol. XIII. pp. 1-13).

XXXI. ŚIVA: the same as XXX, in back view.

XXXII. ŚIVA (VIRATEŚVARA) : dancing figure, eight-armed.

Amongst the symbols held are the *triśūla*, skull-cup, and axe.
The figure is framed by the skin of an elephant, the right foot resting on the separated head ; the left foot raised. The head dress with a skull (*kapāla*).
The whole forms part of a monolithic column, carved below with dwarfs, and above in the usual late Dravidian style.
Granulite ; about seventeenth century (Dravidian).
Śaiva temple at Perūr, S. India.

XXXIII. ŚIVA (BHAIRAVA) : dancing figure, eight-armed.

Amongst the symbols held there are recognisable on the proper right, the drum (*ḍamaruka* or *uḍukkai*) and mace or axe. The upper left hand is raised to support the sky. On the proper left, Pārvatī with a child ; on the proper right, three musicians with flute and drums, and between these and the figure of Śiva, partly hidden by the right leg, a semi-skeleton figure of Kālī.
Trap-rock ; eighth century A.D.
Elūrā.
(Havell, 'Ideals of Indian Art,' Pl. XXIX).

XXXIV. GANESHA : seated figure, four-armed.

The upper proper right hand with rosary; the trunk taking food from a cup held in the lower left hand.
Volcanic rock ; about thirteenth century A.D.
In Java.
(Havell, 'Ideals of Indian Art,' Pl. X).

XXXV. GANESHA : seated figure, four-armed.

Upper hands with axe and rosary ; a cup in each of the lower hands ; skull seat and skulls in head-dress, etc. (as the son of Bhairava).

Volcanic rock; height 4ft. 9¾in.; fourteenth century A.D.
Ruins of Singasari, Java; now in the Ethnographische Reichsmuseum, Leiden.
(Juynboll, 'Katalog des Ethn. Reichsmuseums,' 1909, p. 25; Cat. No. 1681).

XXXVI. DEVĪ (DURGĀ-MAHISHAMARDINĪ:— slaying the demon, eight-armed.

The demon has emerged from the bull-form in the shape of a dwarf, whom Durgā is about to slay.
Volcanic rock; height 5ft. 5½in.; fourteenth century A.D.
(Juynboll, 'Katalog des Ethn. Reichsmuseums,' Leiden, 1909, p. 15; Cat. No. 1622).

XXXVII. DEVĪ (DURGĀ-MAHISHAMARDINĪ):— As XXXVI.

Bronze; height 6⅛in.; ninth to tenth century A.D.
(Juynboll, loc. cit. p. 70; Cat. No. 1875).

XXXIX. DEVĪ (PIḌĀRĪ); seated figure, in sub-active pose, four-armed.

Upper hands with axe and deer, the attributes of Śiva. Earrings diverse, a man's on proper right and woman's on left. Right hand raised in *abhaya mudrā*.
Copper; Twelfth to sixteenth century (Dravidian), now in the Madras Museum.

XL. TRIMŪRTI: rock-cut mask of Brahmā, Vishṇu, Śiva.

Trap-rock; colossal; eighth century A.D.
Elephanta.

XLI. Mask of VISHṆU: detail from XL.

XLII. BRAHMA: four-headed figure.

Elephanta. Eighth to ninth century A.D.
(Now first published).

XLIII. NARASIṂHA: Man-lion avatār of Vishṇu, destroying Hiranyakashipu.

Trap-rock; colossal; eighth century A.D.
Elūrā.
(Coomaraswamy, 'Selected Examples of Indian Art,' Pl. XXXVI.)

XLIV. AYIYANĀR: seated figure in sub-active pose.

Moon and cobra in headdress (as son of Śiva): elephant-goad in right hand.
Copper; sixteenth to eighteenth century.
Musée Cernuschi, Paris.
(For Ayiyanār, see Parker, 'Ancient Ceylon', p. 148, etc.).

XLV. DEVĪ (DURGĀ): at war with the Asuras, rock-cut.

Granulite; colossal; eighth century A.D. (Pallava).
Māmallapuram.

XLVI. TRIMŪRTI: seated figure.

Copper gilt; about fourteenth or fifteenth century A.D.
Nepal; now in the Calcutta School of Art collection.
(Havell, 'Indian Sculpture and Painting,' Pl. XIX)

XLVII. Jaina Tīrthaṅkara, perhaps PARŚVANĀTHA: standing nude figure.

Black stone; about fifteenth century A.D.
Indian Museum, London.

XLVIII. PATTINĪ : standing figure.

Wearing a *dhotī* and high headdress. Right hand in *vara*, left in *vitarka mudrā*.
Pale bronze; height 4ft. 9½in.; perhaps seventh century A.D.
Ceylon, between Trincomalee and Batticaloa. Now in the British Museum.
(Coomaraswamy, 'Selected Examples of Indian Art,' Pl. XXXIII. For the cult of Pattinī, see also Parker, 'Ancient Ceylon,' p. 631, etc.).

XLIX. BĀLA-KRISHṆA : dancing figure.

Copper; about the sixteenth century A.D. (Dravidian).
Collection of M. Victor Goloubew.

L. ŚIVA; standing figure, four-armed.

Bronze; height 2ft. 10⅝in.; about the twelfth century A.D. (Khmer).
Cambodia. Now in a private collection in Paris.

MEN, WOMEN AND NĀGAS

LI. A SAGE: standing rock-cut figure.

With matted locks, bearded; wearing a *dhotī*; reading a palm-leaf book. Possibly representing Mānikka Vāçagar (4th century), less probably (but in accordance with tradition) Parākrama Bāhu the Great (12th century).
Granulite; colossal; perhaps, ninth or tenth century A.D.
Polonnāruva, Ceylon.
(Coomaraswamy, 'Selected Examples of Indian Art,' Pl XXXII).

LII. KAPILA : rock-cut seated figure.

Seated in '*mahārājā-līlā āsana.*' Behind the figure, on the proper right, the head of a horse.
Granulite; over life size; eighth century.
Isurumuniya, Anurādhapura, Ceylon.
(Coomaraswamy, 'Selected Examples of Indian Art,' Pl. XXVI).

LIII. TORSO and base of seated figure.

Sandstone; eleventh to twelfth century A.D. (Pāla).
Sārnāth; now in the Calcutta Museum.

LIV. TORSO and base of seated figure.

Sandstone; eleventh to twelfth century A.D. (Pāla).
Sārnāth; now in the Calcutta Museum.

LV. A WOMAN.

Sandstone; thirteenth century.
Bhuvaneśvara; Collection of Mr. Ponten-Möller, Calcutta.

LVI. A WOMAN.

Sandstone; thirteenth century.
In situ on the Sun temple, Konārak.

LVIII. DEVADĀSĪ with *vīnā.*

Granulite (monolithic column); seventeenth century A.D. (Dravidian).
Great Temple at Madurā.

LIX. KRISHṆARĀYA and two queens.

Brass figures, with inscription.
The date of Krishṇarāya of Vijayanagar is 1510-1529 A.D.; the figures are clearly contemporary.
Śrī Nivāsa Perumal temple, Tirumalai, Tirupati, N. Arcot.
(Vincent Smith, 'History of Fine Art in India and Ceylon,' Pl. XLVIII).

LX. LOVE SCENE.

Stone relief in Gupta style built into wall at Isurumuniya Vihāra, Anurādhapura.
Fifth to sixth century A.D.
(Coomaraswamy, 'Arts and Crafts of India and Ceylon,' fig. 26).

LXI. ARJUNA as hermit.

The central figure of the composition known as 'Arjuna's Penance,' of which further details are given in Pls. LXIV, and LXXXII to LXXXVII.
Mamallapuram.
Seventh to eight century A.D. (Pallava).
(Havell, 'Ideals of Indian Art,' Pls. XVIII, XIX and XX, and pp. 147-151).

LXII. MĀNIKKA VĀÇAGAR.

Śaiva saint and psalmist. Standing figure, reading from a palm-leaf MS.
Copper; height 21⅜in.; tenth to thirteenth century A.D.
Polonnāruva, Ceylon; now in the Colombo Museum.
(Coomaraswamy, 'Bronzes from Ceylon, chiefly in the Colombo Museum,' 1914, Pl. IX, figure 19).

LXIII. SUNDARA MŪRTI SVĀMI.

Śaiva saint and psalmist. Youthful figure in rapture.
Copper; height 25in.; tenth to thirteenth century A.D.
Polonnāruva, Ceylon; now in the Colombo Museum.
(Coomaraswamy, 'Bronzes from Ceylon, chiefly in the Colombo Museum,' 1914, Pl. VIII, figs. 15 and 16: and 'Selected Examples of Indian Art,' Pl. XXXI and p. 15).

LXIV. FIGURE OF A WOMAN.

Possibly the Earth Goddess, or a Yakshī.
In the style of the Bharhut reliefs. Cf. also Pl. XXVI.
Sandstone; height 6ft. 7in.; third century B.C. (Mauryan).
Besnagar, Bhopal: now in the Indian Museum, Calcutta.
(Vincent Smith, 'History of Fine Art in India and Ceylon, Pl. XIV).

LXV. Rock-cut Column and Capital.

From rock-cut Vaishnava temple.
Sixth century (Late Gupta).
Bādāmī, Bijāpur district.
(*Indian Antiquary*, VI, pp. 354-66; Vincent Smith, 'History of Fine Art in India and Ceylon,' Pl. XLII).

LXVI. FLYING FIGURES.

Carved slabs outside 'Durgā' (Vaishnava) temple, Aihole, Bijāpur district.
(Arch. Sur. Western India, I. Pl. 54).

LXVII. YAKSHĪ (tree-devī or dryad).

Sandstone; second century B.C.
From *toraṇa*, Sānchī.
(Havell, 'Indian Sculpture and Painting,' Pl. XXX: Foucher, 'La Porte Orientale du Stūpa de Sānchi,' Paris, 1910).

LXVIII. APSARAS: dancing figure.

From interior doorway of Kunwar Maṭh temple, Khajurāho.
About twelfth century A.D.
(Griffin, 'Famous Monuments,' Pl. 61).

LXIX. Dancing ṚISHI.

Wood ; South India ; seventeenth to eighteenth century A.D.
Collector of M. Victor Goloubew.
(Now first published).

LXX. Four Architectural Figures.

Mediæval.
Bhojpur, Bhopal.
(Now first published.).

LXXI. NĀGA king, with PATTINĪ.

Wood ; possibly eleventh century A.D.
Nikavẹva, Ceylon.
(Parker, 'Ancient Ceylon,' p. 631 and fig. 272).

LXXII. NĀGA and NĀGINĪ ; seated figures.

Trap rock ; fifth to sixth century (Gupta).
(Havell, 'Ideals of Indian Art,' Pl. XXIV).

LXXIII. NĀGINĪ.

Detail from the Mukteśvara temple at Bhuvaneśvara ; tenth to twelfth century A.D.
(Now first published).

LXXIV. NĀGINĪ, and another NĀGA and NĀGINĪ.

Granulite ; eighth century.
Arjuna's Penance, Māmallapuram (see No. LXI).

LXXV. NĀGA, Dvārapāla (door-guardian).

Granulite ; sixth to eighth century A.D.
Anurādhapura, Ceylon.

For LXXI A, LXXII A, LXXIII A, see end of list.

ANIMALS, INCLUDING ANIMAL AVATĀRS

LXXVI. A LED HORSE.

Sandstone; colossal; thirteenth century A.D.
War horse, led by a warrior, and trampling an *asura*. Konārak.
(Havell, 'Indian Sculpture and Painting,' Pl. XLIII).

LXXVII. ELEPHANT.

Lifting an *asura*.
Sandstone; colossal; thirteenth century A.D.
Konārak.

LXXVIII. HEAD OF A HORSE.

Sandstone; thirteenth century A.D.
Konārak.

LXXIX. GRYPHON.

Trampling and goring *asuras*.
Sandstone; thirteenth century A.D.
Konārak.

LXXX. AŚOKAN capital.

Four lions; below elephant, bull and horse.
Polished sandstone; third century B.C. (Mauryan).
Sārnāth.
(Vincent Smith, 'The Edicts of Asoka,' Oxford, 1909, frontispiece).

LXXXI. AŚOKAN capital.

Four lions; below, affronted chimeras.
Polished sandstone; height of lion and pedestal about 4ft. 6in.; third century B.C. (Mauryan).
Sānchī.
(Maisey, 'Sānchī and its Remains,' Pl. XIX).

LXXXII. DEER.

LXXXIII. MONKEYS.

LXXXIV. MONKEY.

LXXXV. CAT AND MICE.

LXXXVI. ELEPHANT.

LXXXVII. ELEPHANTS.

Nos. LXXXII-LXXXVII from Māmallapuram; eighth century. (See No. LXI).

LXXXVIII. Above, BULL.

Śiva's Bull Nandi.
Copper; height 16½in.; tenth to thirteenth century A.D.
Polonnāruva, Ceylon. Now in the Colombo Museum.
('Bronzes, chiefly in the Colombo Museum,' Pl. XXII, 109 and p. 16).

LXXXIX. DEER and HORSE.

Brass castings (toys); about $\frac{4}{5}$ original size; seventeenth to nineteenth century A.D.
Rājputāna.
Collection of Dr. Coomaraswamy.

XC. Above, 'MOONSTONE' (a monastery doorstep.)

Carved in low relief, as an expanded lotus (half) with three bands of ornament beyond the petals, viz., a row of *hamsas*, a band of *liya vela* floral pattern, a procession of elephants, horses, lions and bulls, and a narrow fringe of *liya pata*.
Granulite; about the sixth century A.D.
In situ at Anurādhapura, Ceylon.

Below, MAN with Bull and Winged Chimera.

Fragment of marble frieze; second century A.D.
Amarāvatī.

XCI. HORSE and ELEPHANT.

Details of Plate LXXX.

XCII. HORSE: rearing above a *yāli.*

Wood; seventeenth century A.D.
Collection of M. Victor Goloubew.

XCIII. VARĀHA.

The Boar avatār of Vishṇu, raising the Earth, (holding to the tush) above the Primal waters; Mediæval.
Sagar, Eran.

XCIV. SARASVATĪ (?), with Peacock; fragment.

Sandstone; second to third century A.D. (Kushaṇa)
Mathurā; in the Museum.

XCV. NAGA.

Coiled, with seven heads; the guardian of a dāgaba.
Granulite; about second century A.D.
(Vincent Smith, 'History of Fine Art in India and Ceylon,' Pl. XX B).

XCVI. Capital.

Mediæval; in the Fort at Gwalior.

XCVII. LION, with seated archer.

Granulite; above life-size; about eighth century.
Māmallapuram, near the shore temple.

XCVIII. ELEPHANT.

Granulite, rock-cut; life-size; perhaps eighth century A.D.

Kaṭupilana, N.C.P., Ceylon.
(Vincent Smith, 'Journal of Indian Art,' Vol. XVI, p. 29 and Pl. 6B).

XIC. VARĀHA.

The Boar-Avatār of Vishṇu, raising the Earth from the primal waters; Śesha-nāga beneath his feet.
Sandstone; colossal; fourth to fifth century A.D. (Gupta).
Udayagiri, Bhopal.
('Archæological Survey of India Report,' Vol. X, p. 48 and Pl. XVIII.)

C. HANUMAN; standing figure, on pedestal.

A representation of the Himālayan mountain formerly rested on the hands.
Copper; height 21in.; perhaps tenth to thirteenth century A.D.
Ceylon; in the Indian Museum, London, formerly in the collection of William Morris.
('Eleven Plates,' Pl. VII).

SUPPLEMENT.

LXXI A. Two Figures of Women.

Sandstone; about 18in.; about second century A.D. (Kushaṇa).
Mathurā; in the Museum.

LXXII A. Vaishṇava GURU and disciples.

Black slate; thirteenth century A.D.
Konārak; Indian Museum, London.
('Eleven Plates,' Pl. III).

LXXIII A. Figure of ĀNANDA, disciple of Buddha.

With crossed arms.
Granulite; colossal; mediæval.
Polonnāruva, Ceylon.
(Vincent Smith, 'Journal of Indian Art,' Vol. XVI, p. 26 and Pl. I A).

EDITORIAL NOTE.

The List of Plates above printed aims to be no more than a list. While no endeavour has been made to give exhaustive references, those mentioned may be of use to students in search of further information. In any case, those who require a history of Indian Sculpture, will find the material elsewhere. The present series is mainly intended for those who are interested as artists in Indian art. The illustrations have in no case been selected solely for archæological interest. The series cannot claim to be exhaustive, but it may well be claimed that it includes at least a considerable proportion of the most important sculptures known or likely to be recovered in the future.

Grateful acknowledgments are made to the following for the use of photographs: The India Office (Under Secretary of State for India), Nos. 16, 23, 25, 32, 33, 38, 43, 45, 57, 58, 64, 65, 66, 68, 70 (lower), 72, 80, 81, 90, 96; M. Victor Goloubew, 7, 30, 31, 40, 41, 49, 69, 82, 83, 84, 85, 86, 87, 92; The Archæological Survey of India (Mr. J. H. Marshall, C.I.E.), Nos. 22, 24, 27, 42, 59, 91, 93; The Director, Colombo Museum No. 91; The Director, Victoria and Albert Museum, Nos. 17, 72A; M. le Comte Gouy d'Arsy, No. 50; Prof. Von le Coq, No. 16; Mr. S. Hadaway, No. 39; Mr. E. B. Havell, Nos. 8, 19, 34, 46; Dr. H. H. Juynboll, Nos. 5, 35, 36, 37; Mr. H. Parker, No. 71; Messrs. Skeen & Co., Colombo, Nos. 1, 15, 51, 52, 60, 75, 73A, 90 (upper), 95; Mr. Vincent Smith, No. 98; M. Ardenne de Tizac, No. 44.

Most of the remaining Plates are from photographs taken or commissioned by myself.

The binder is advised that Plates LXXI A, LXXII A, LXXIII A issued with Part VII are extra numbers, originally printed by oversight, and these should be bound immediately following Plate C. Plate 1 in Part VIII is to replace Plate 1 in Part I.

One thousand copies of the whole edition have been printed, of which five hundred have been prepared for sale in parts, the remainder in one volume.

With the completion of the First Series of One Hundred Plates of Sculptures the publication of Viśvakarmā will be discontinued for the present.

A.K.C.

Britford,
Nr. Salisbury,
September, 1914.

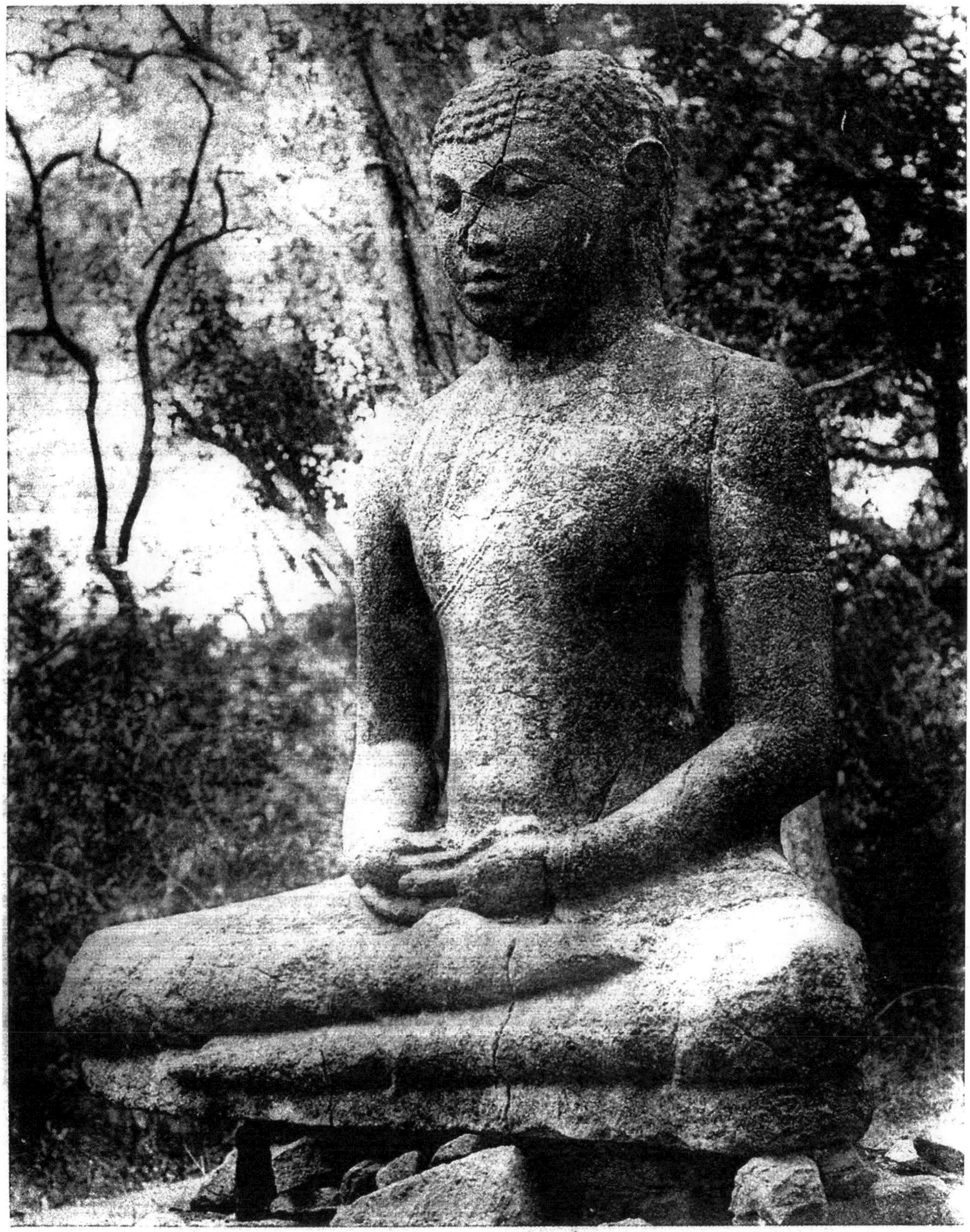

II

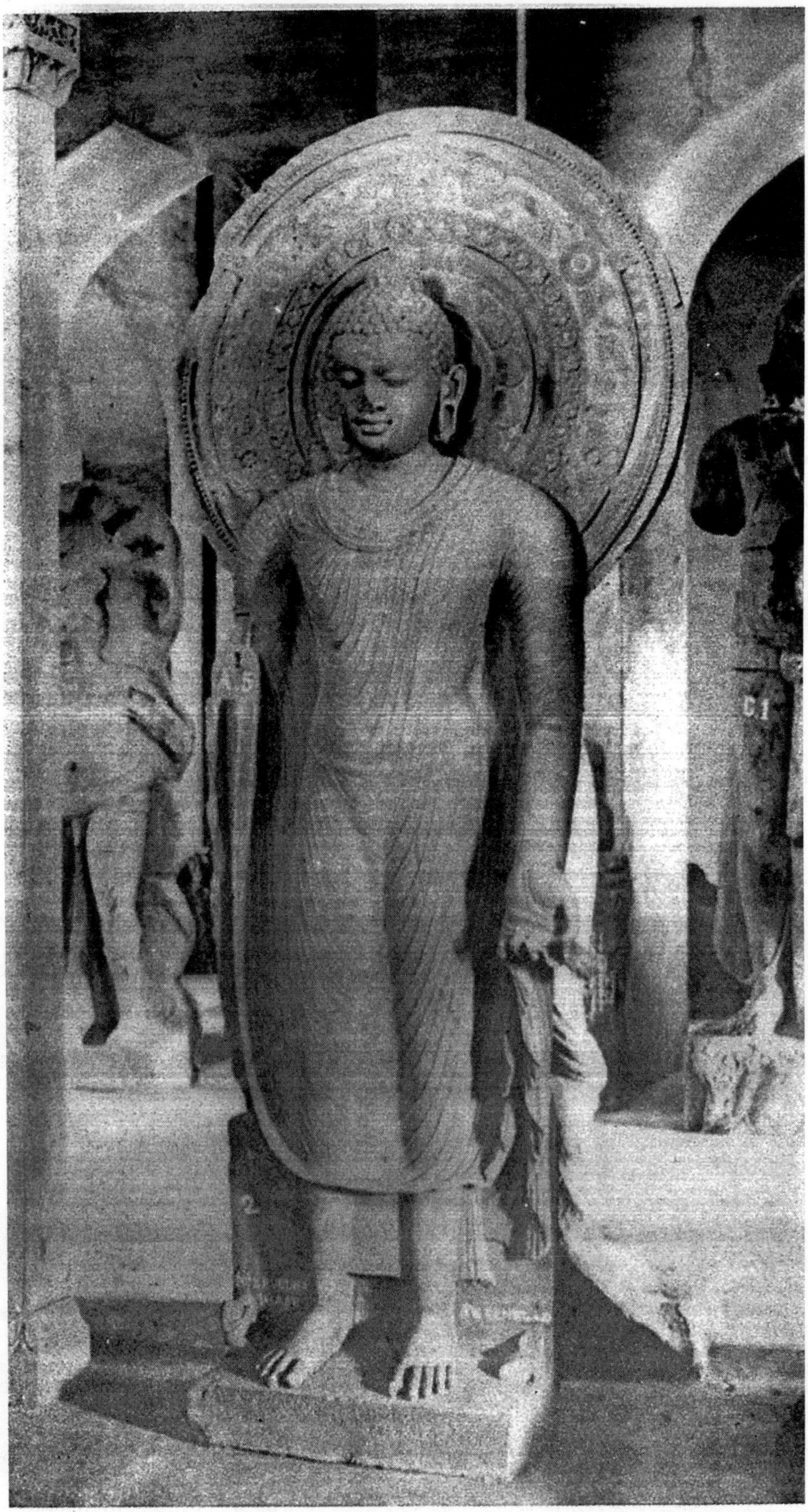

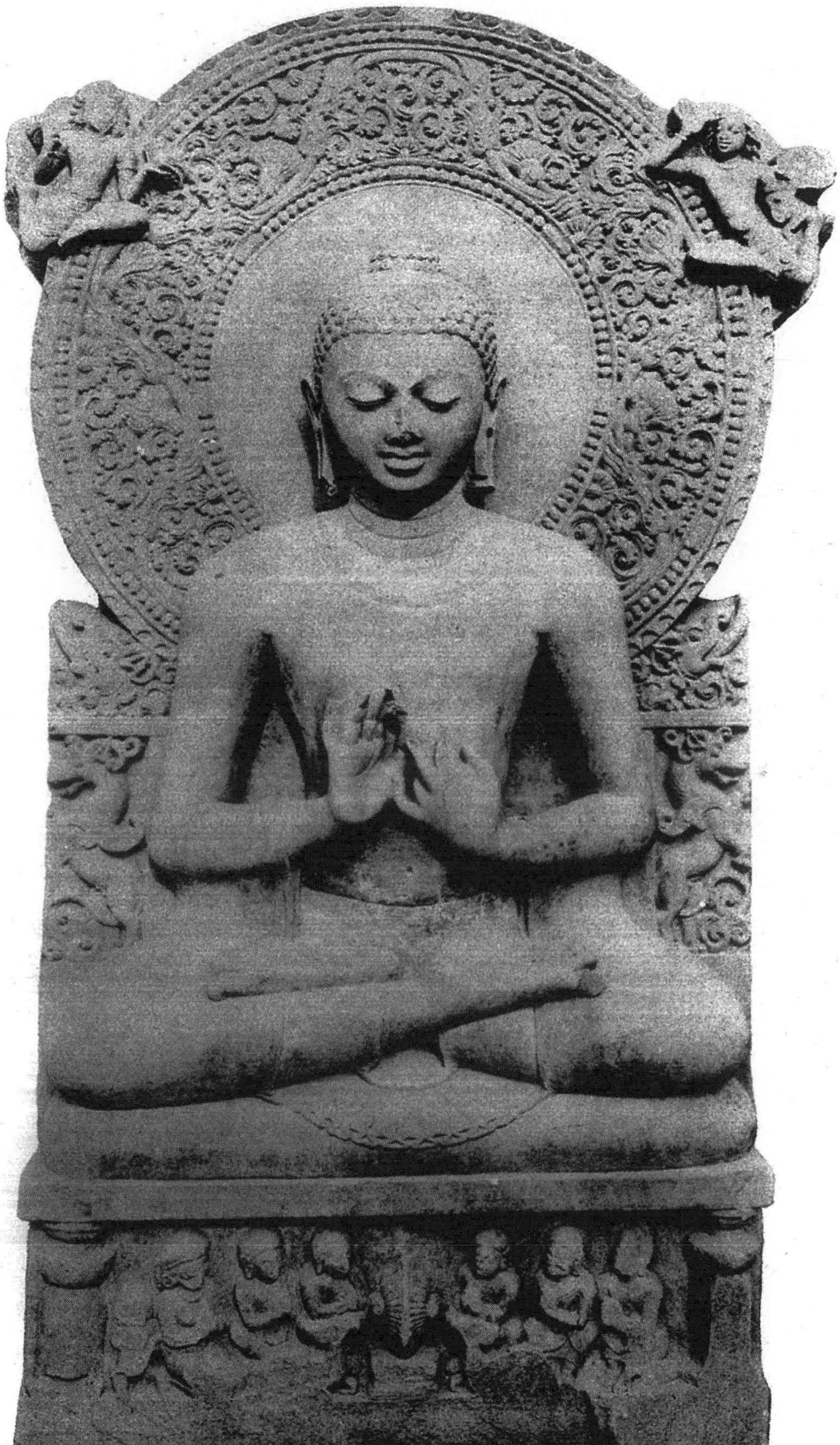

IV

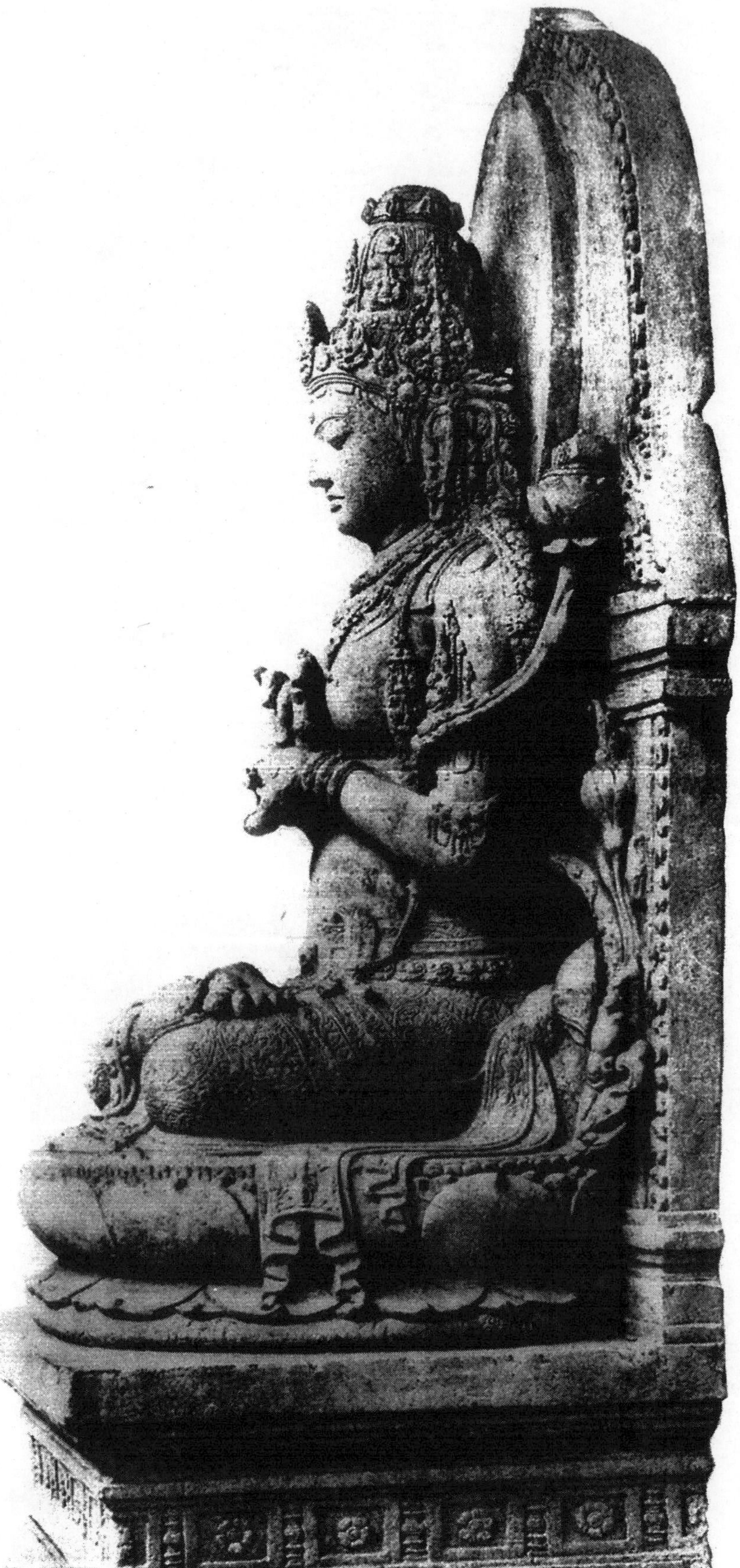

V

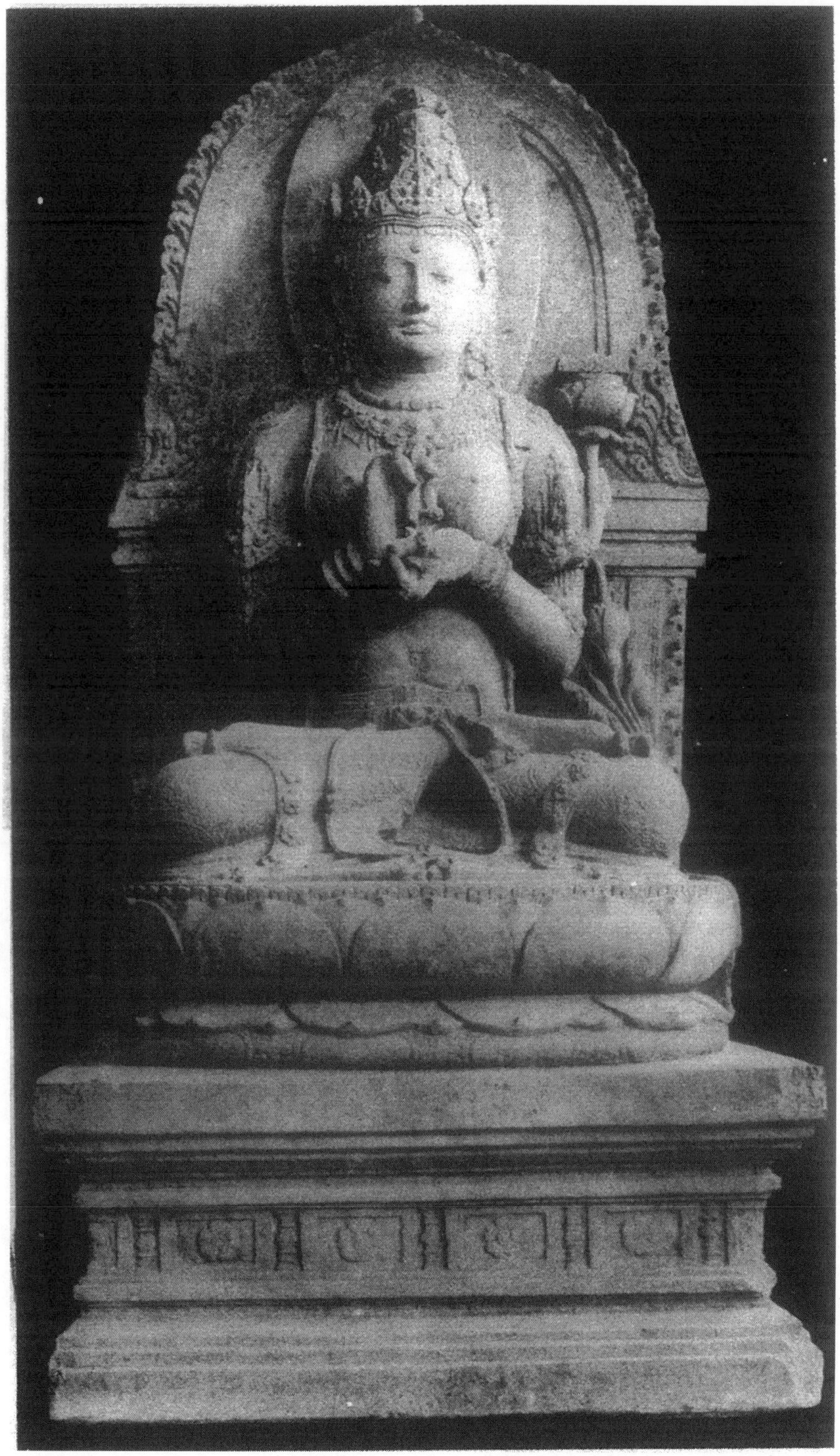

VI

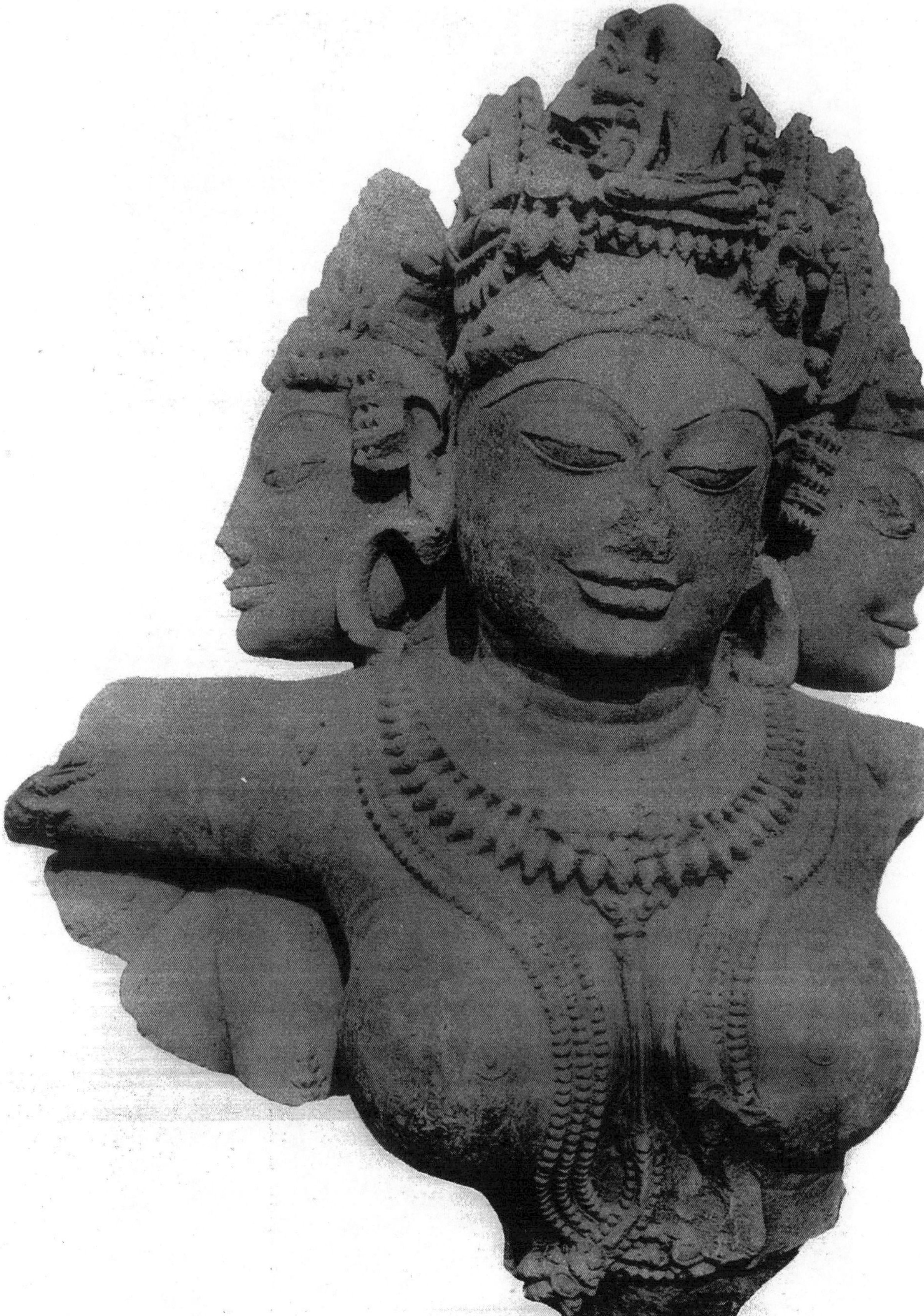

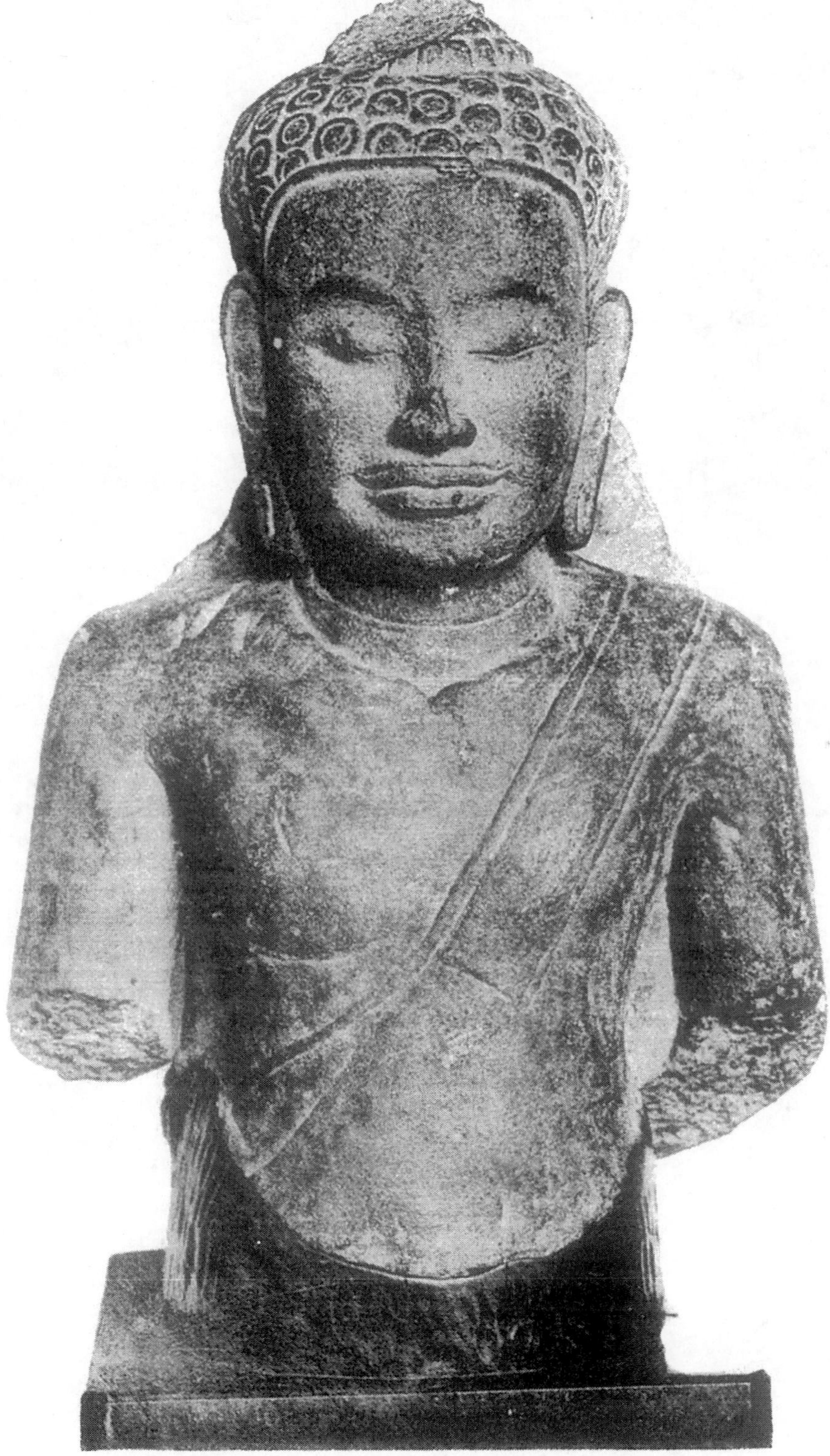

VIII

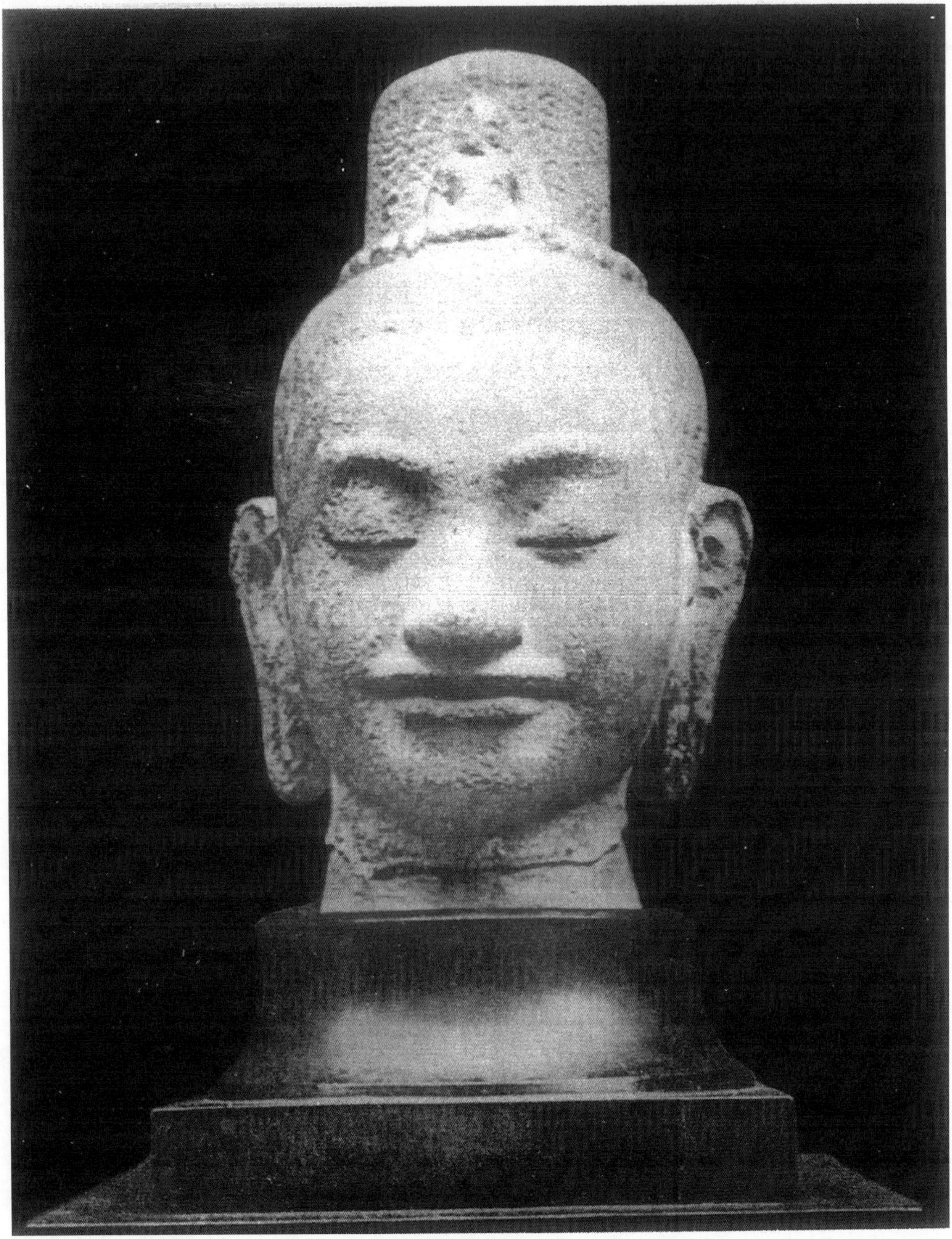

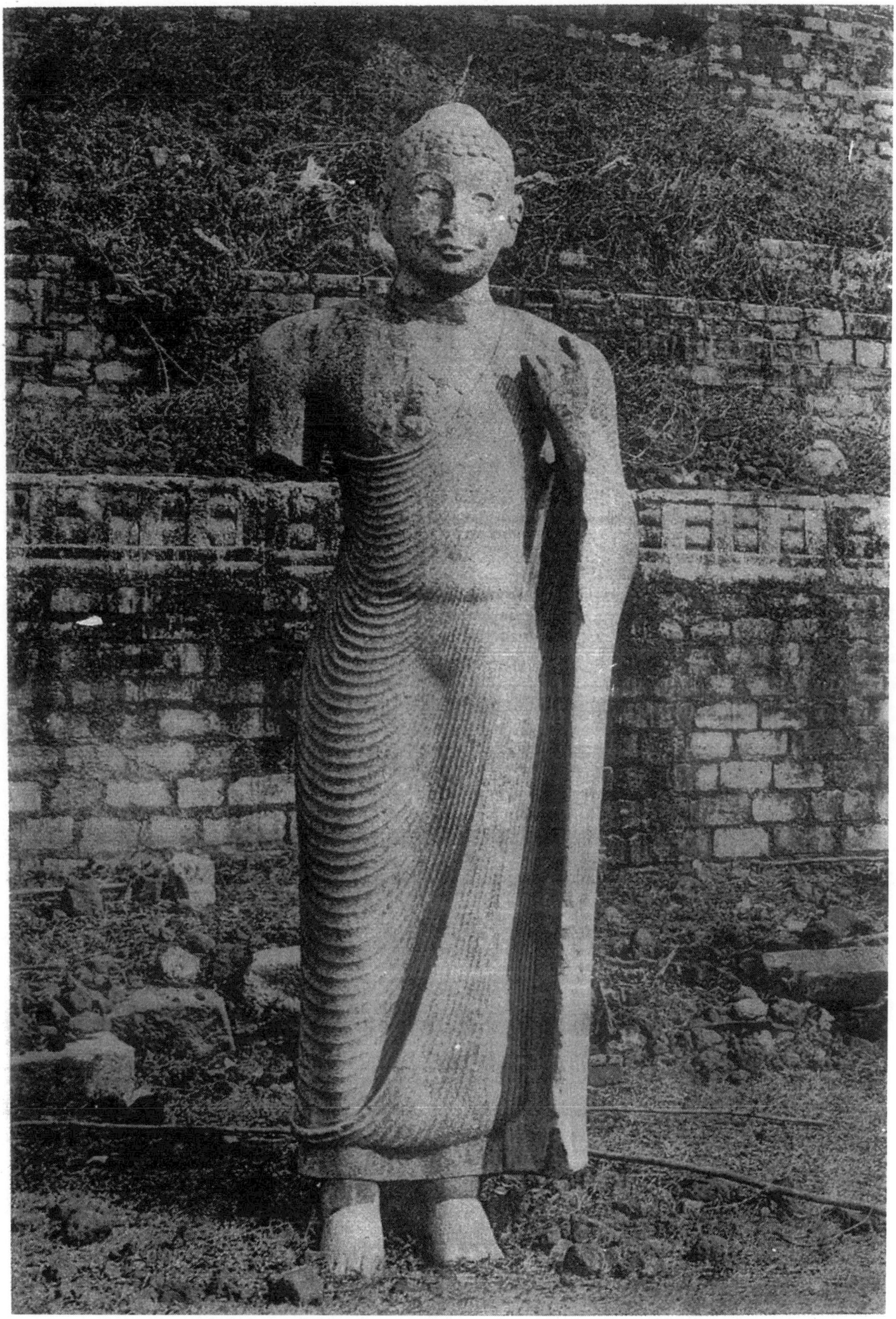

X

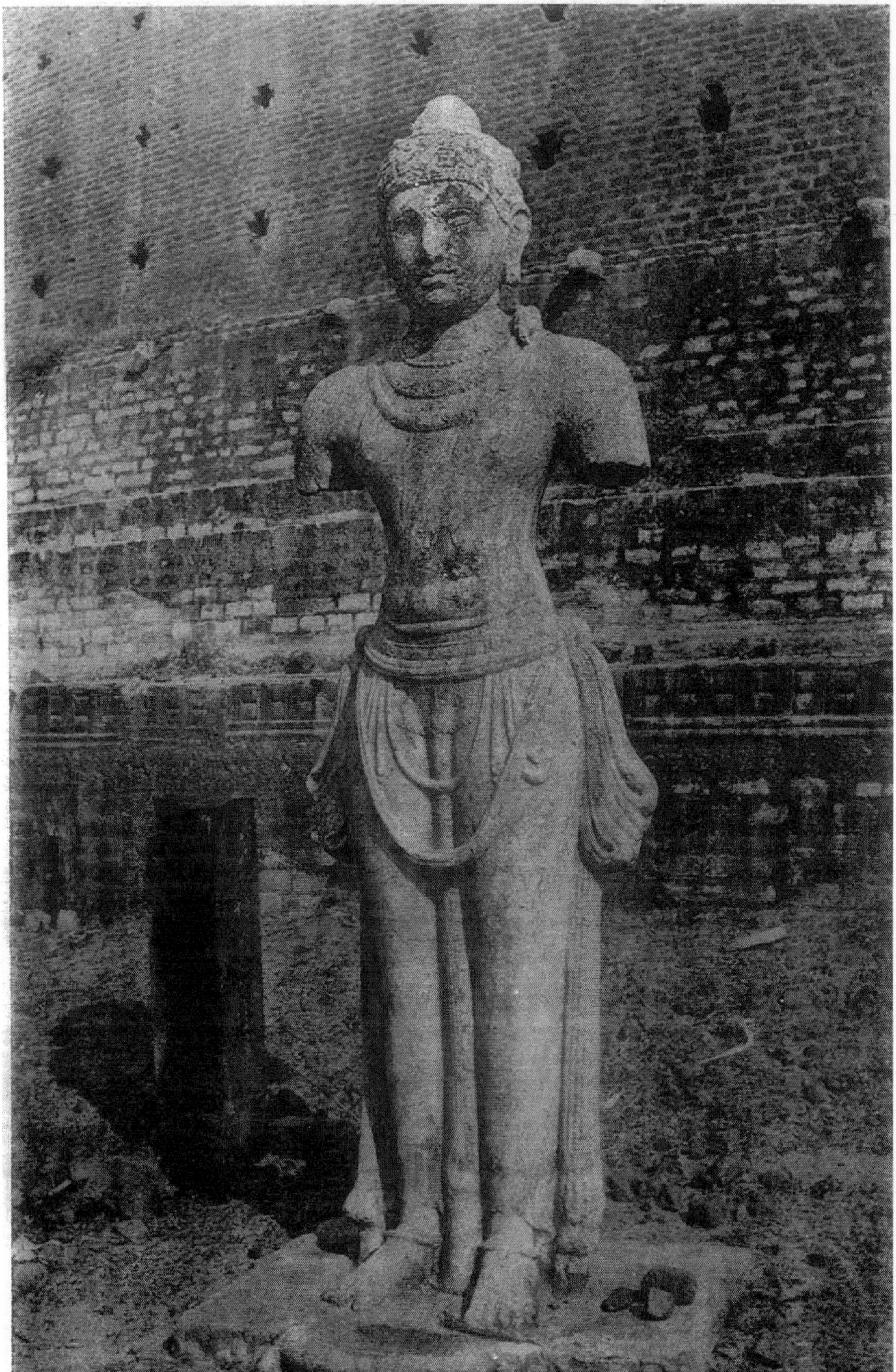

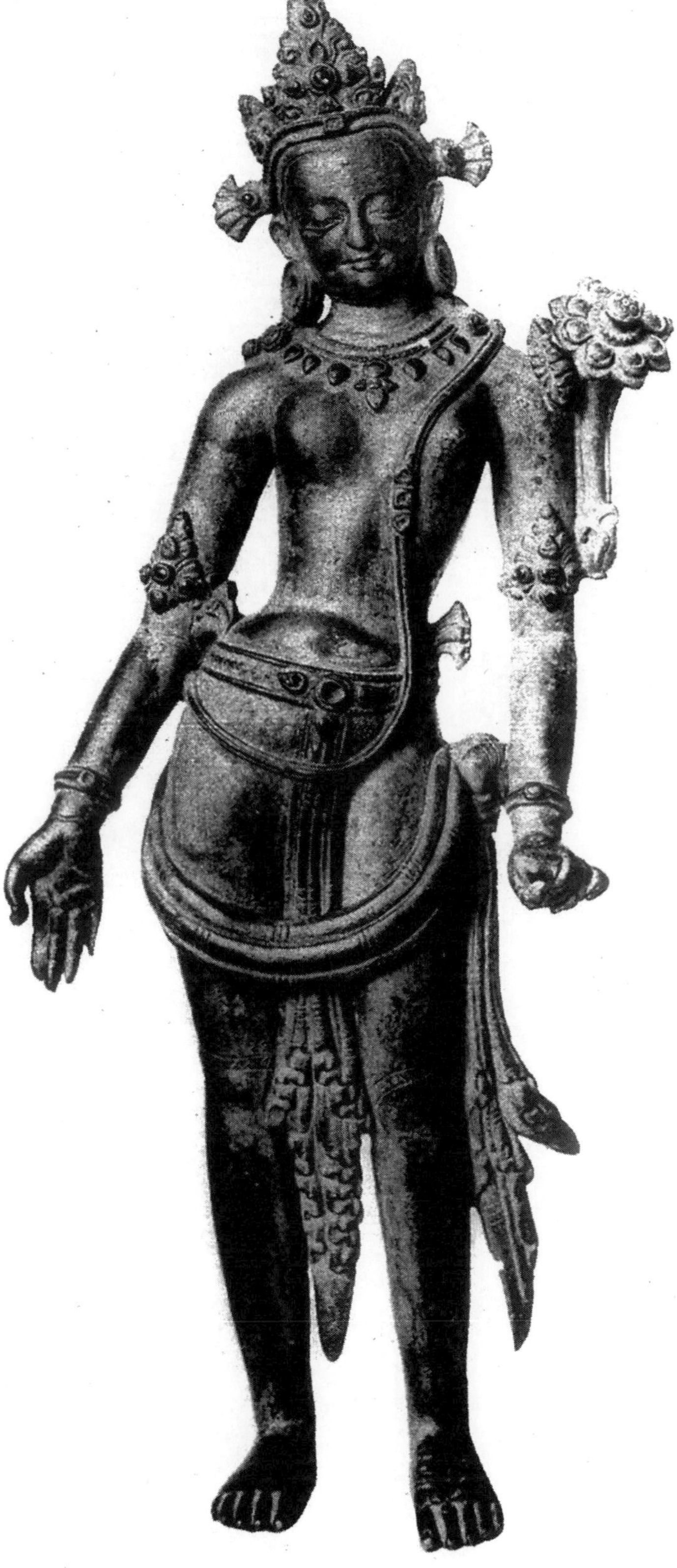

XII

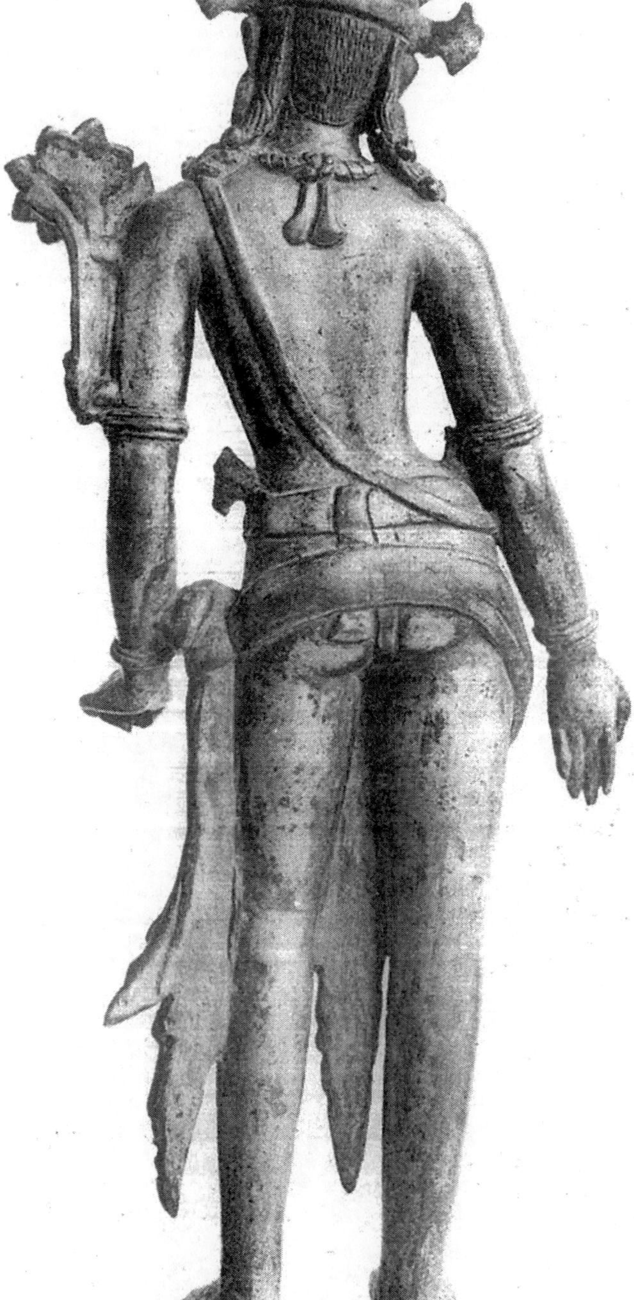

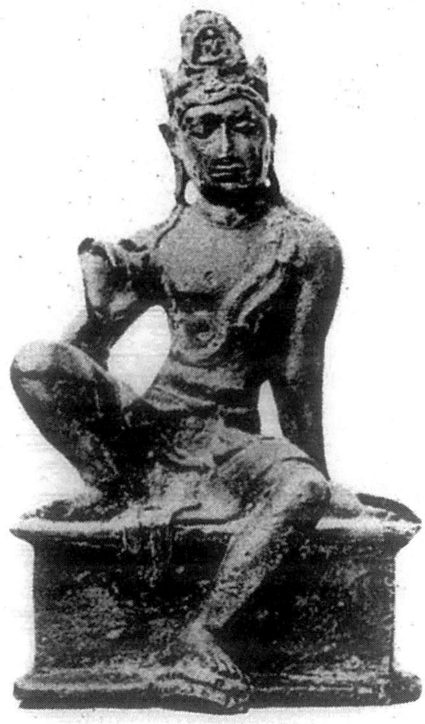

XIV

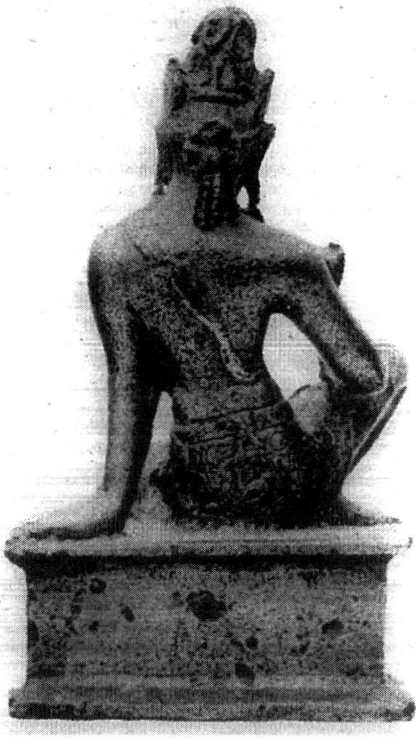

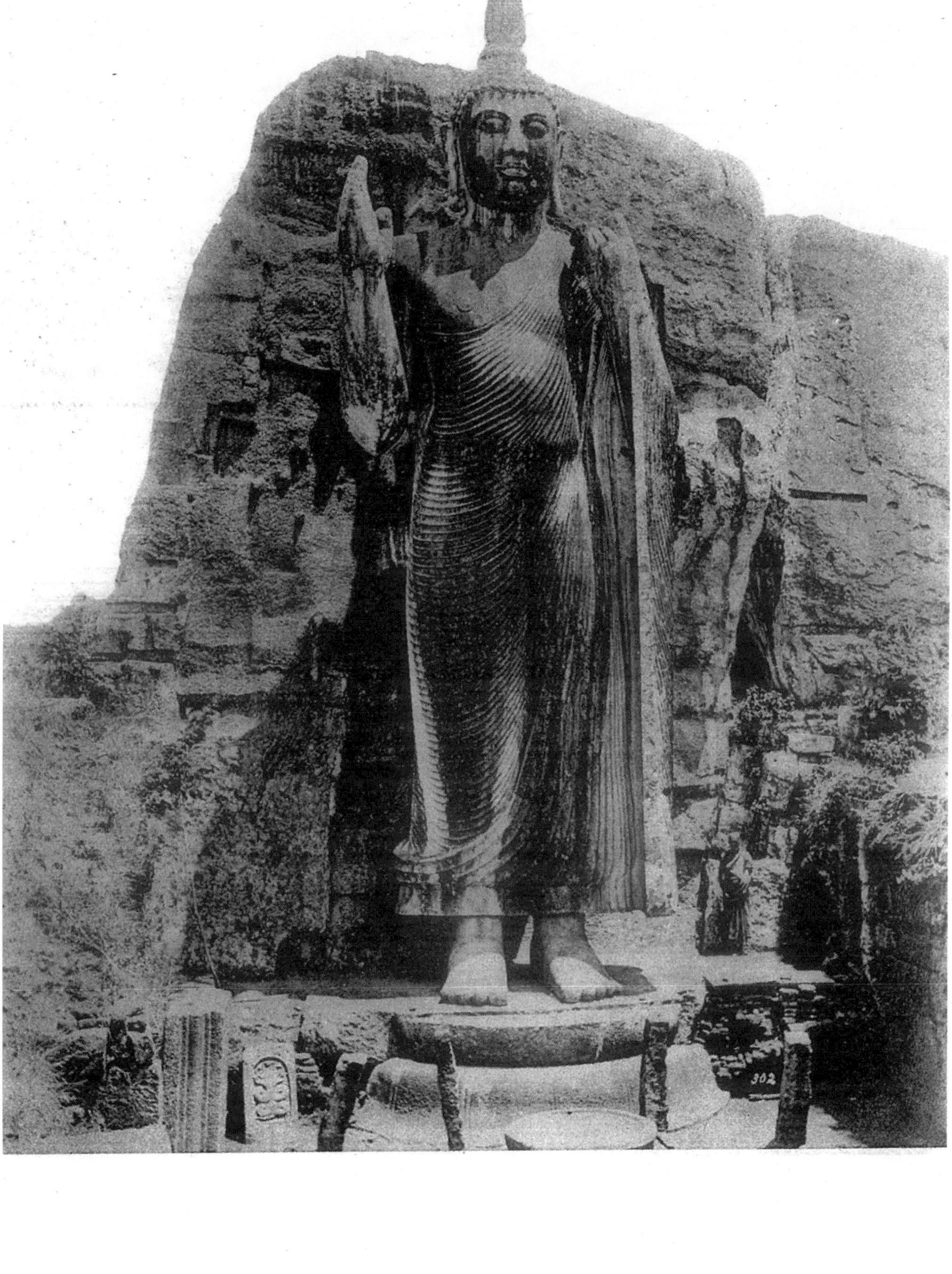

XVI

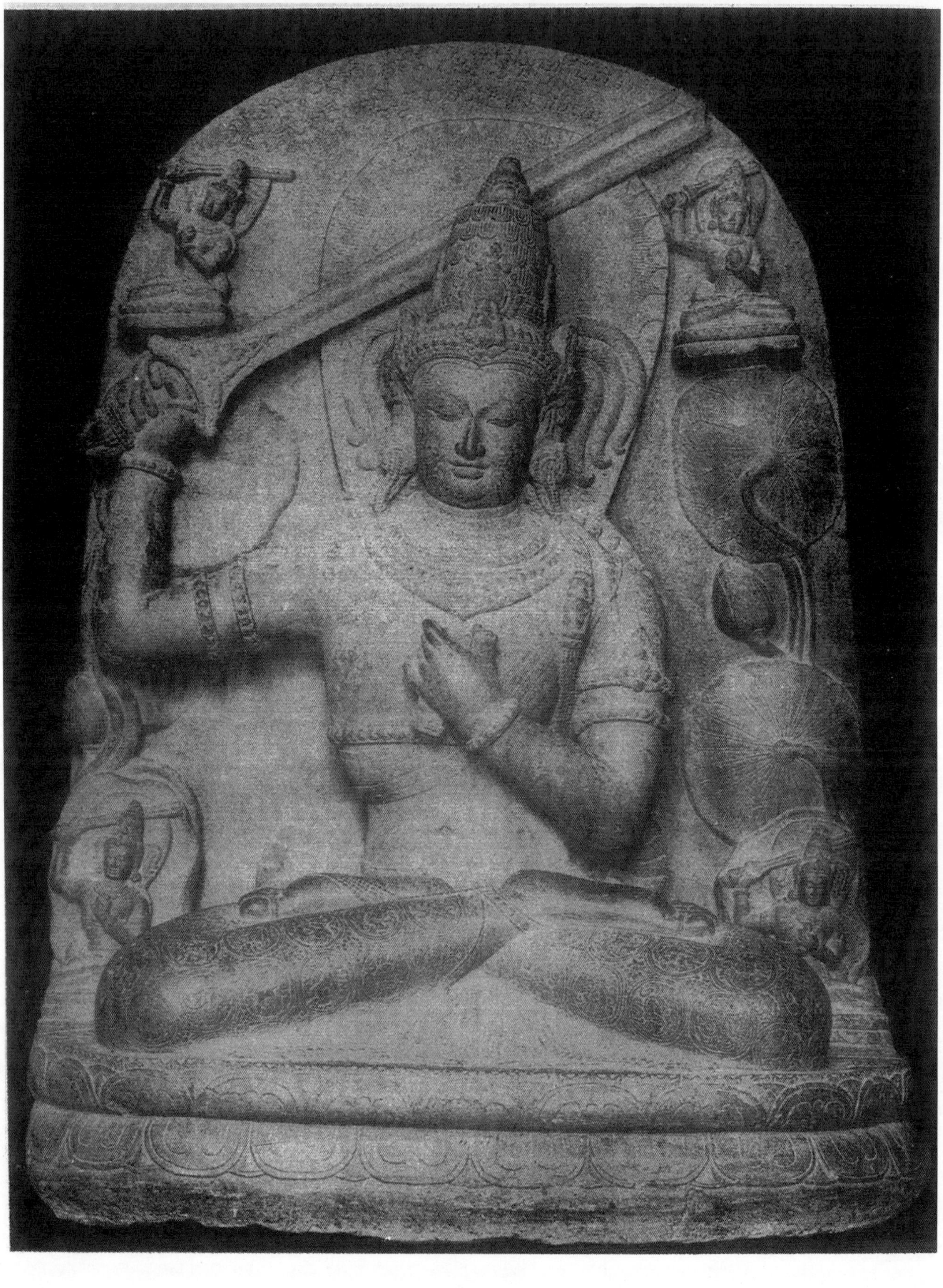

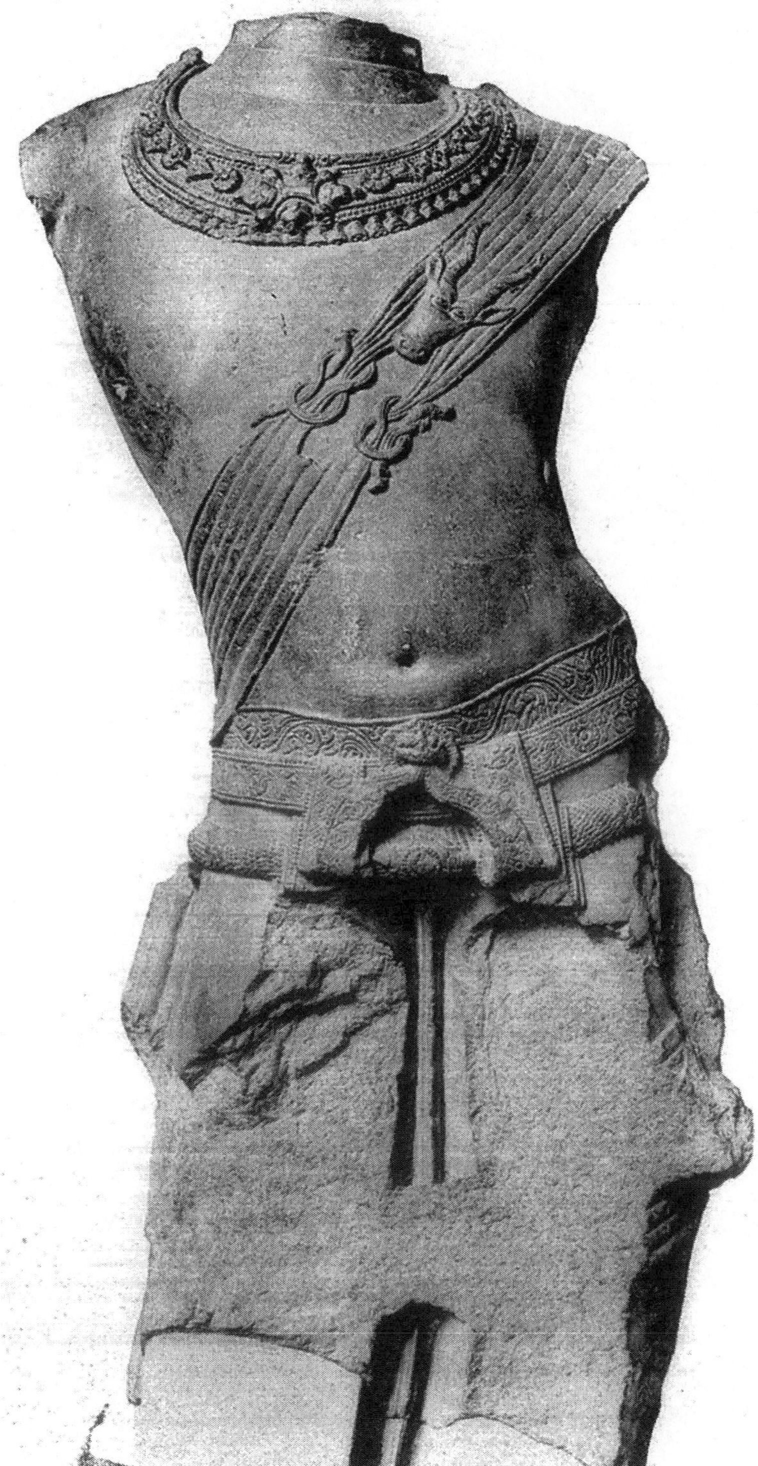

XVIII

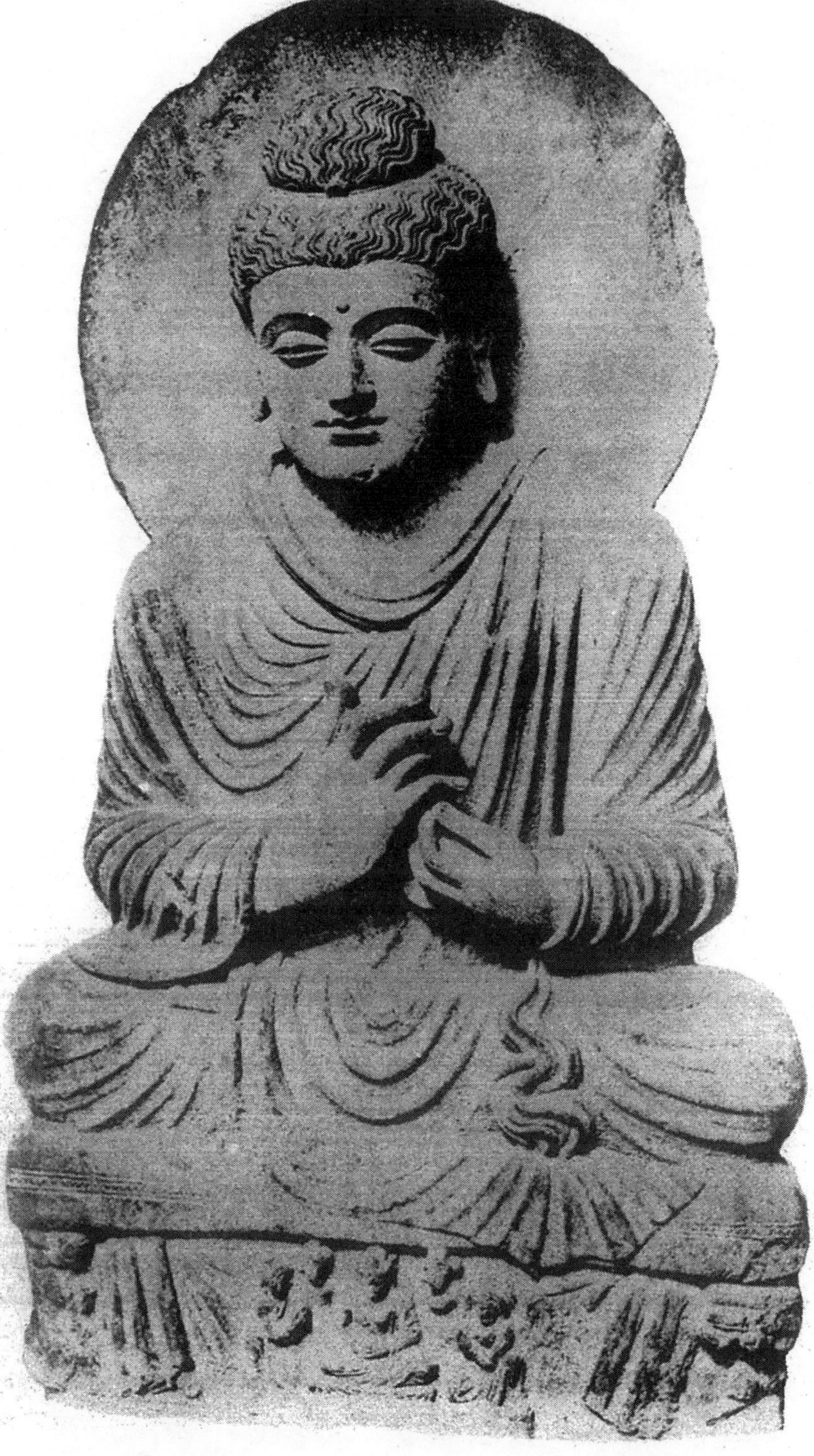

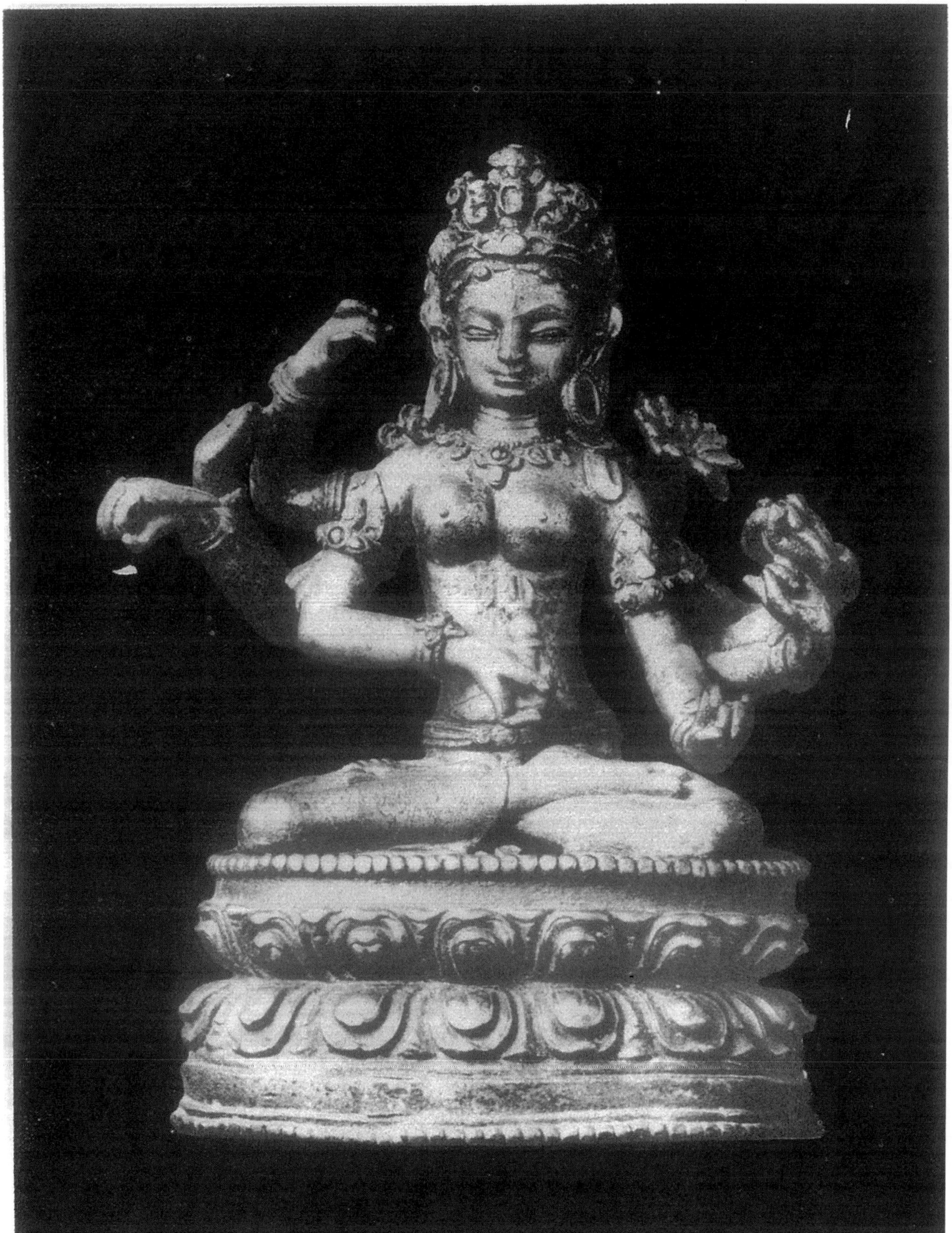

XX

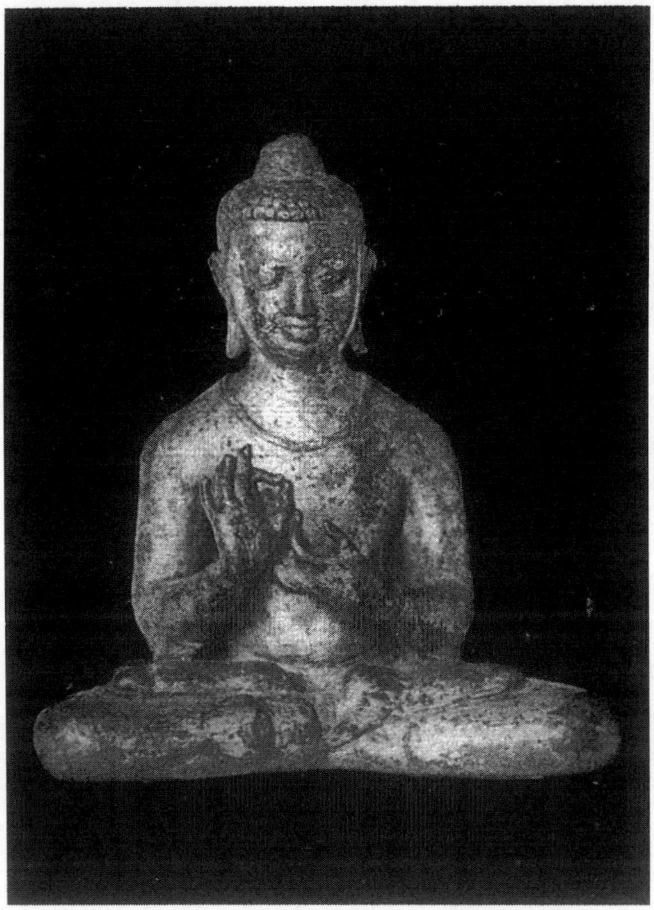

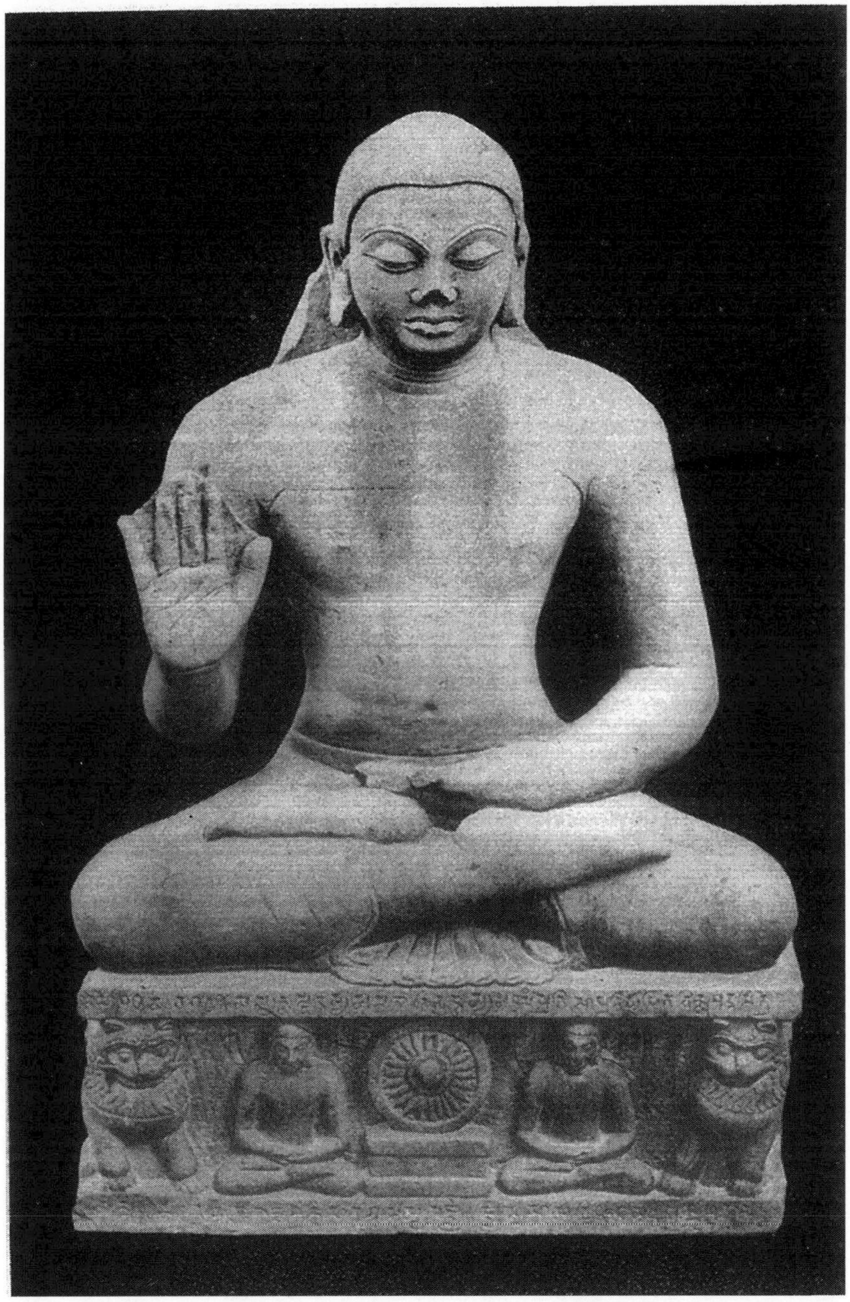

XXII

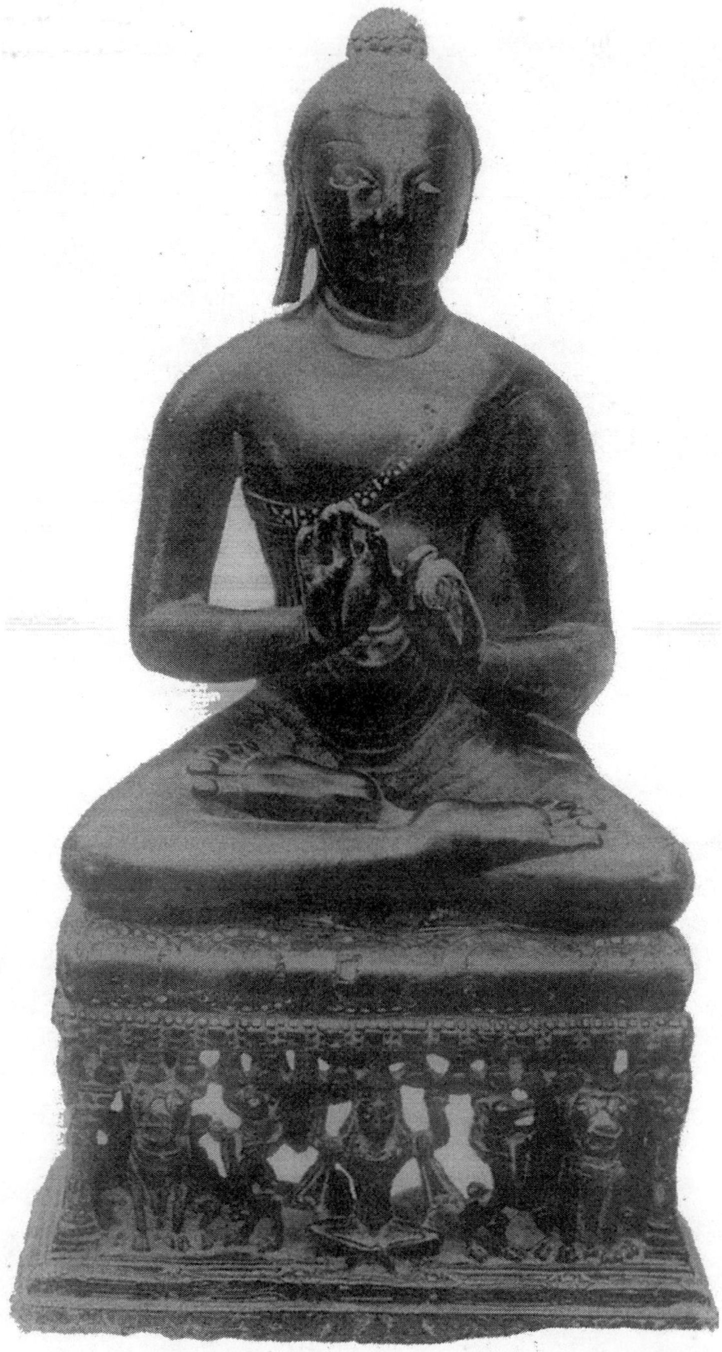

XXIII

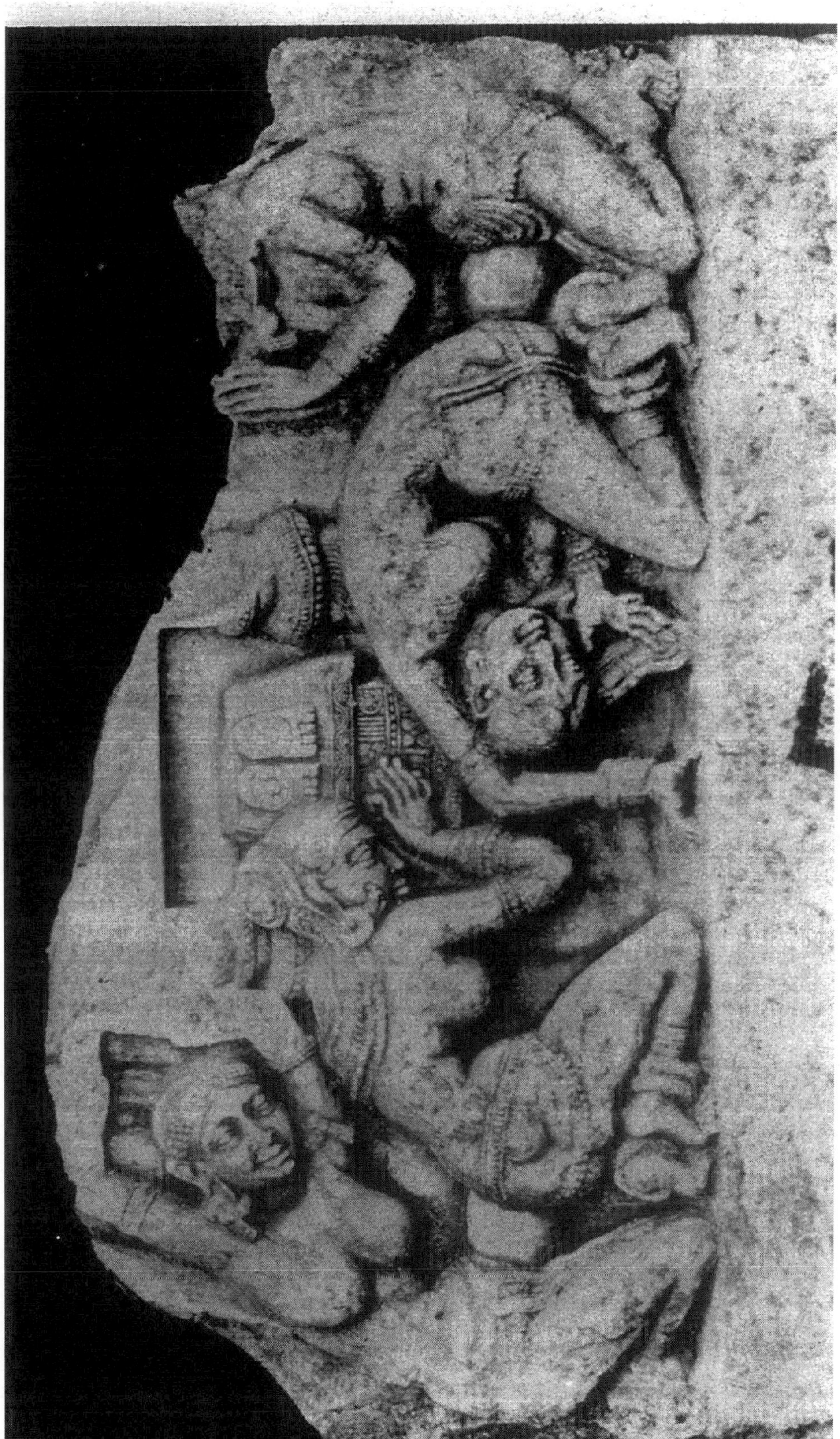

XXIV

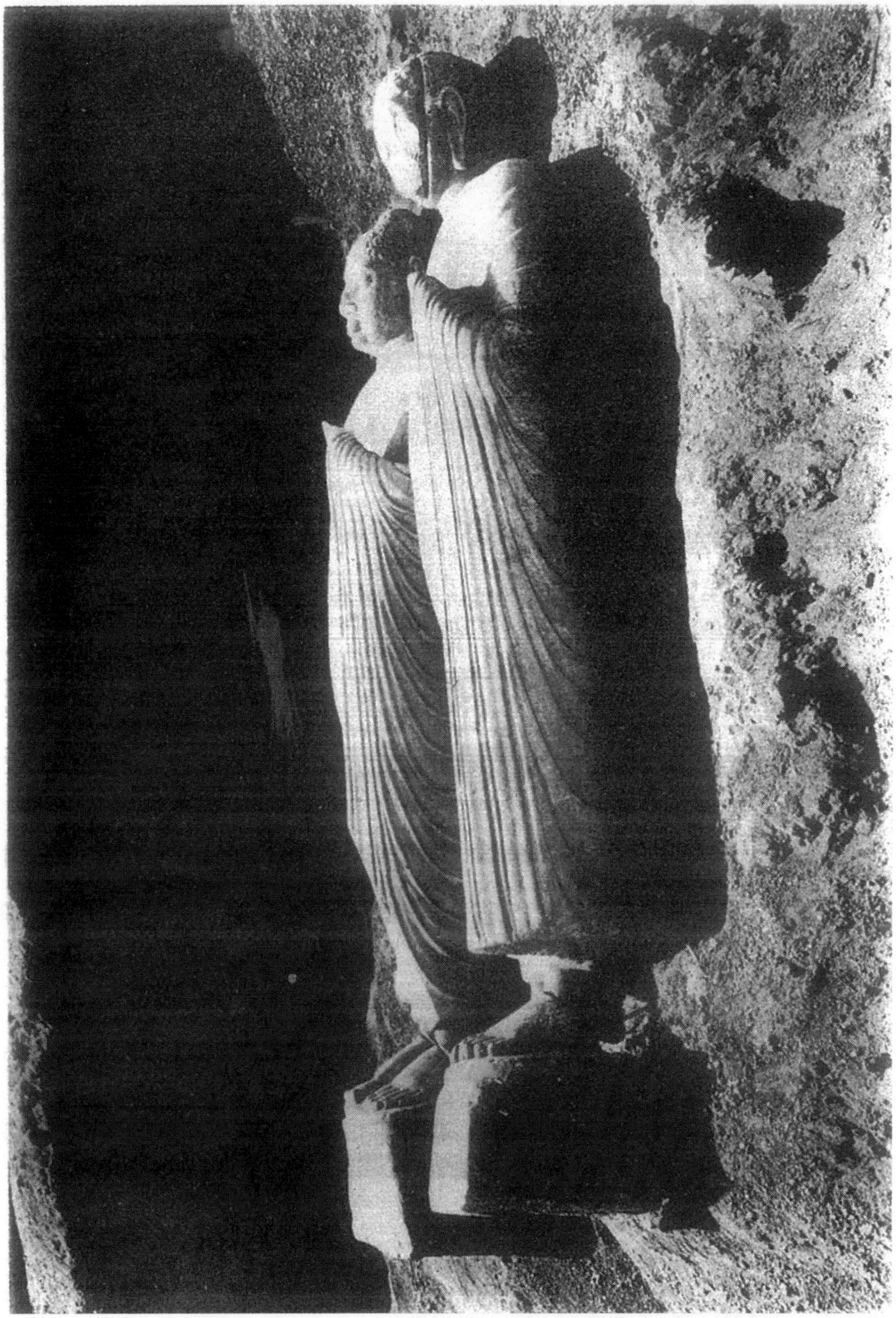

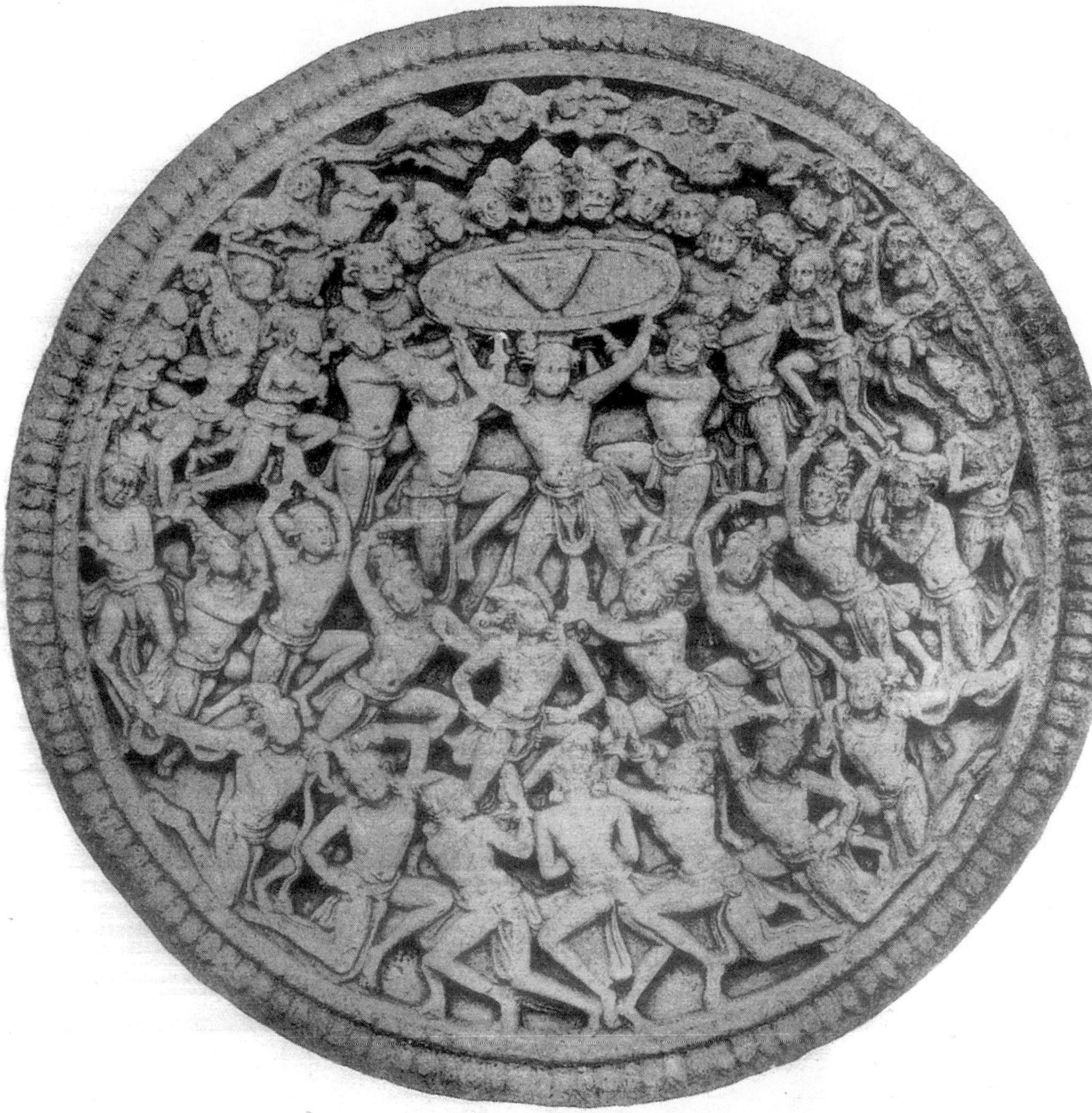

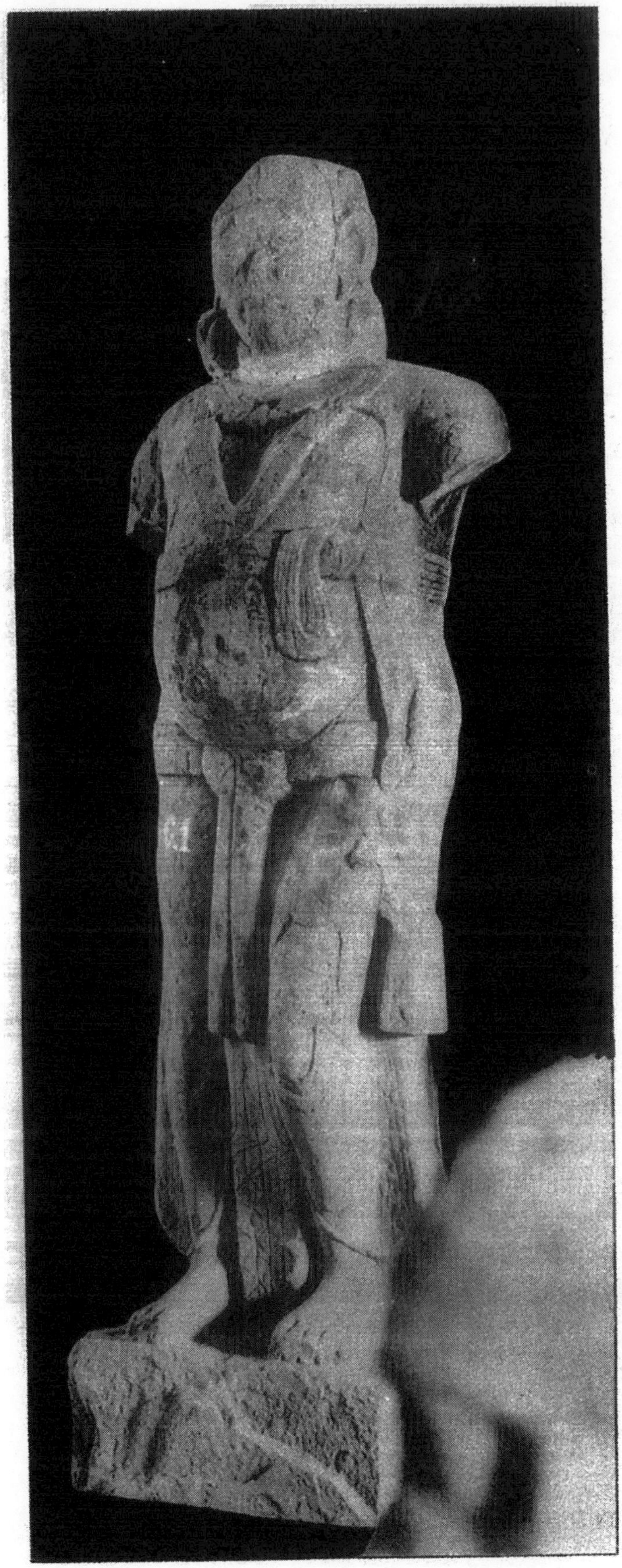

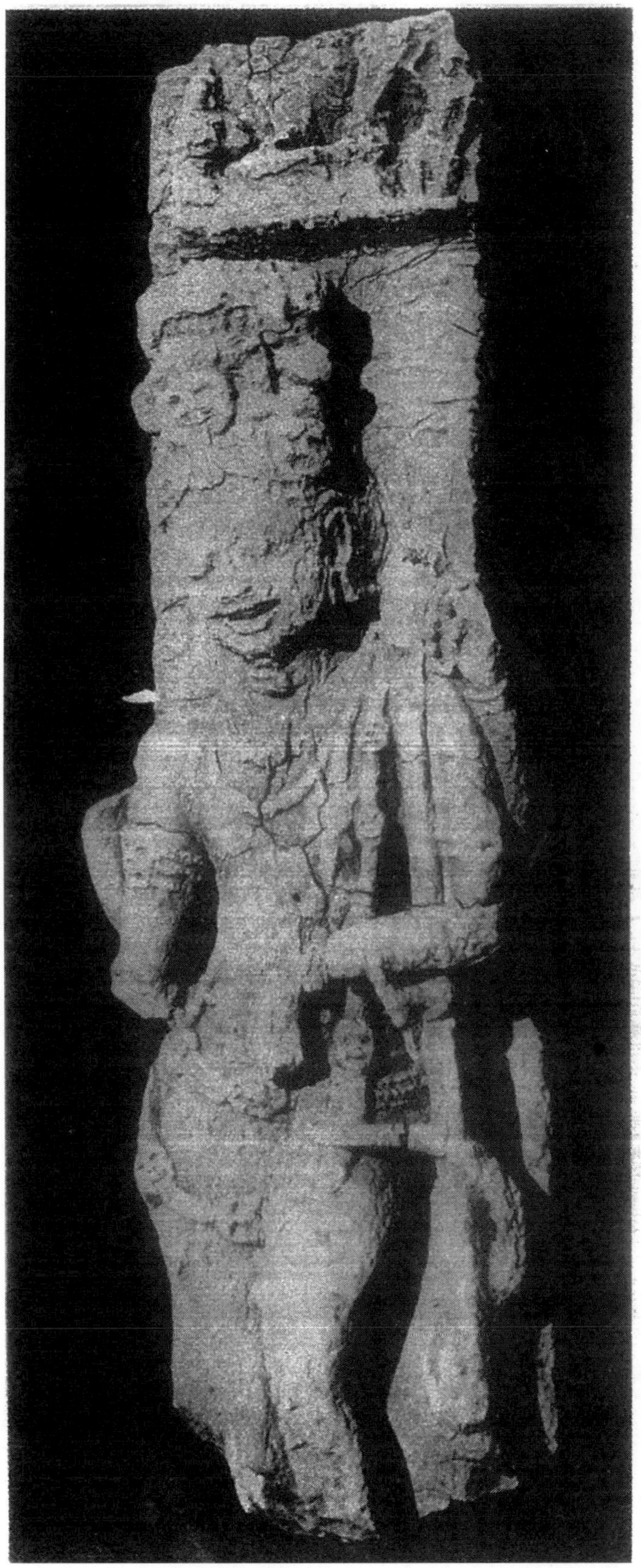

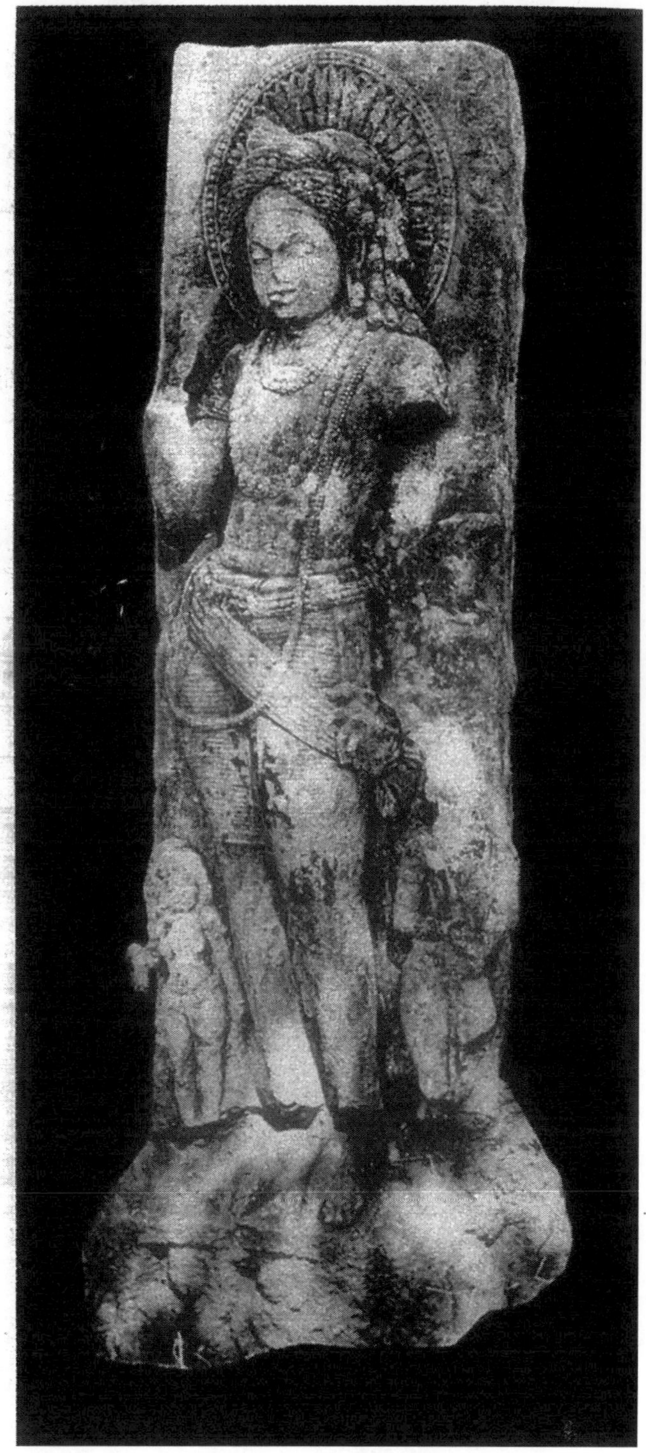

XXVIII

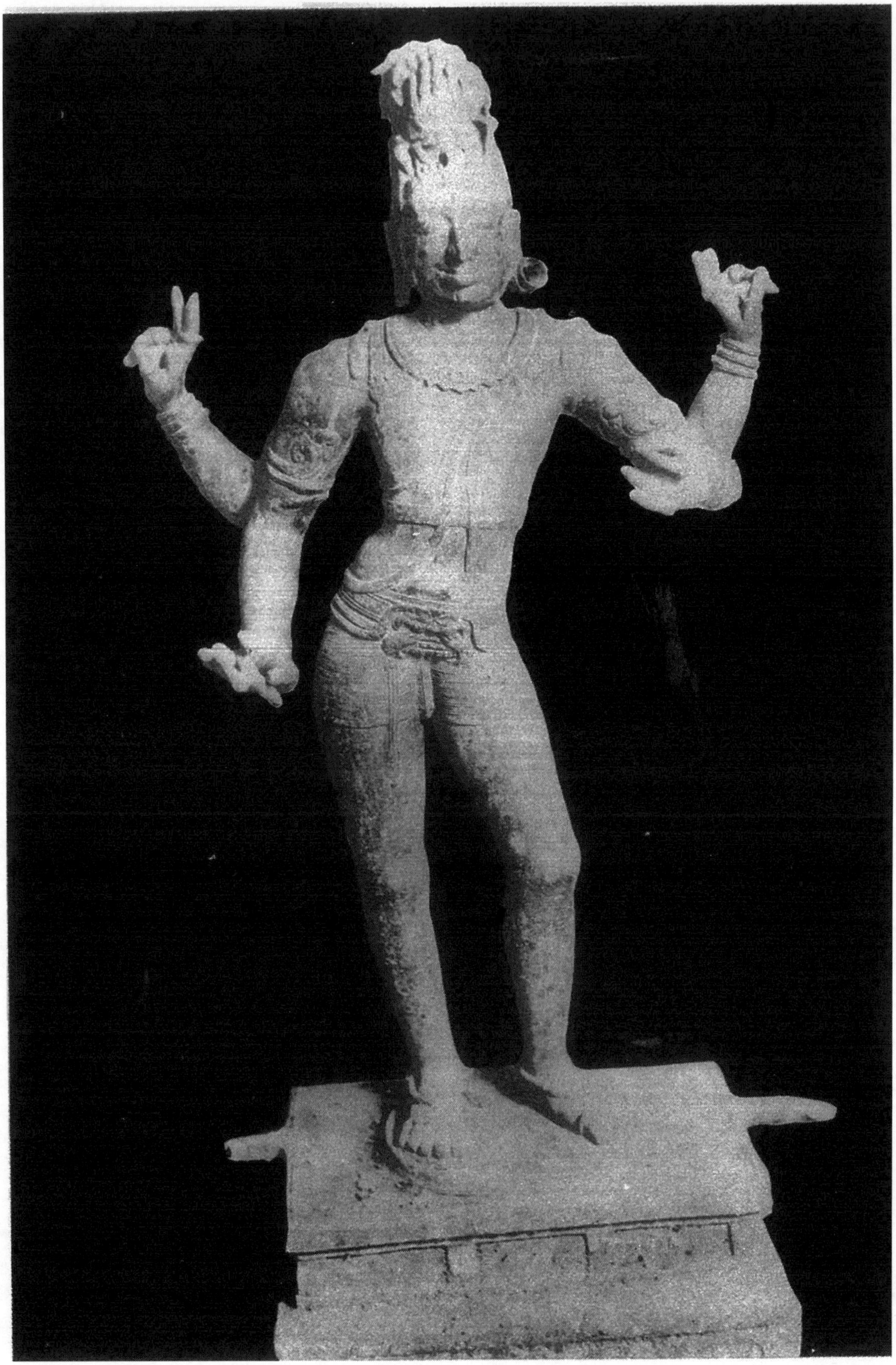

XXIX

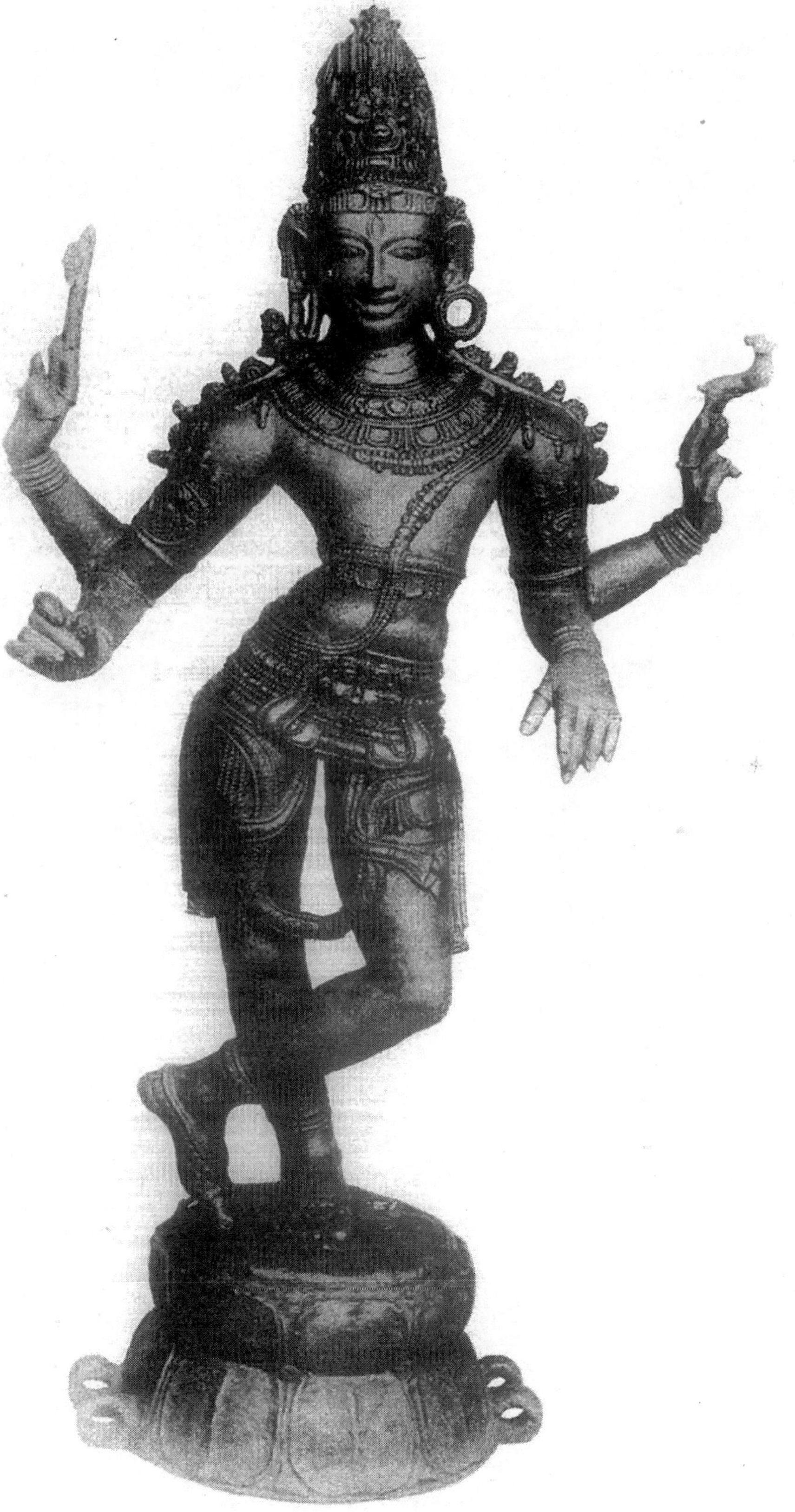

XXX

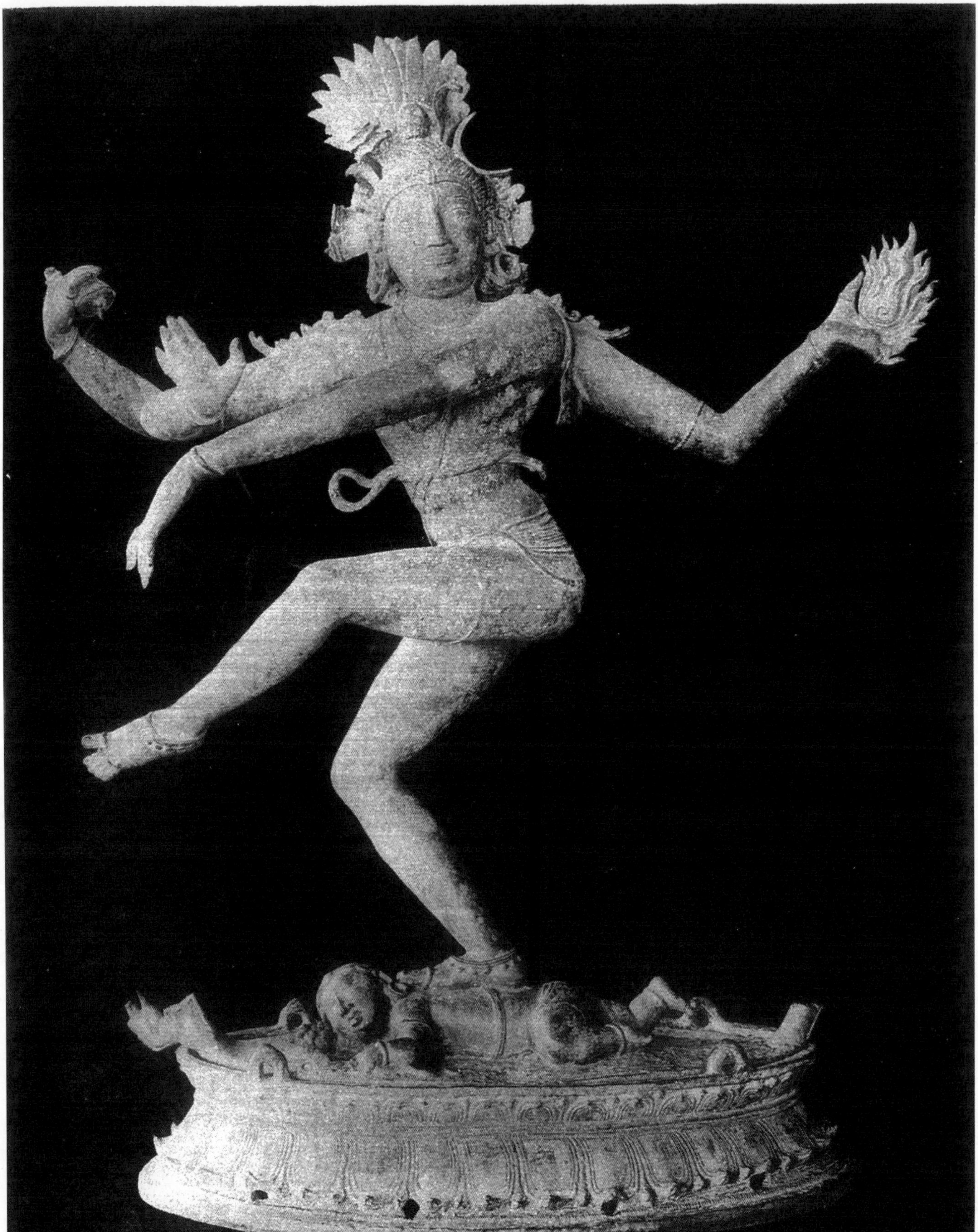

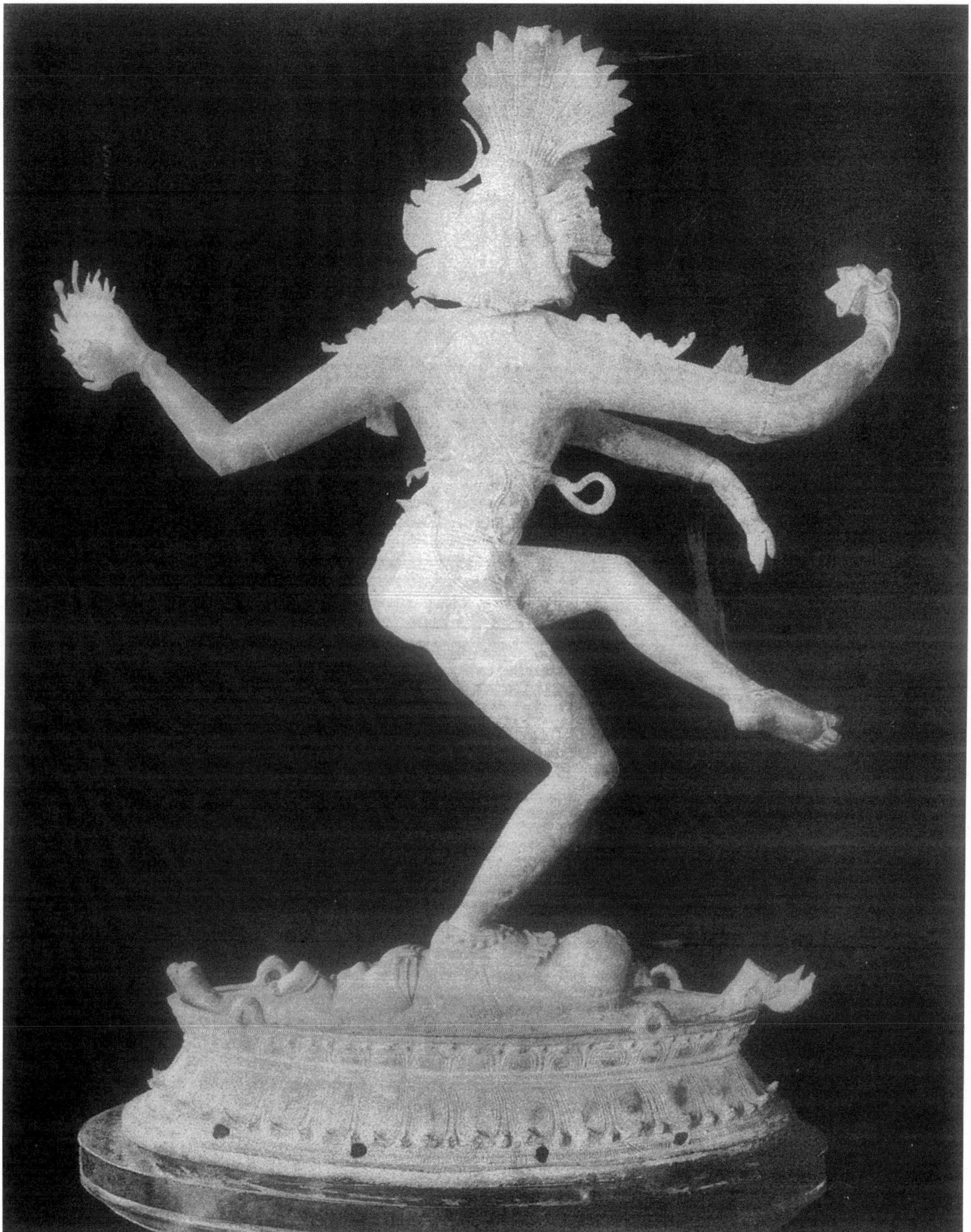

XXXII

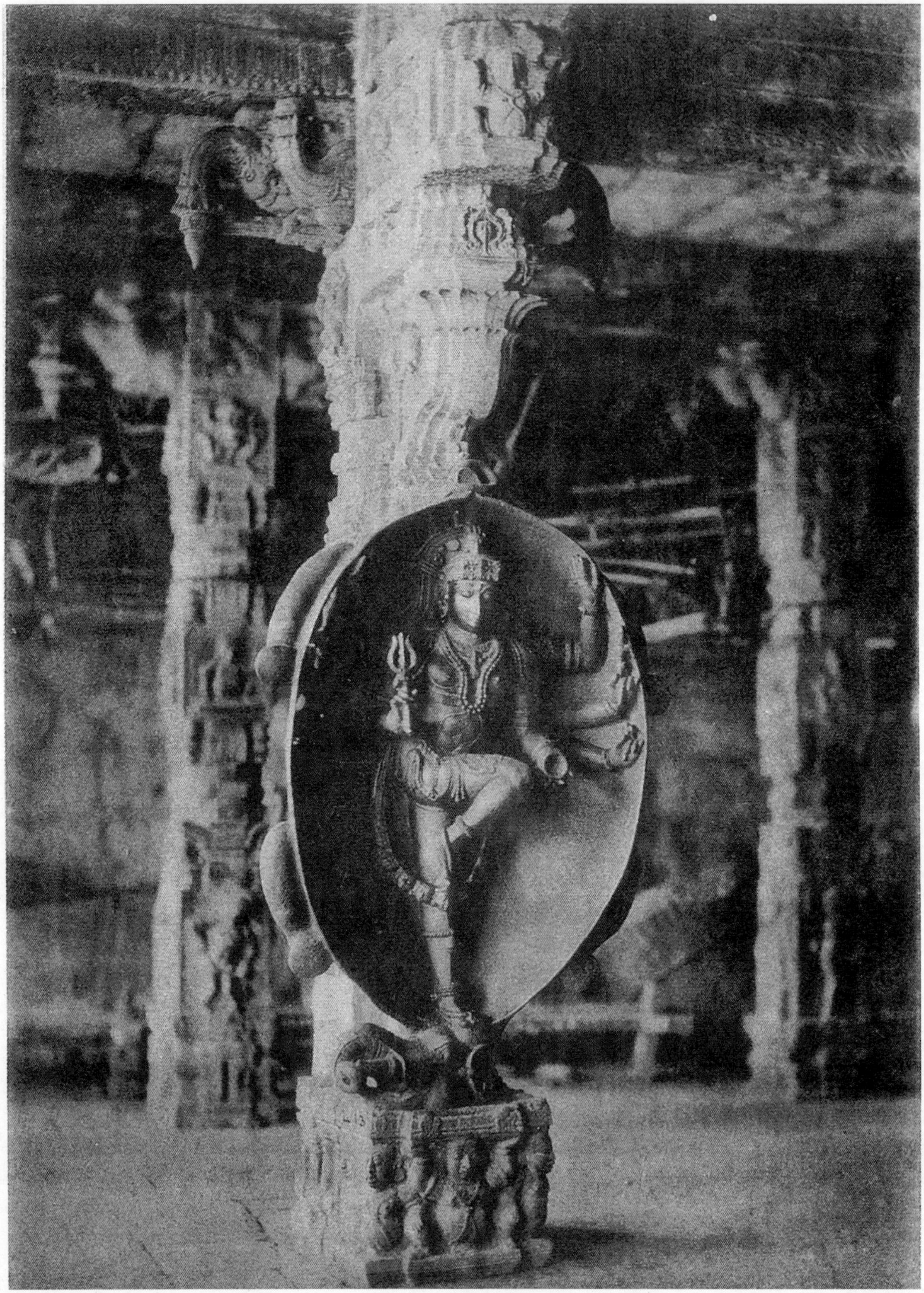

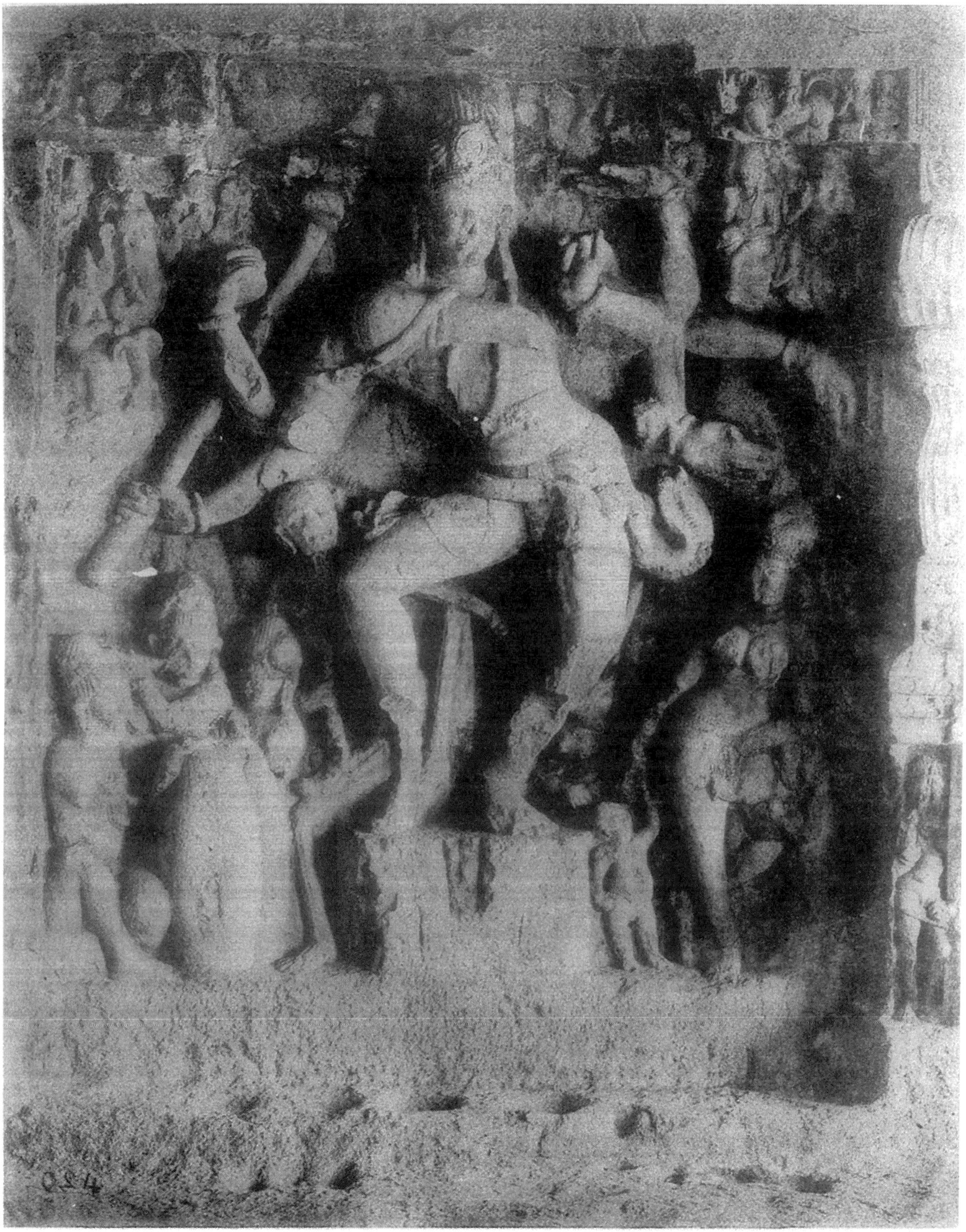

XXXIV

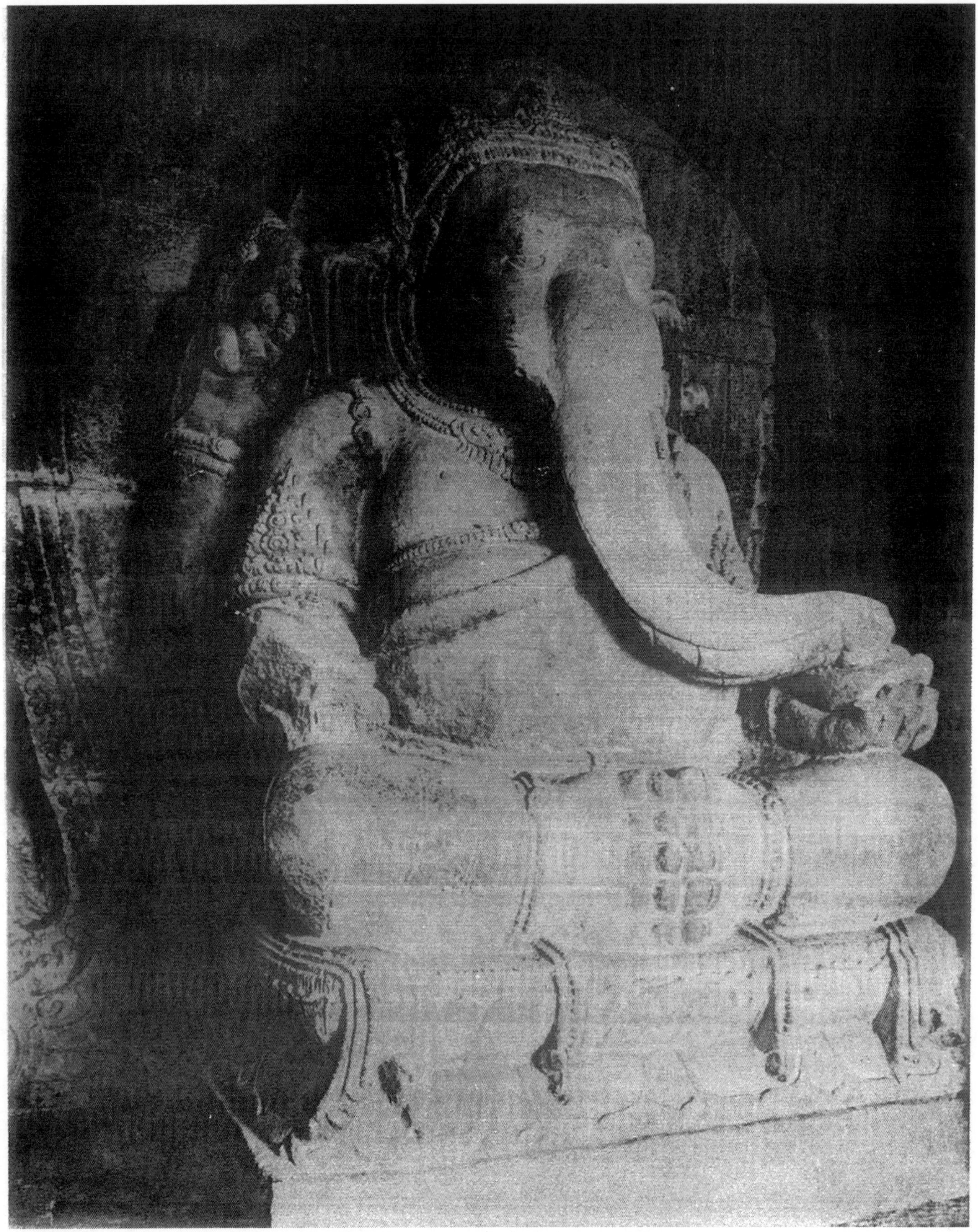

XXXV

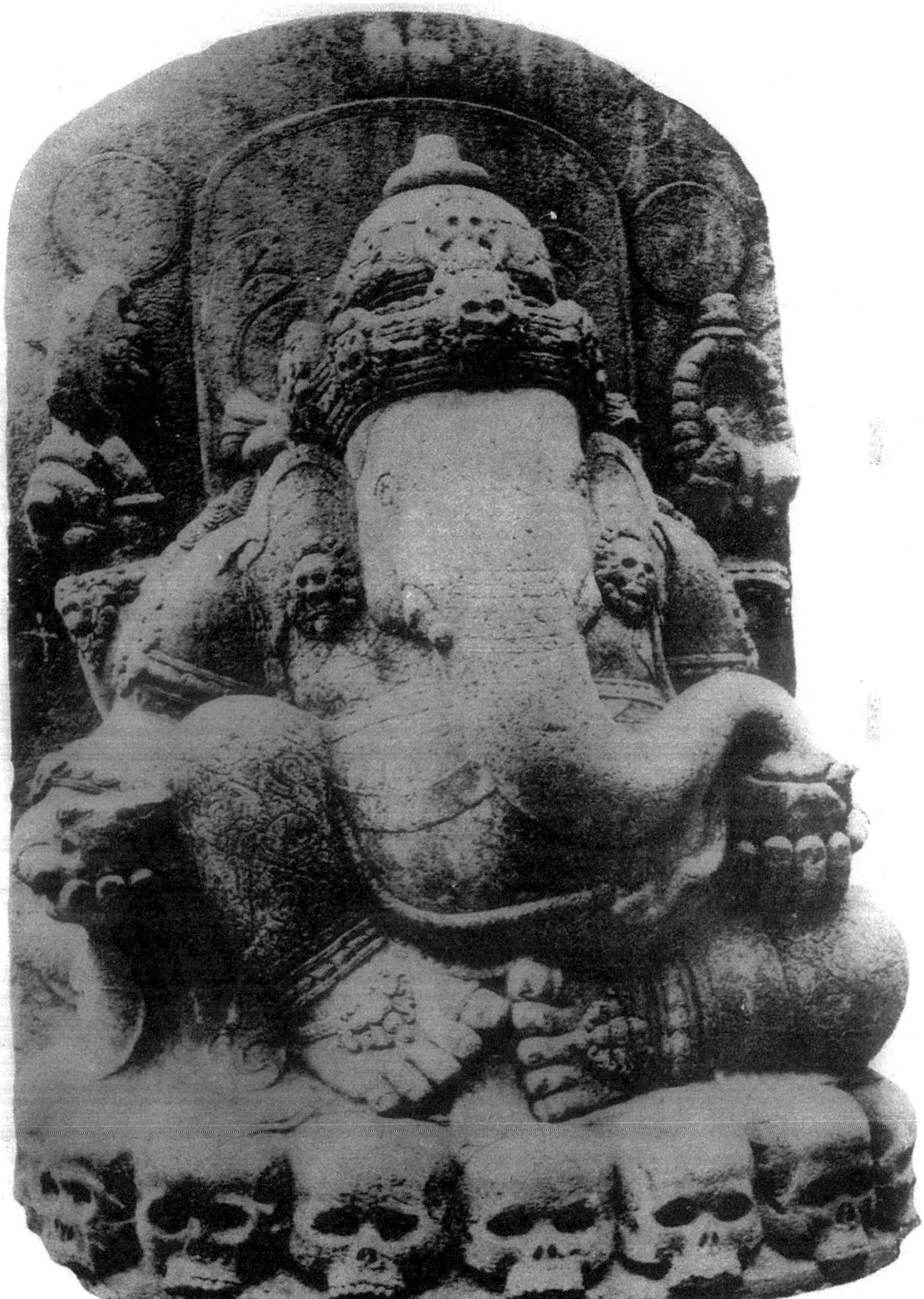

XXXVI

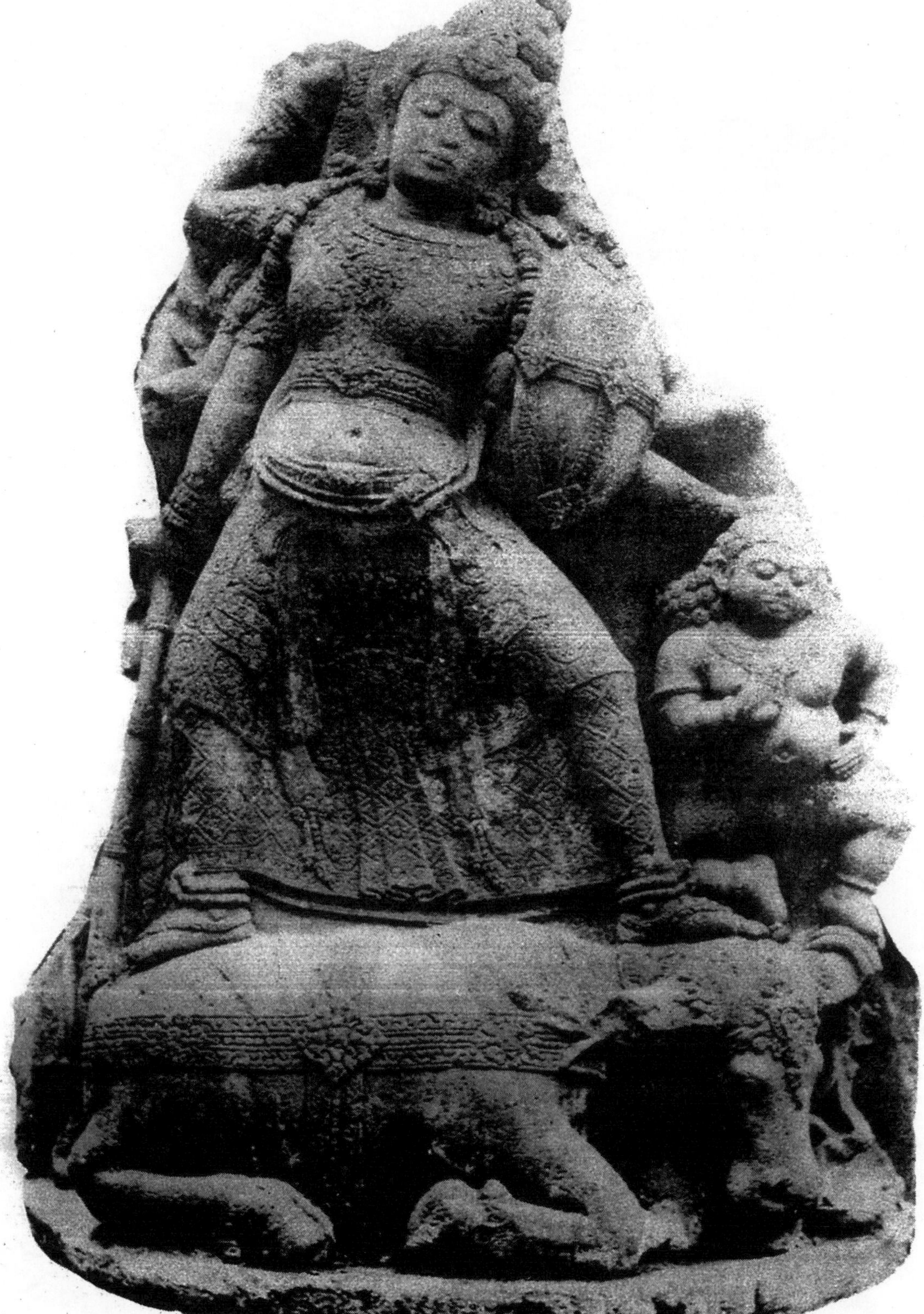

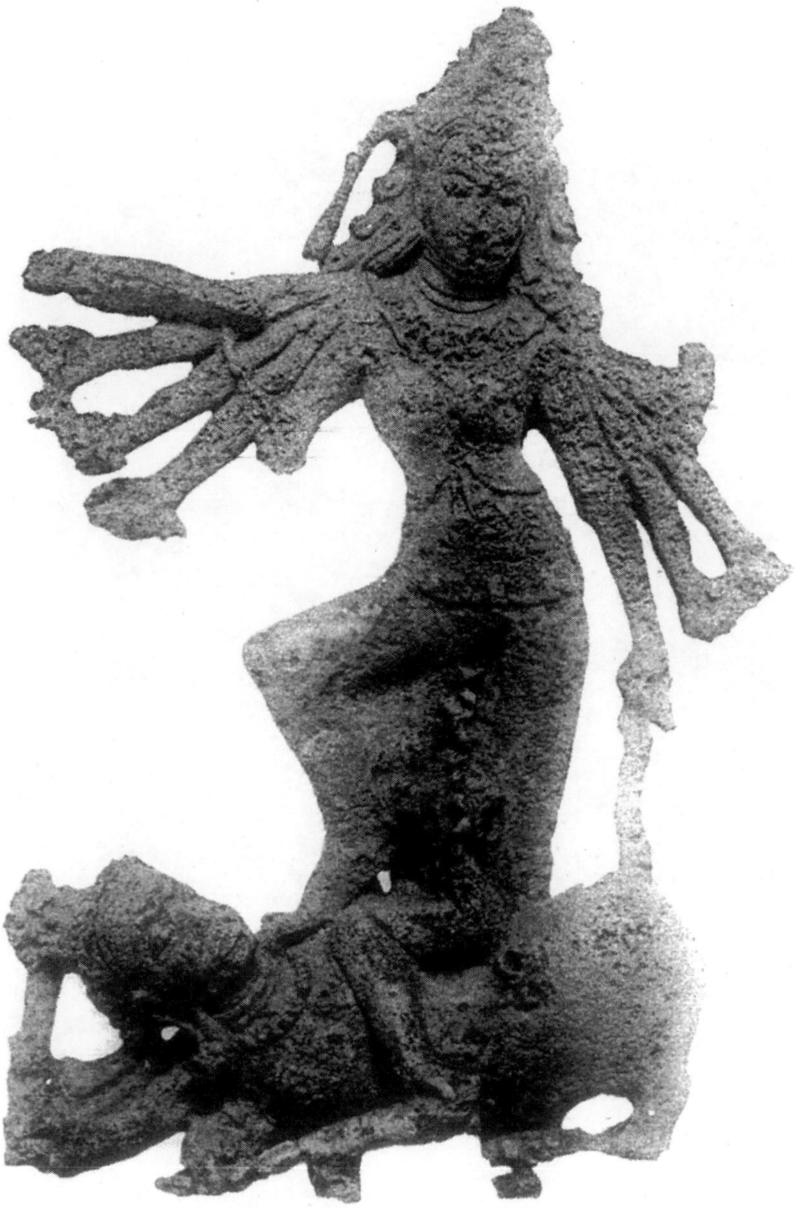

XXXVIII

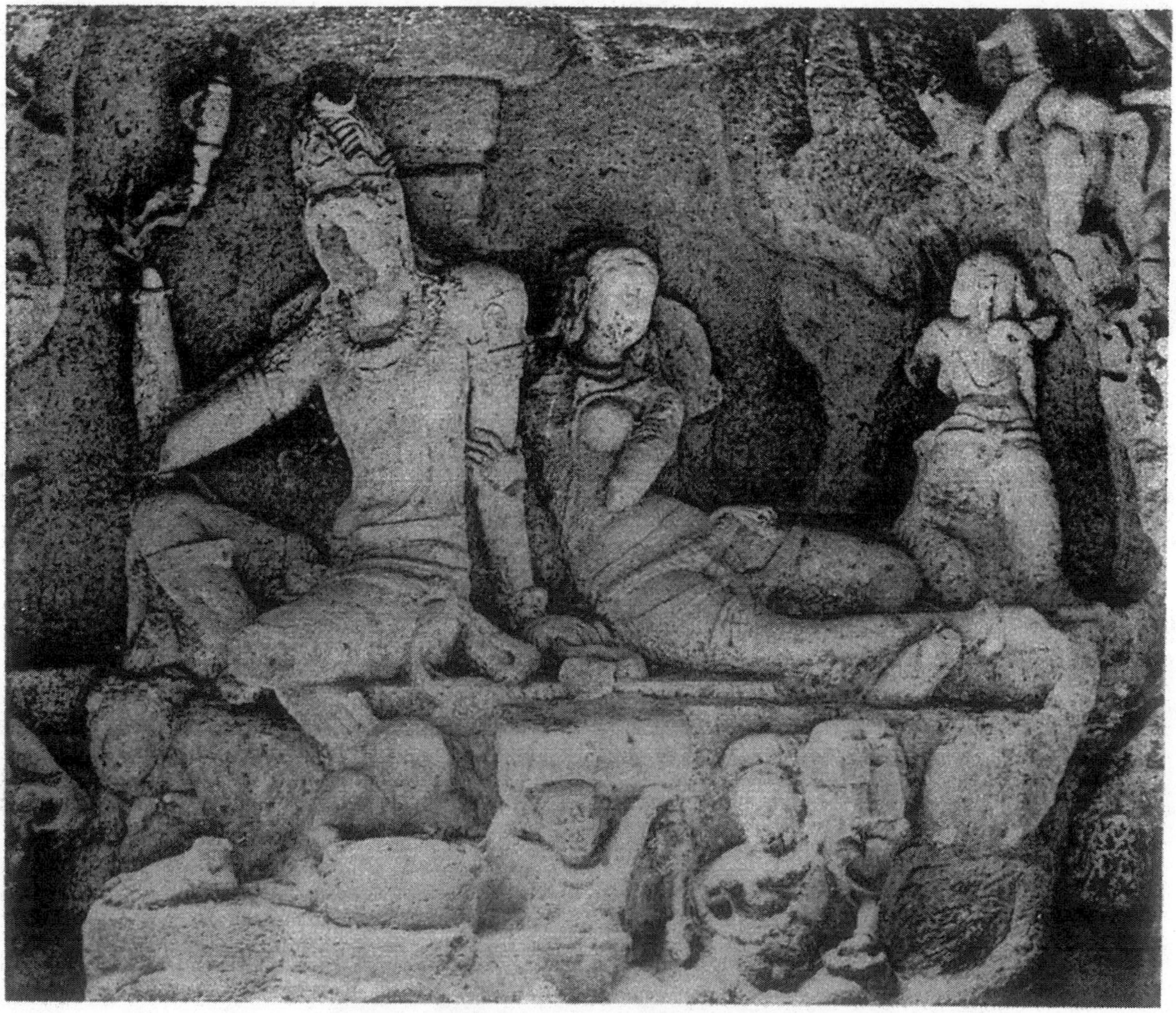

XXXIX

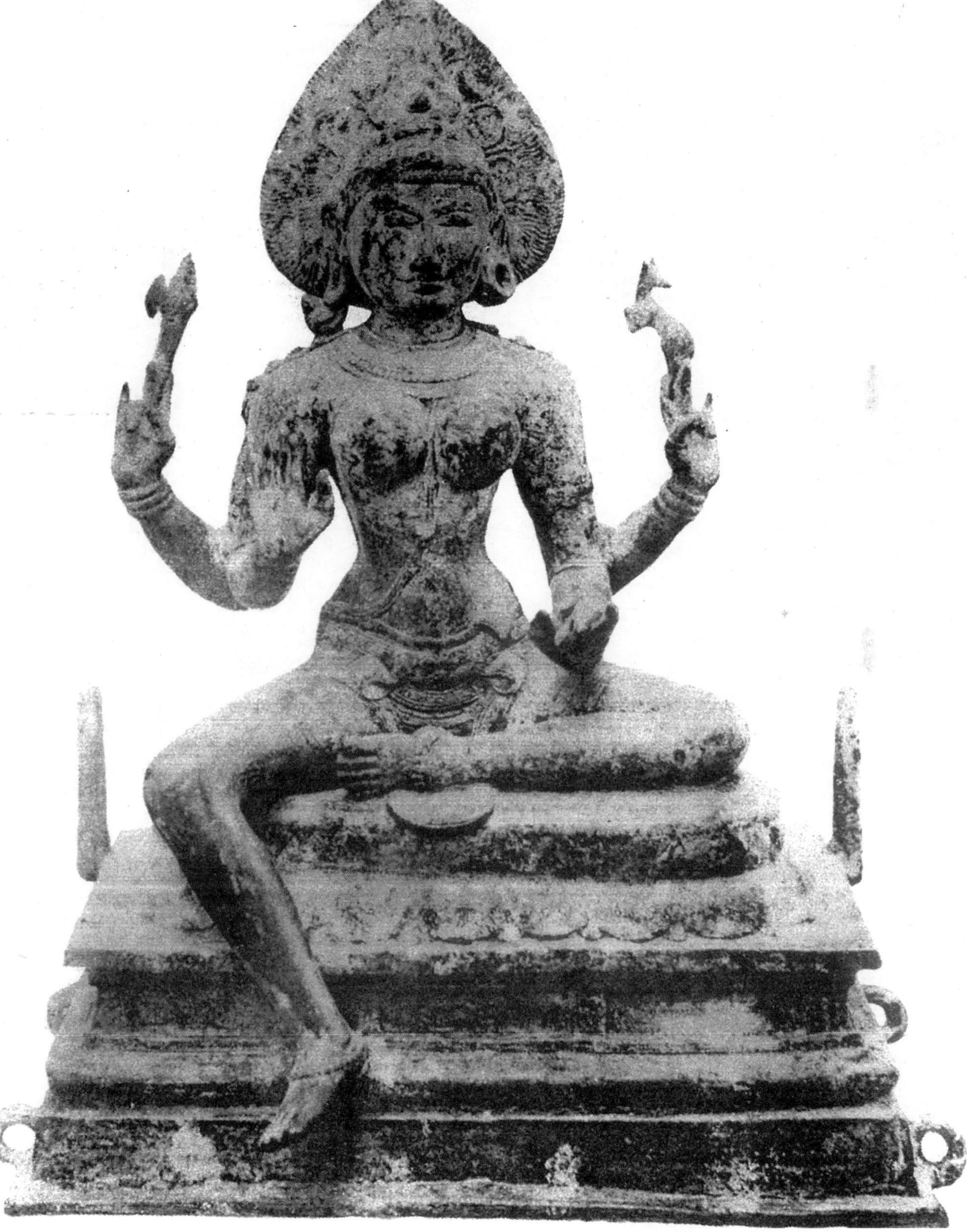

XL

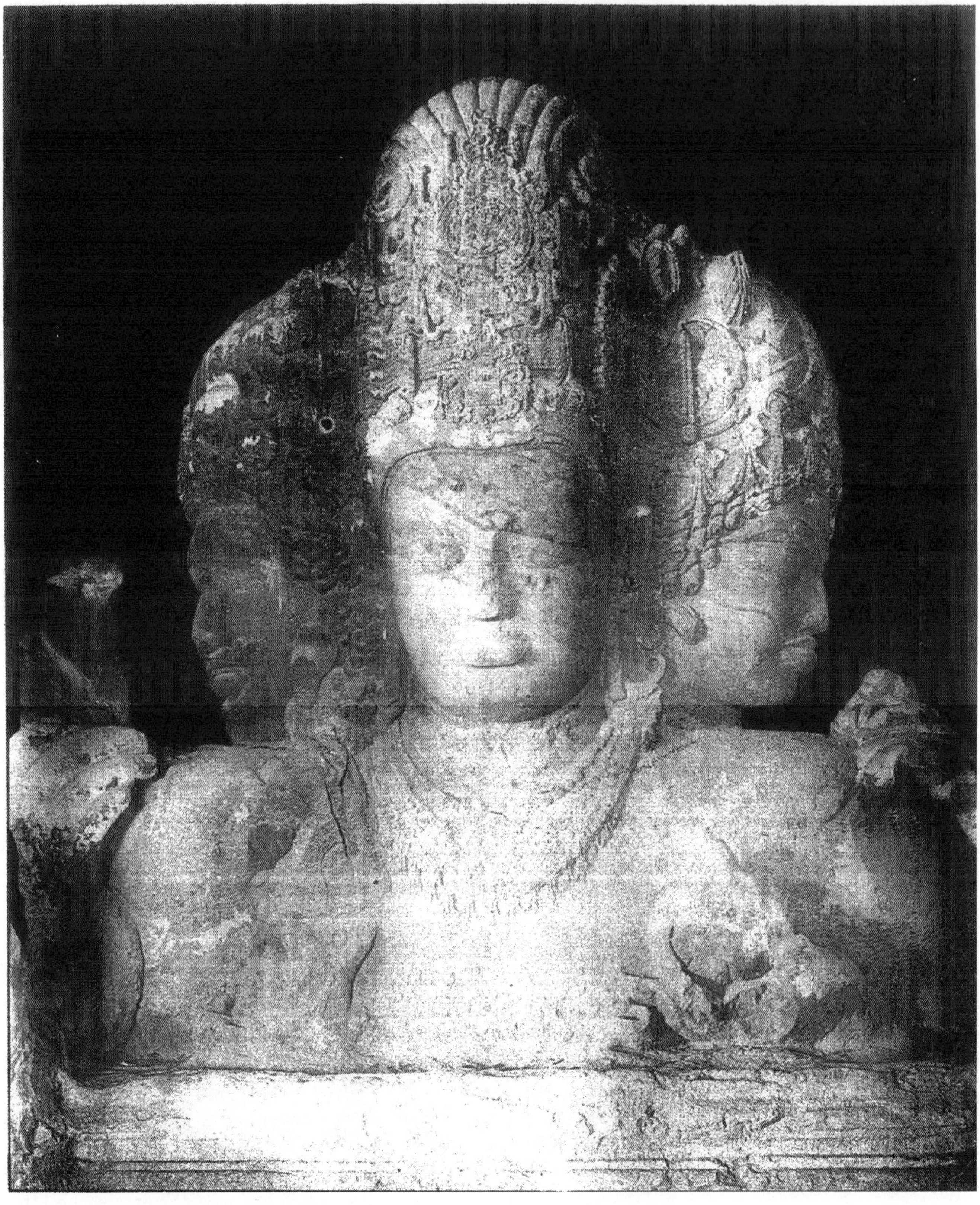

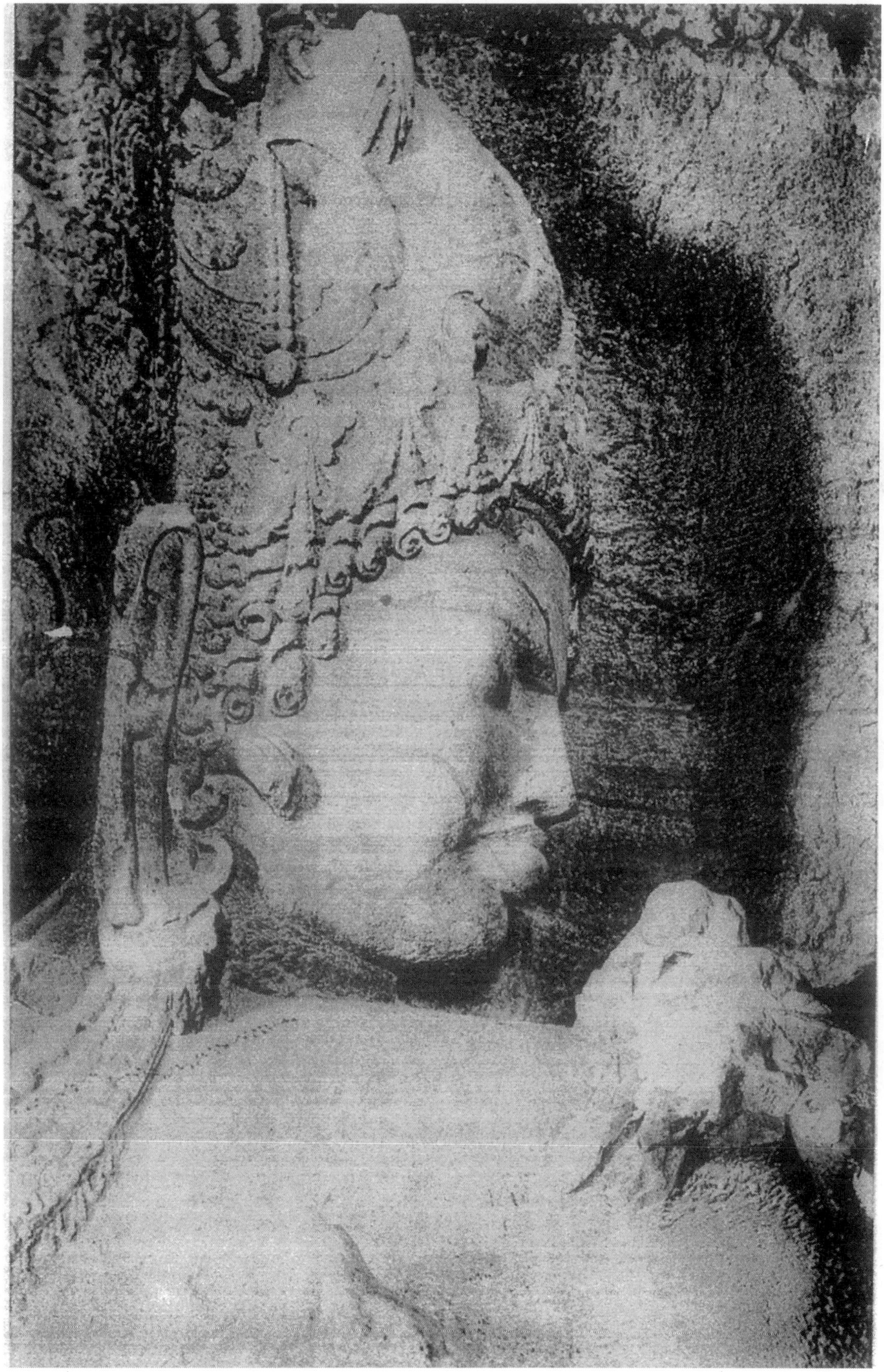

XLII

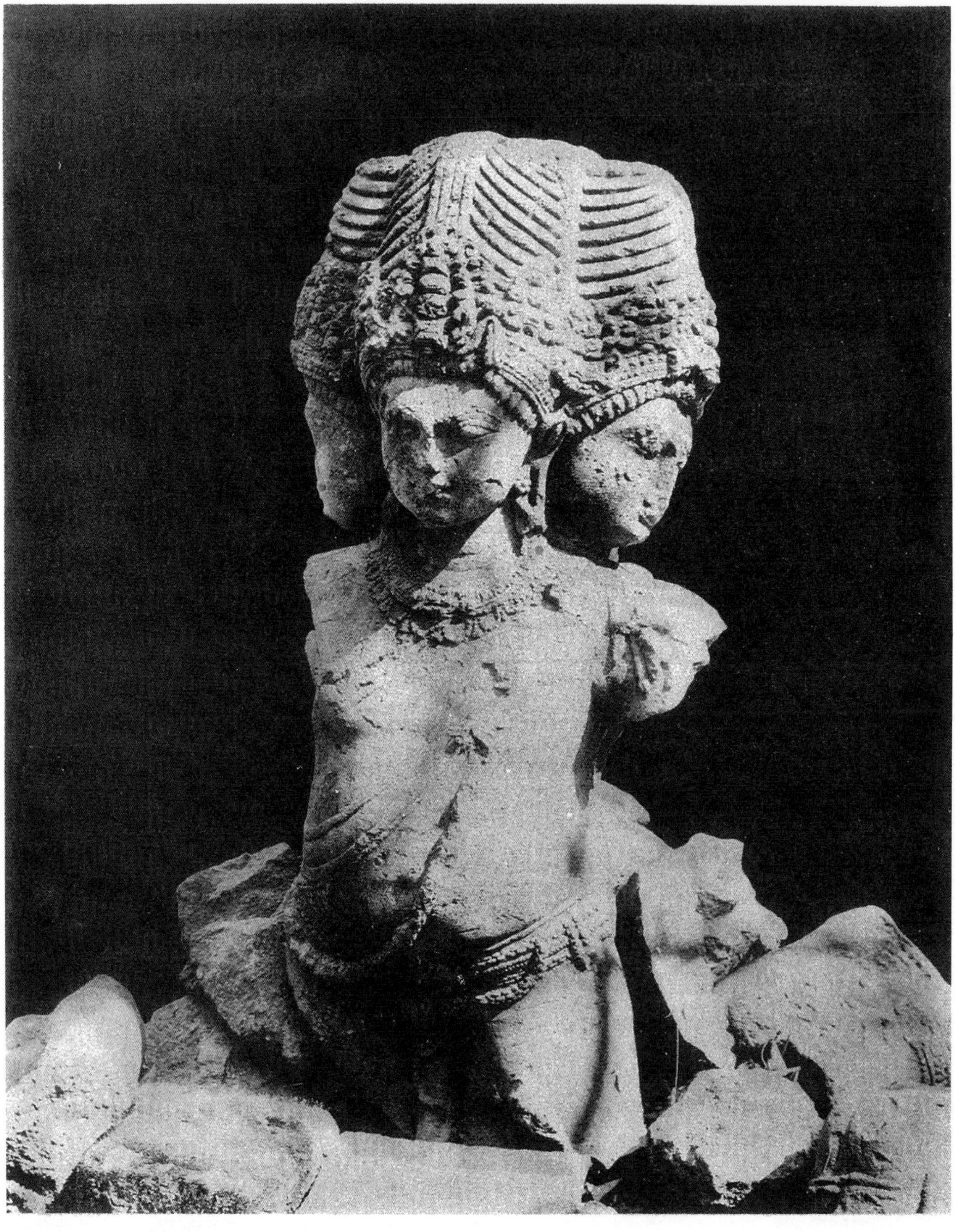

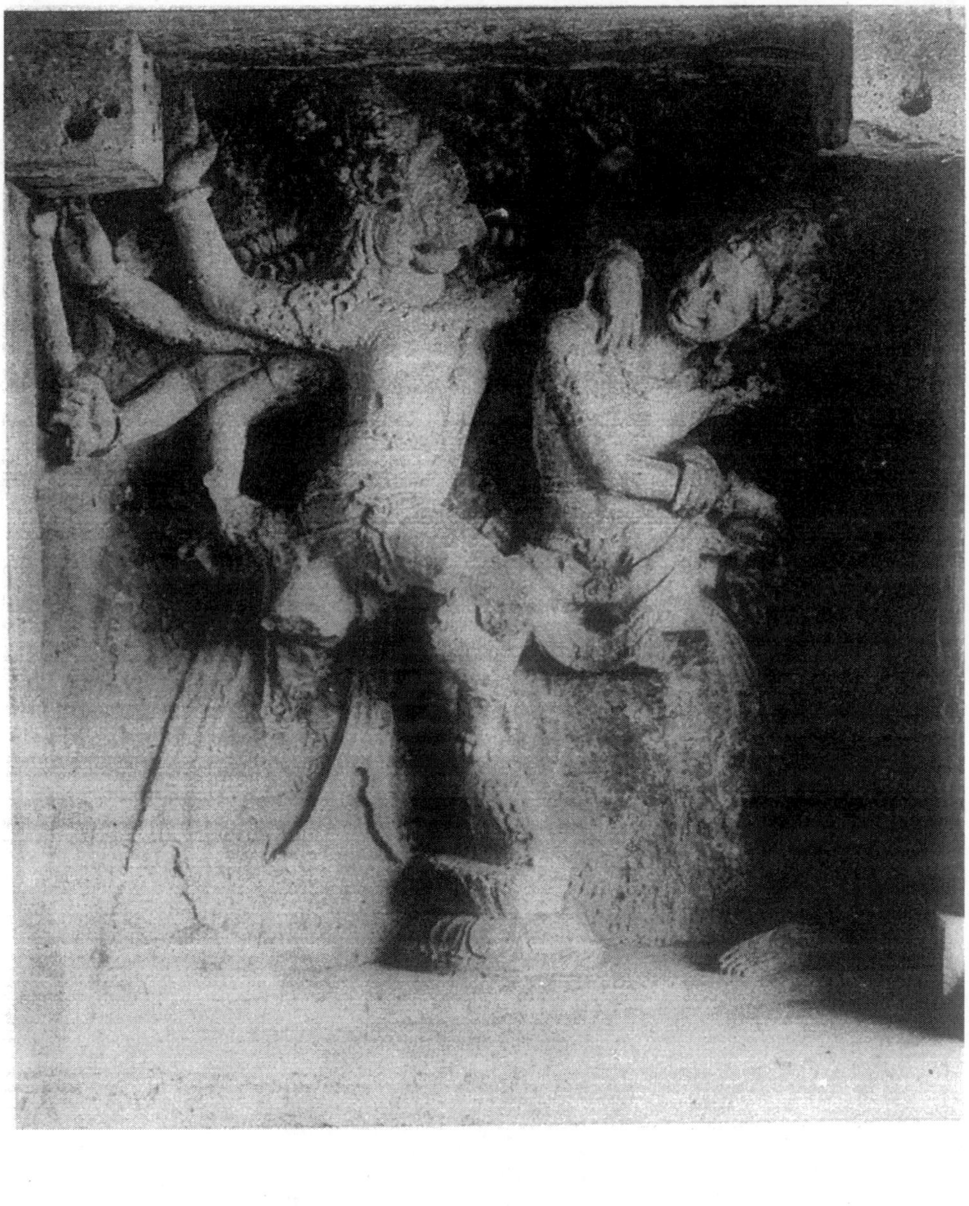

XLIV

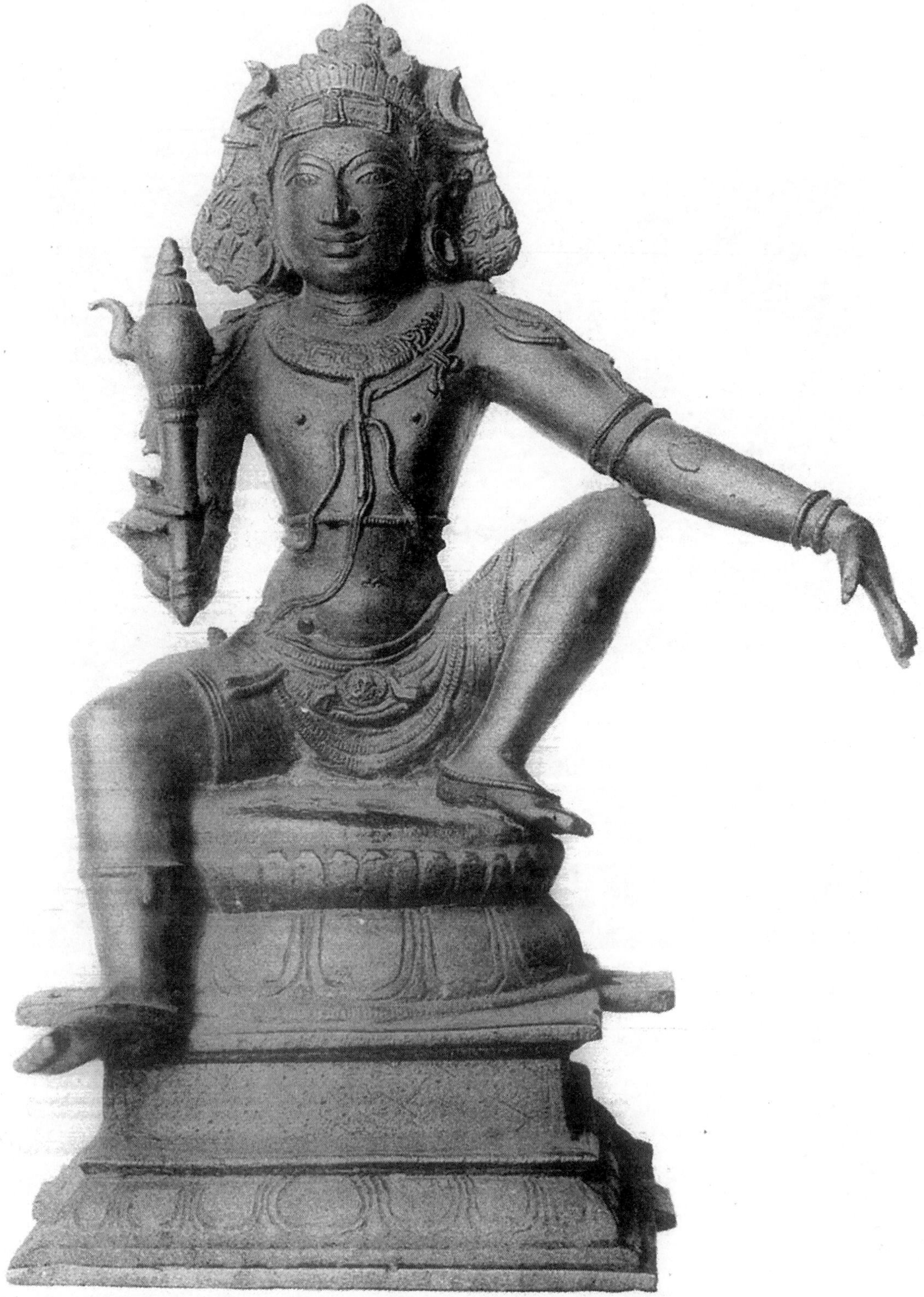

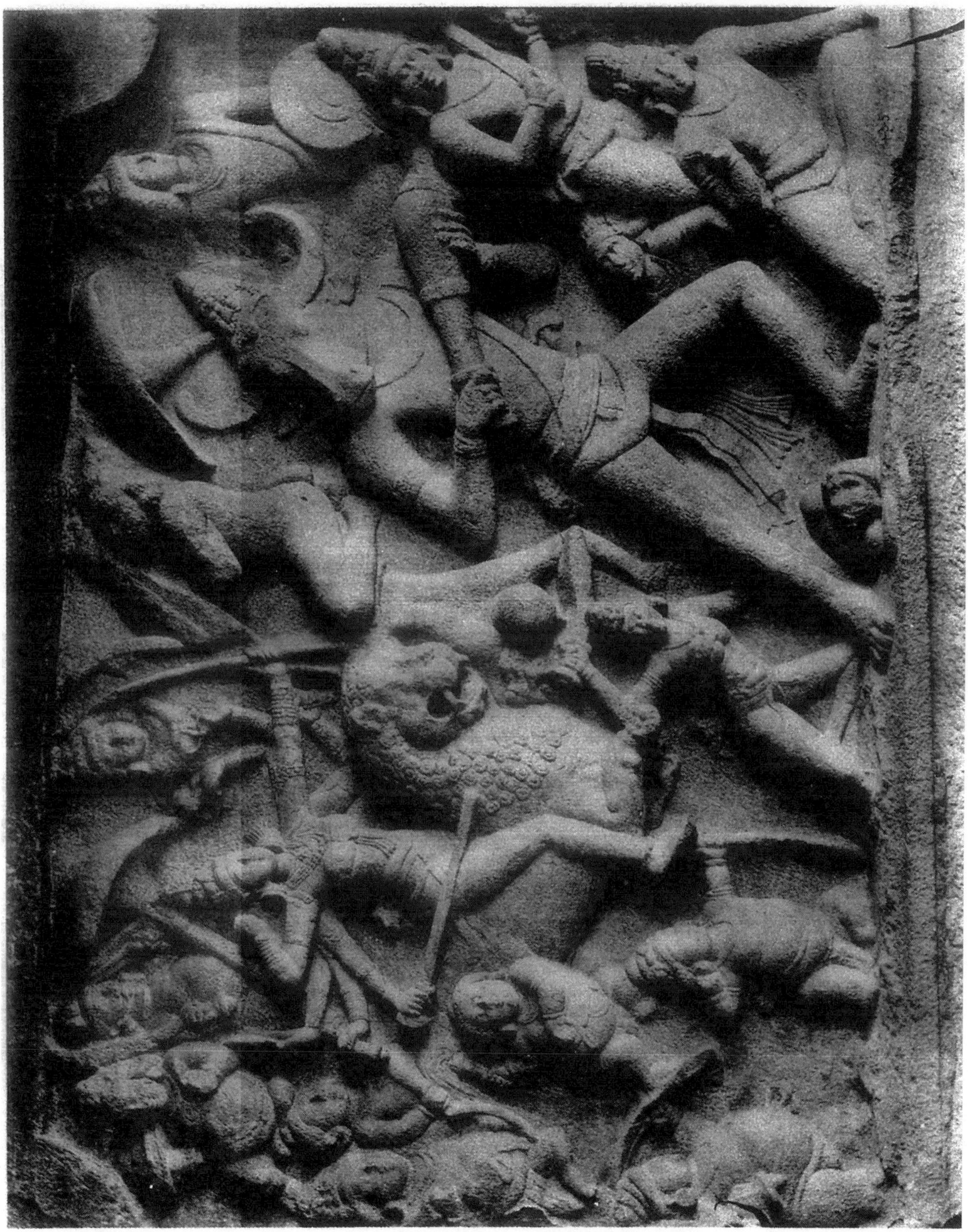

XLVI

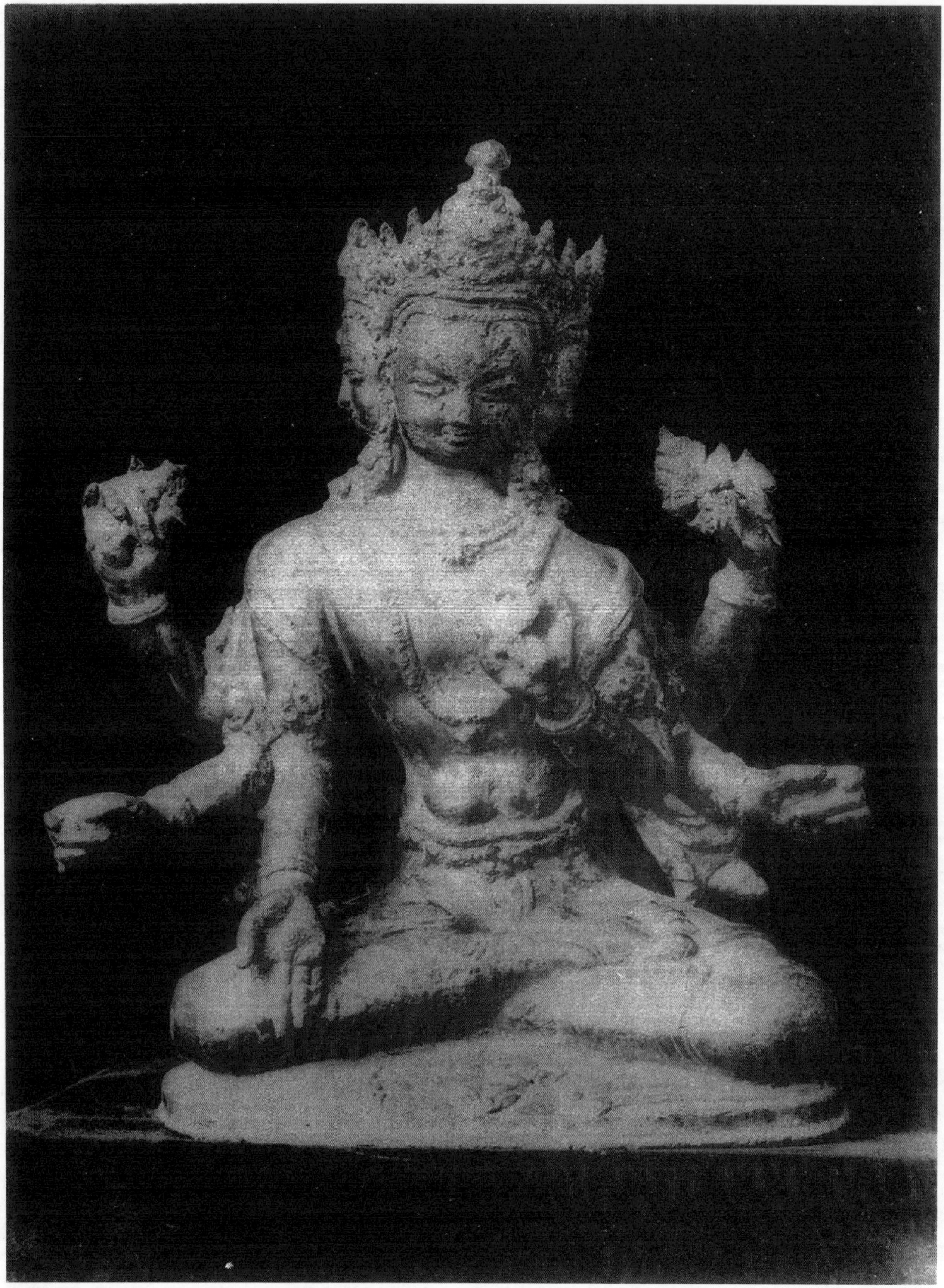

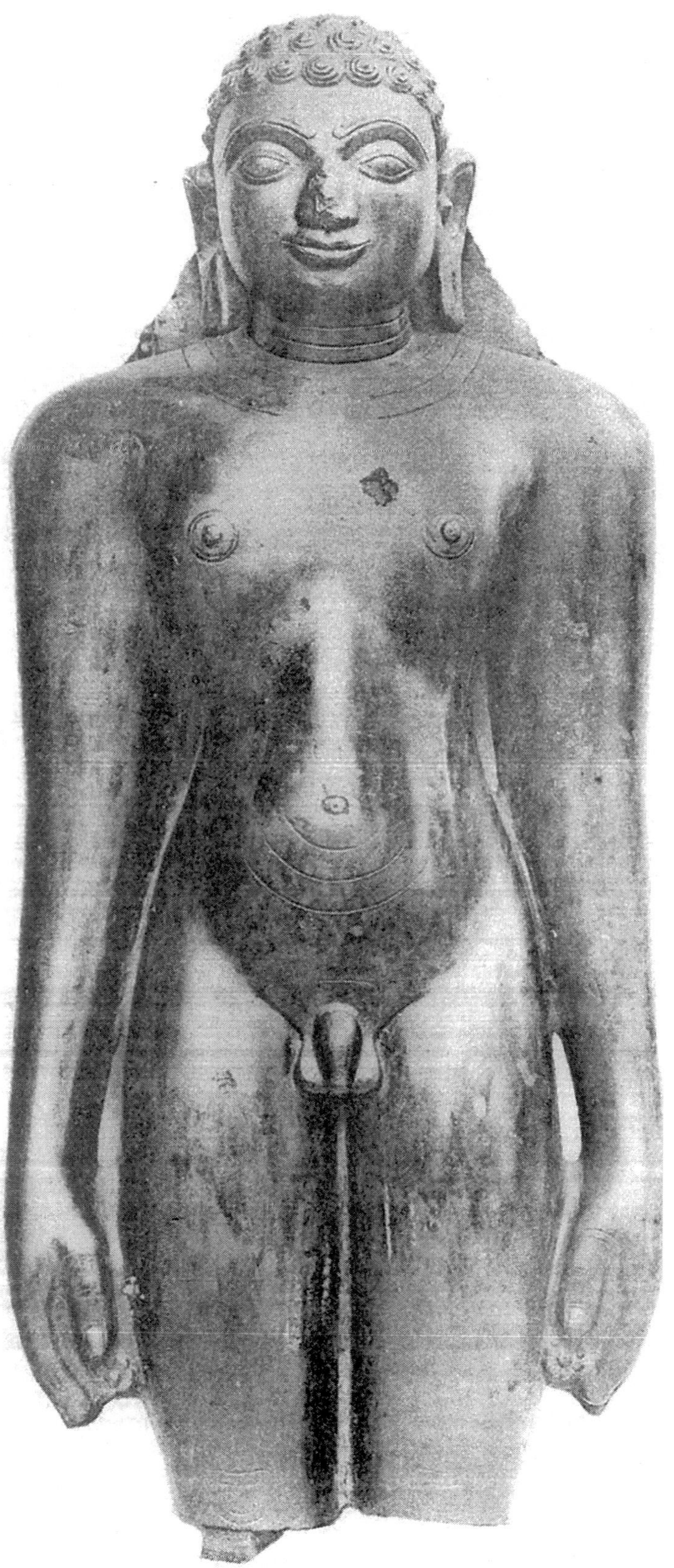

XLVIII

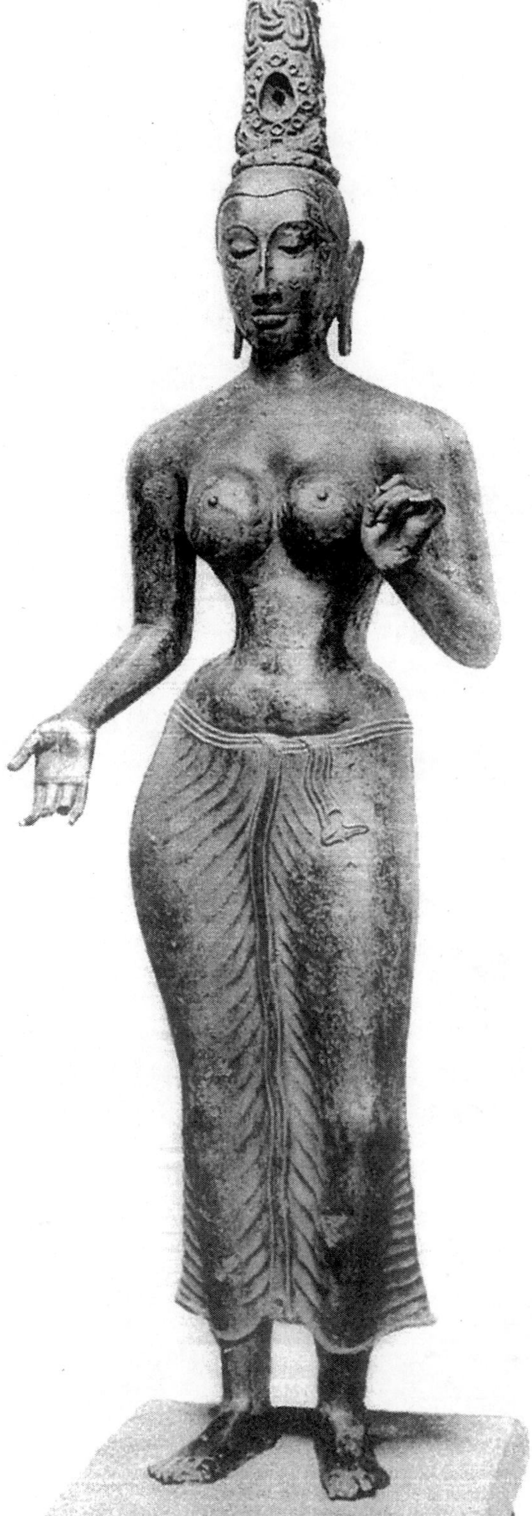

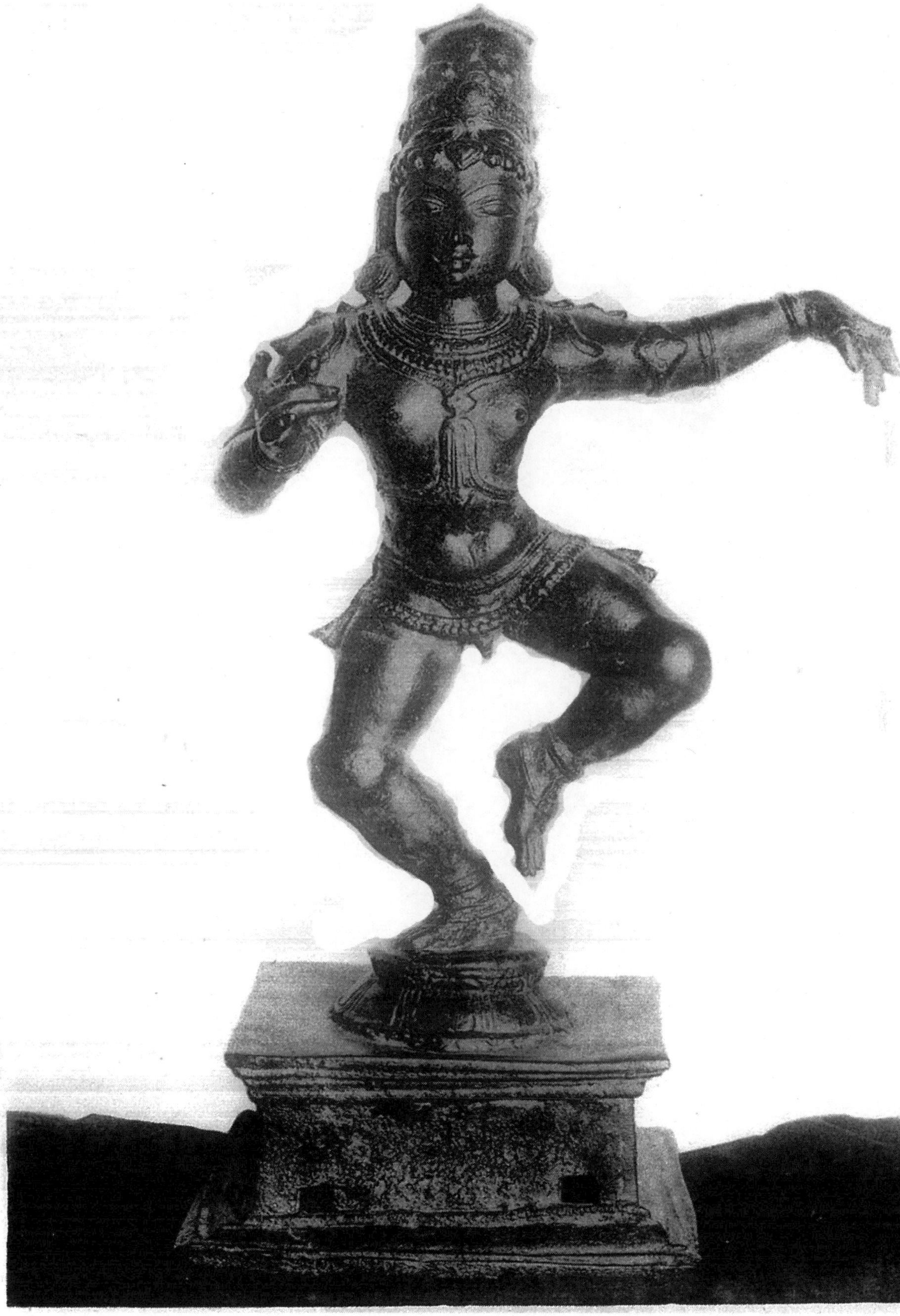

L

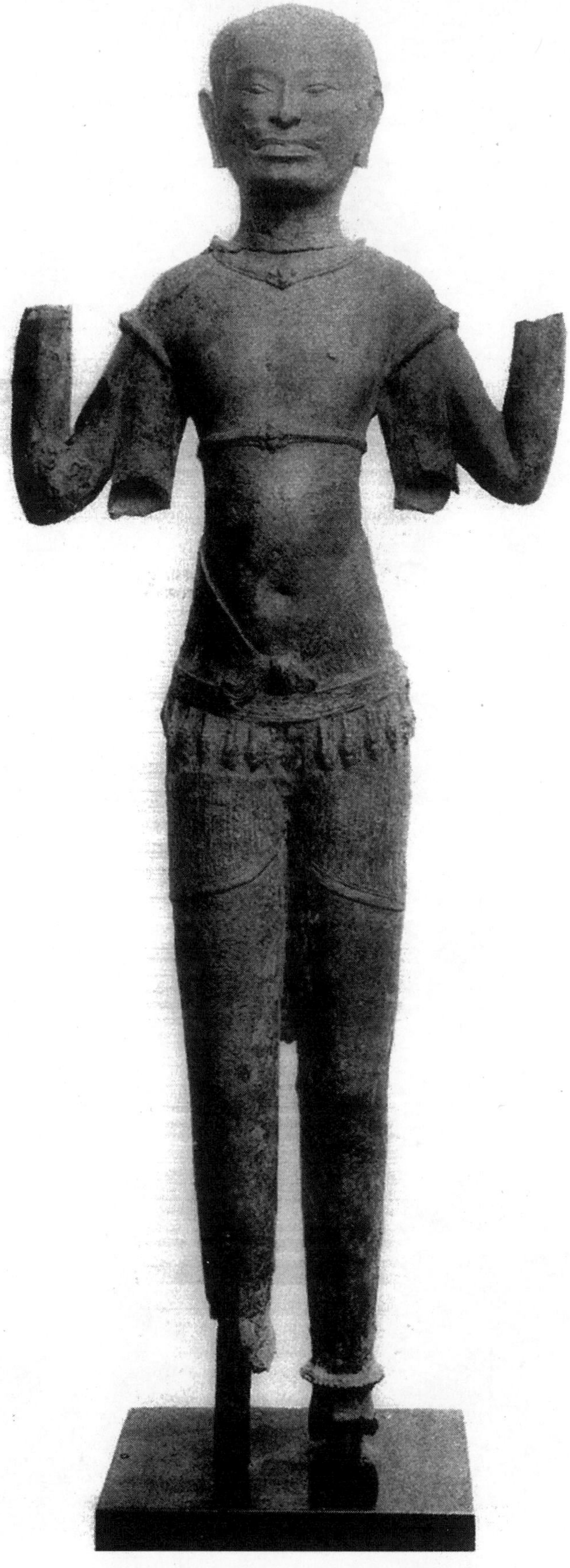

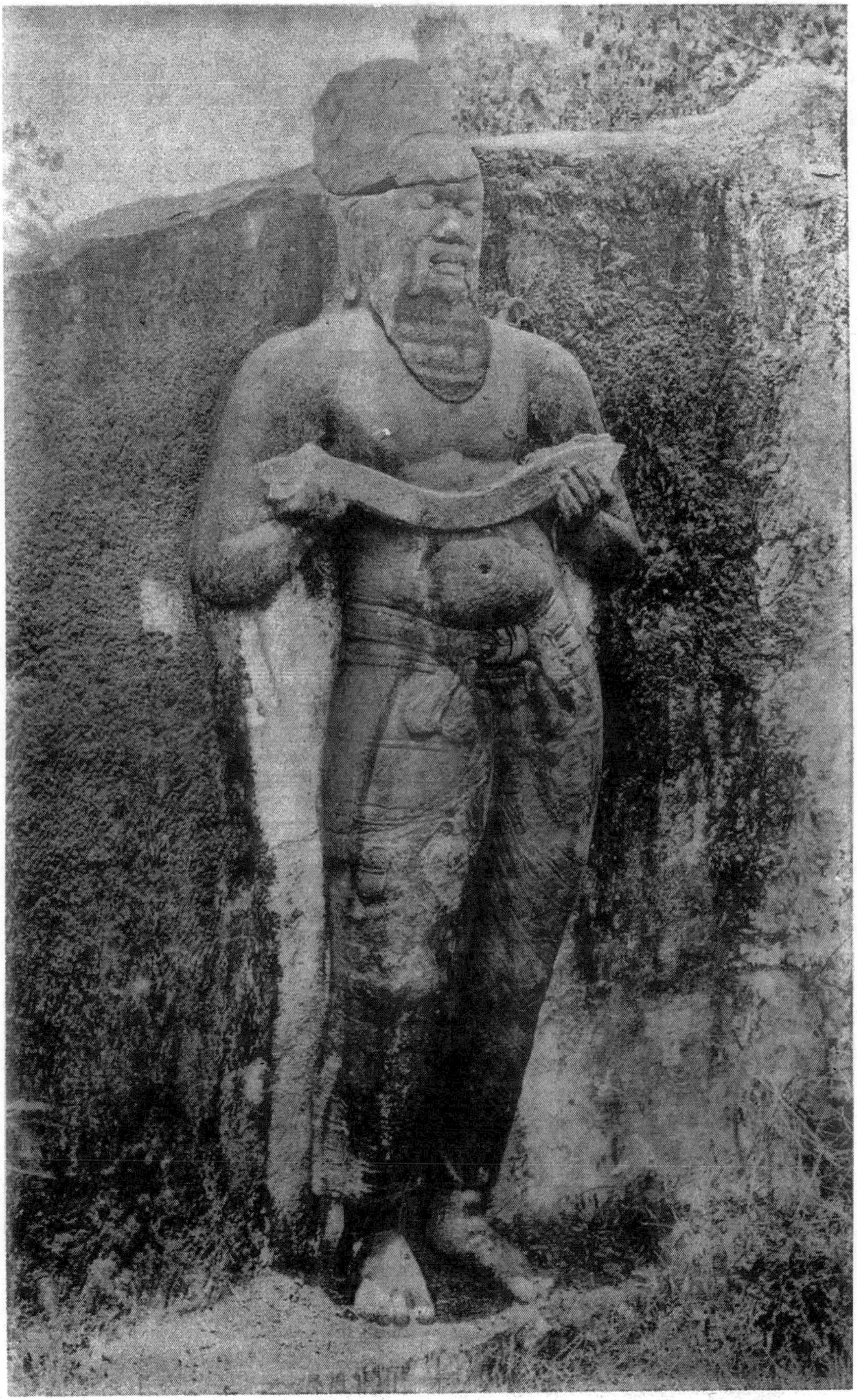

LII

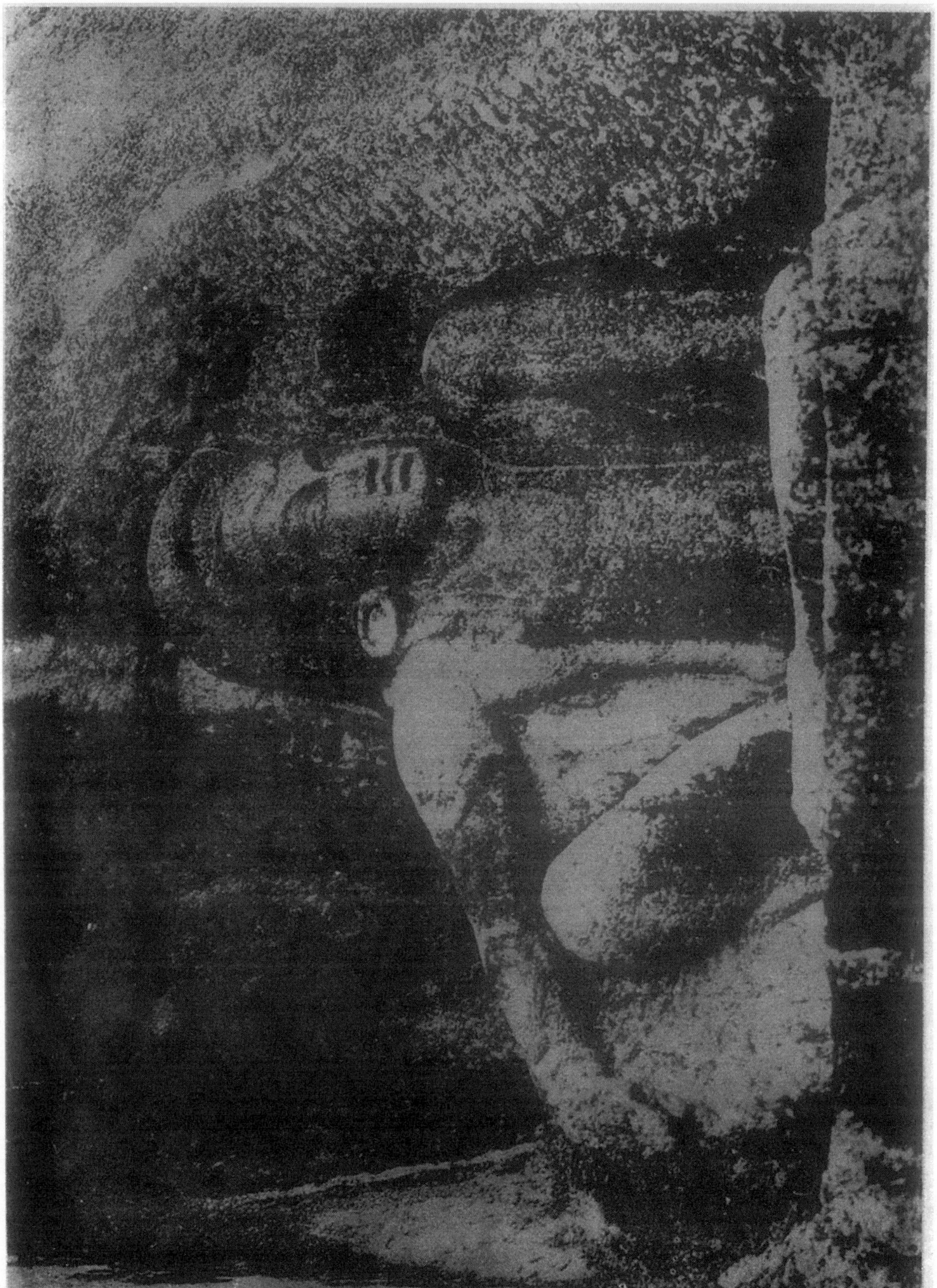

LIII

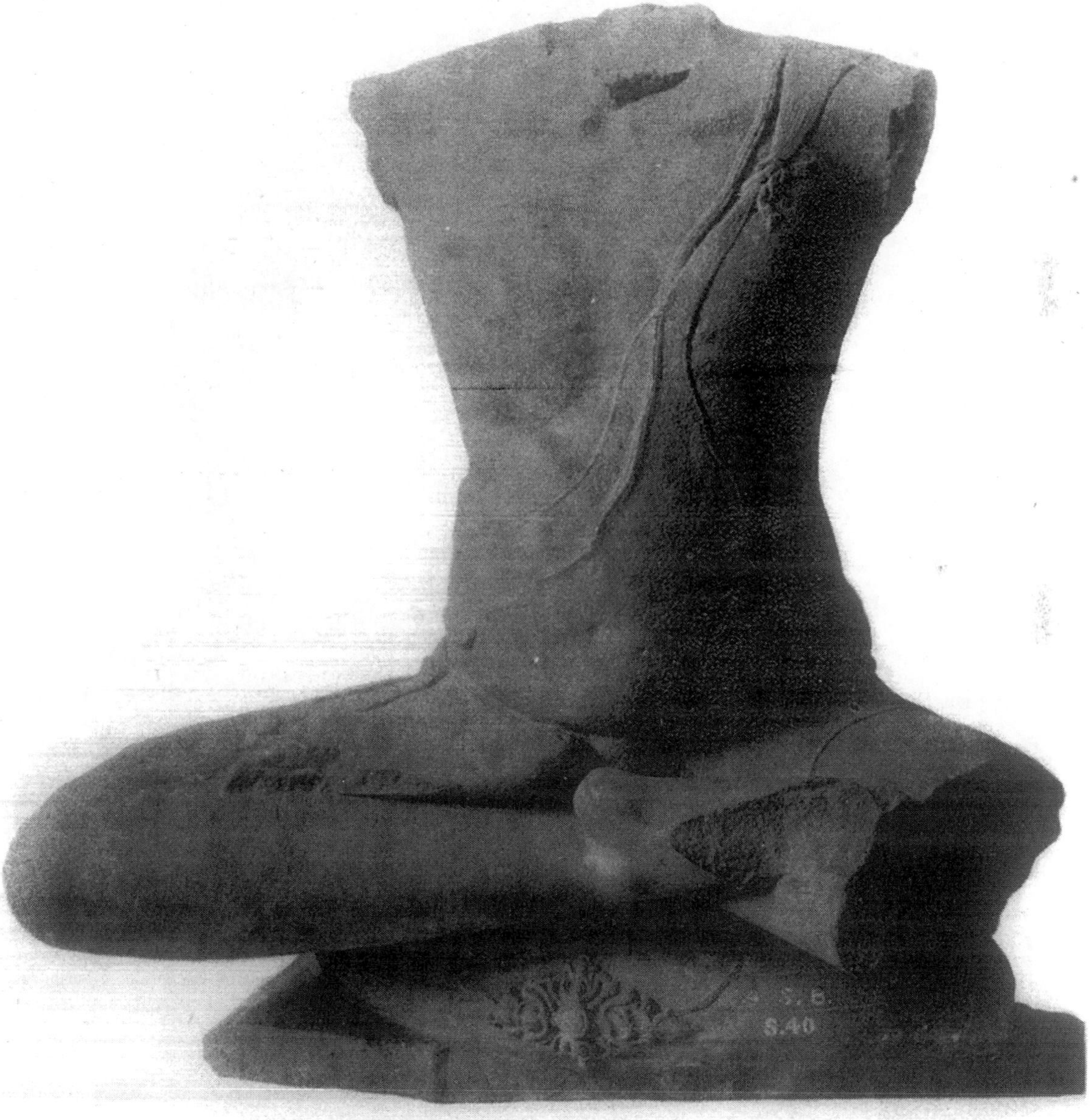

LIV

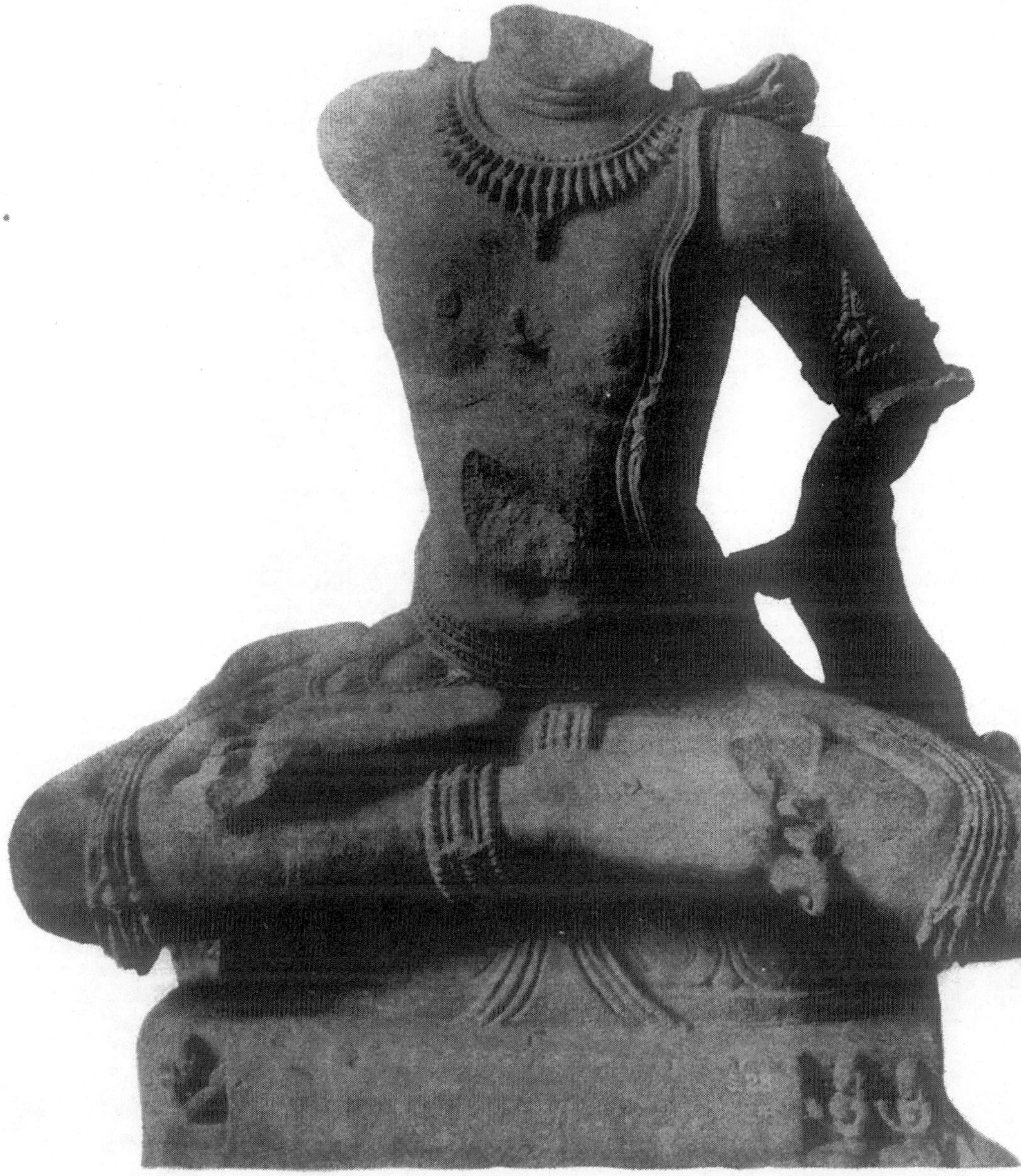

LV

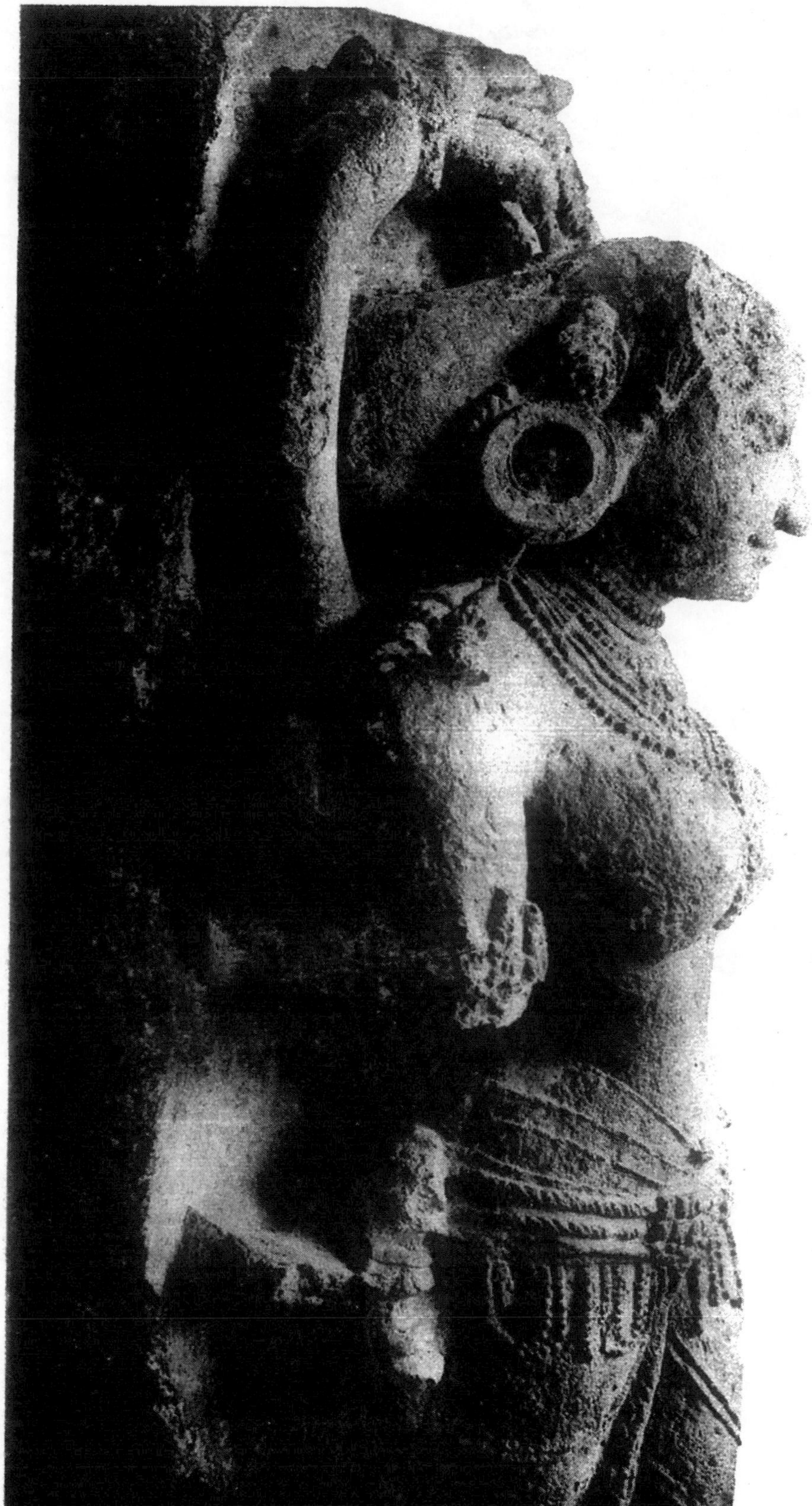

LVI

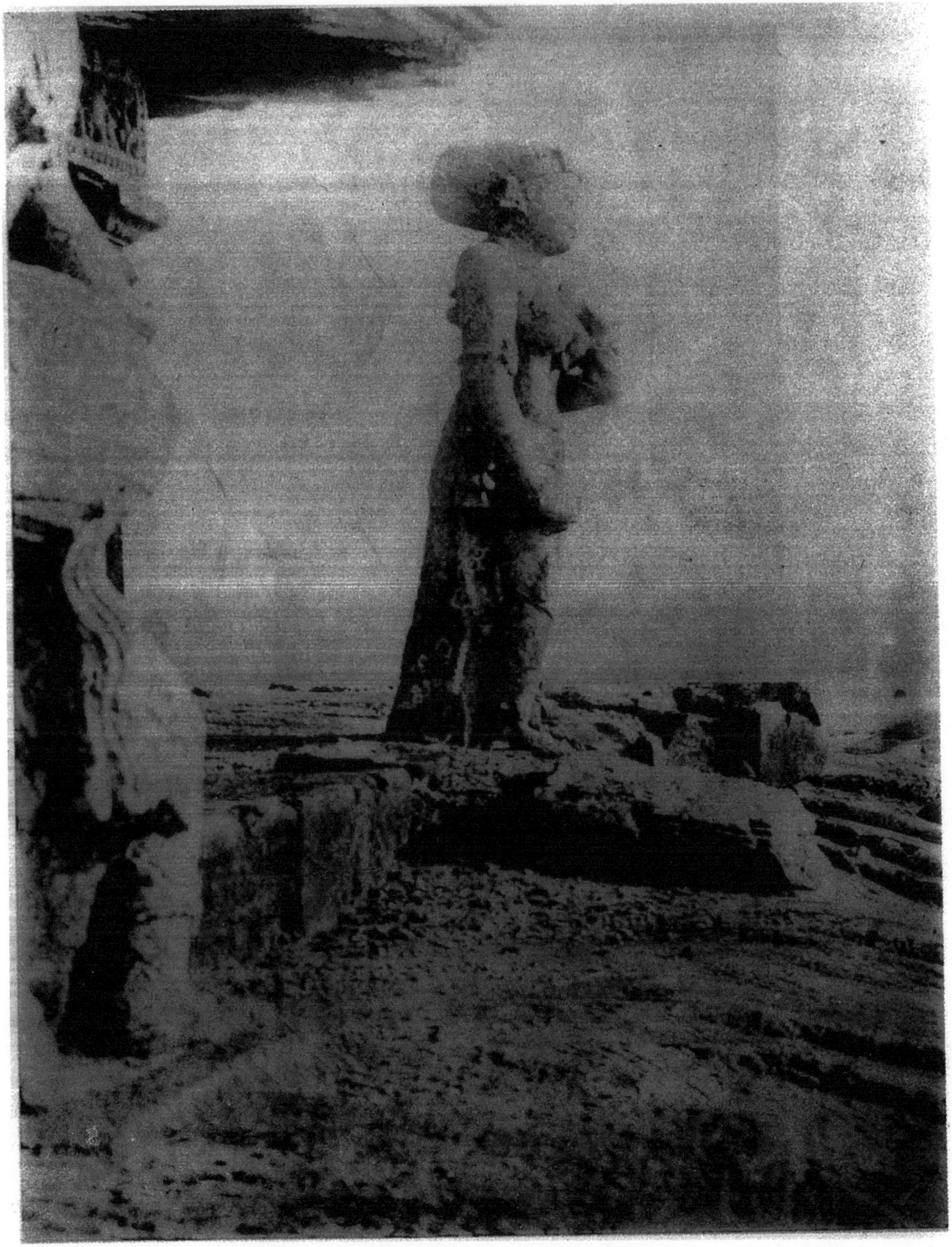

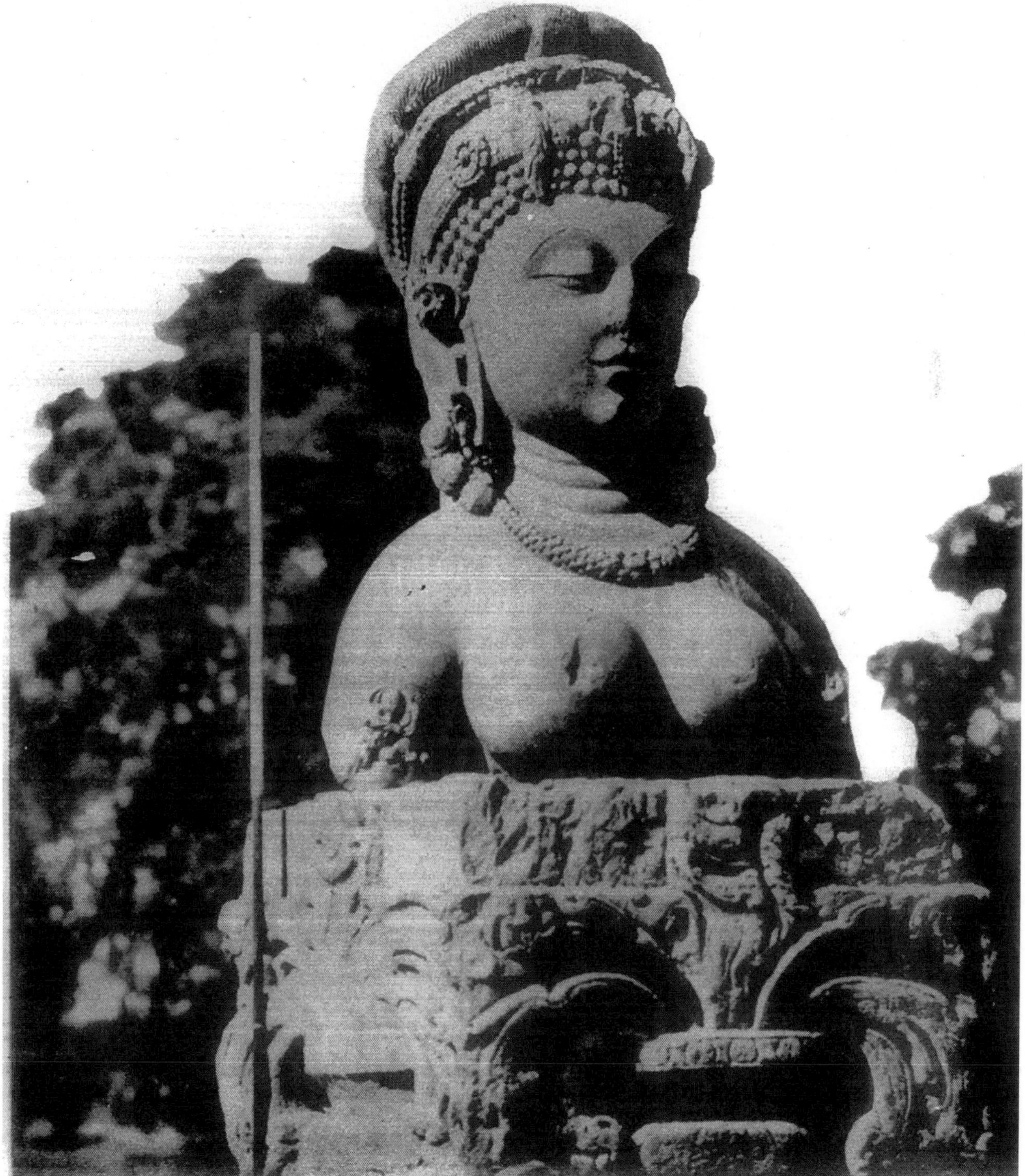

LVIII

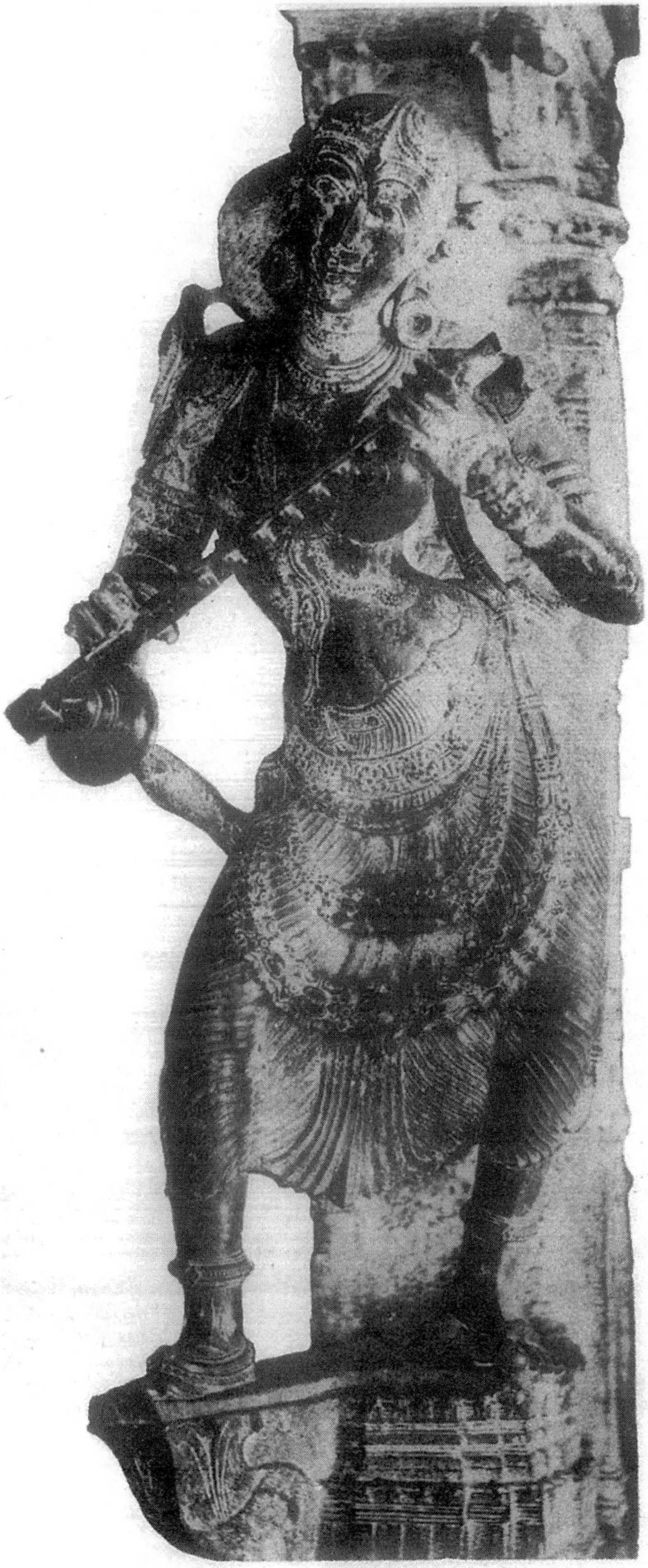

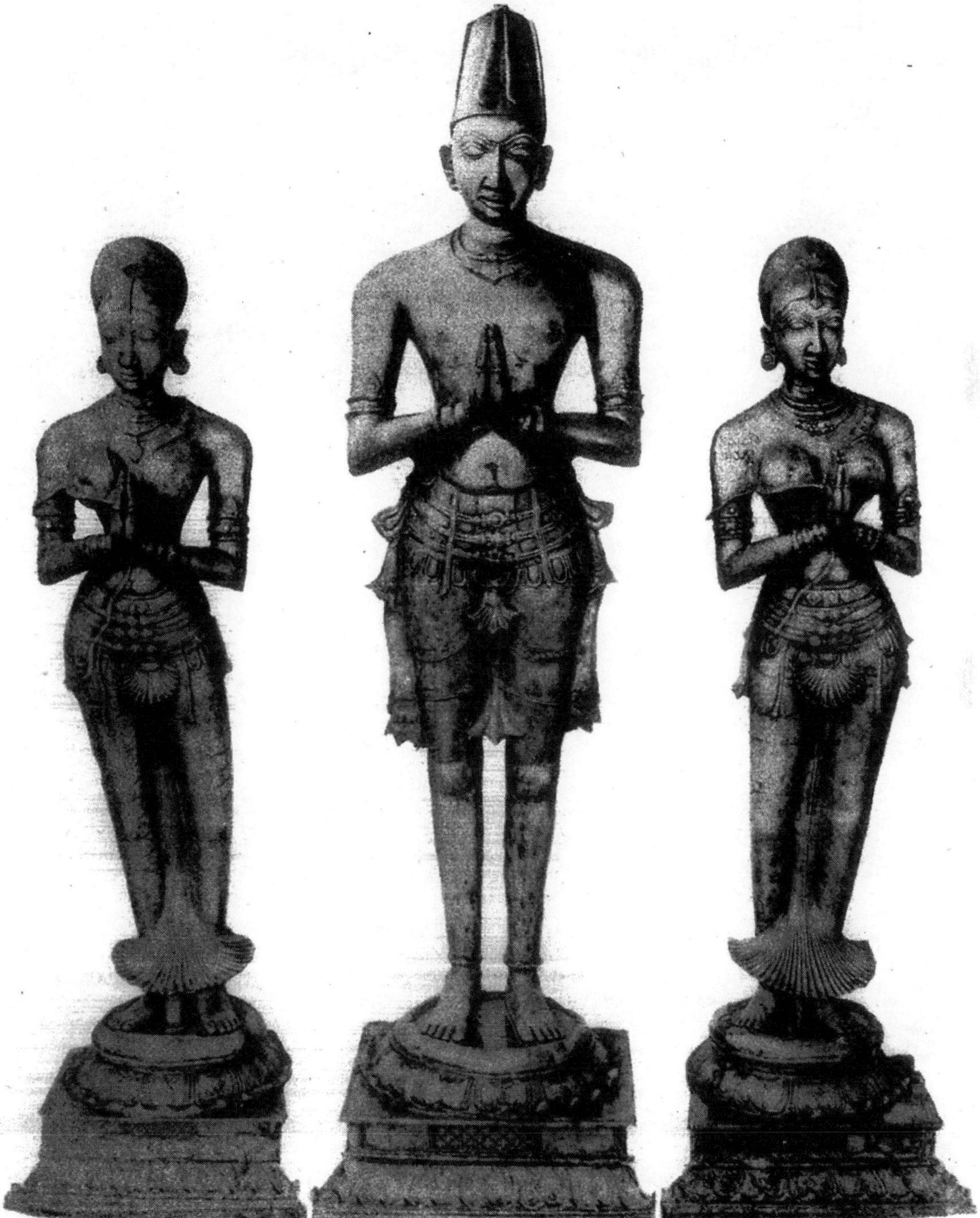

LX

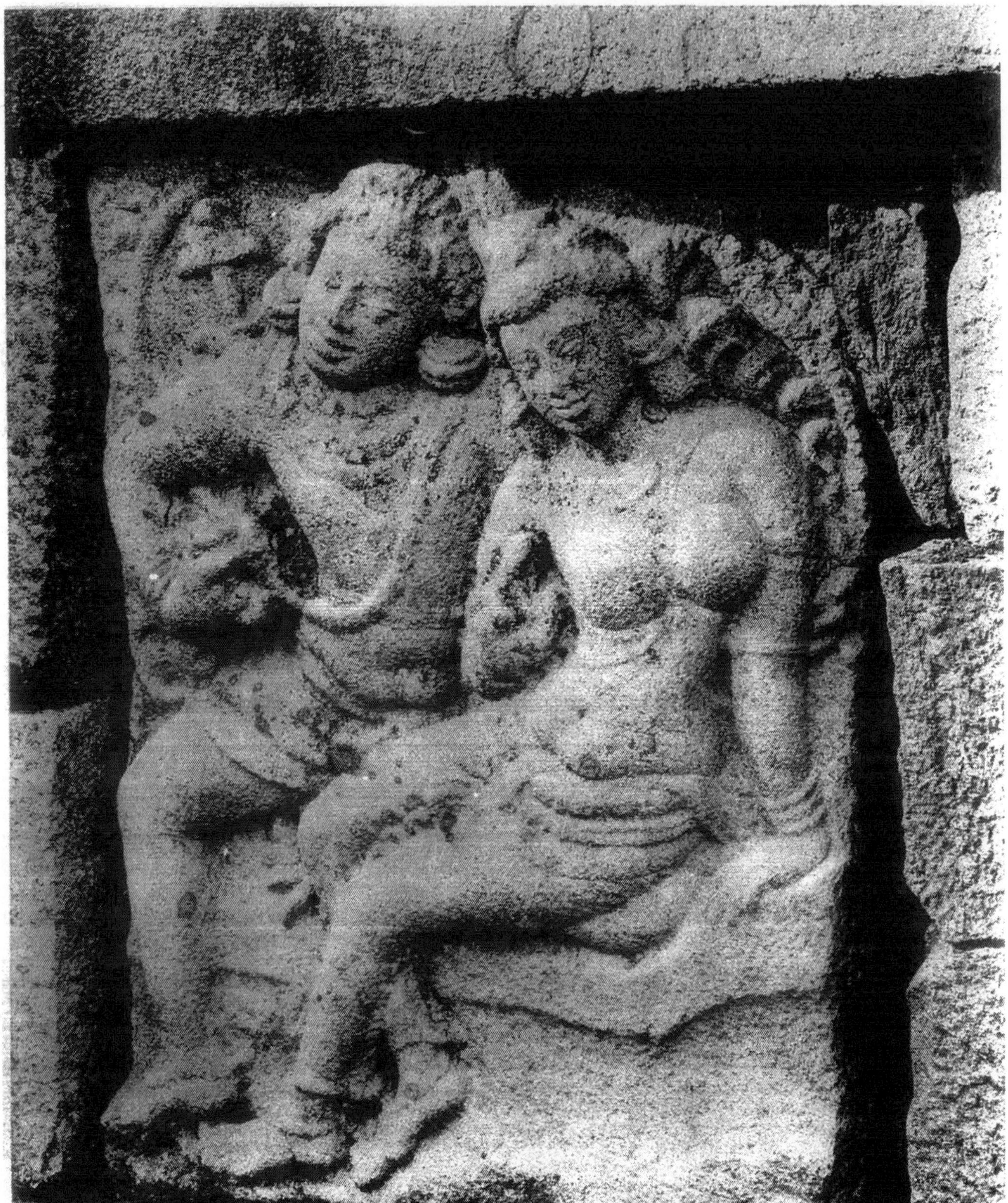

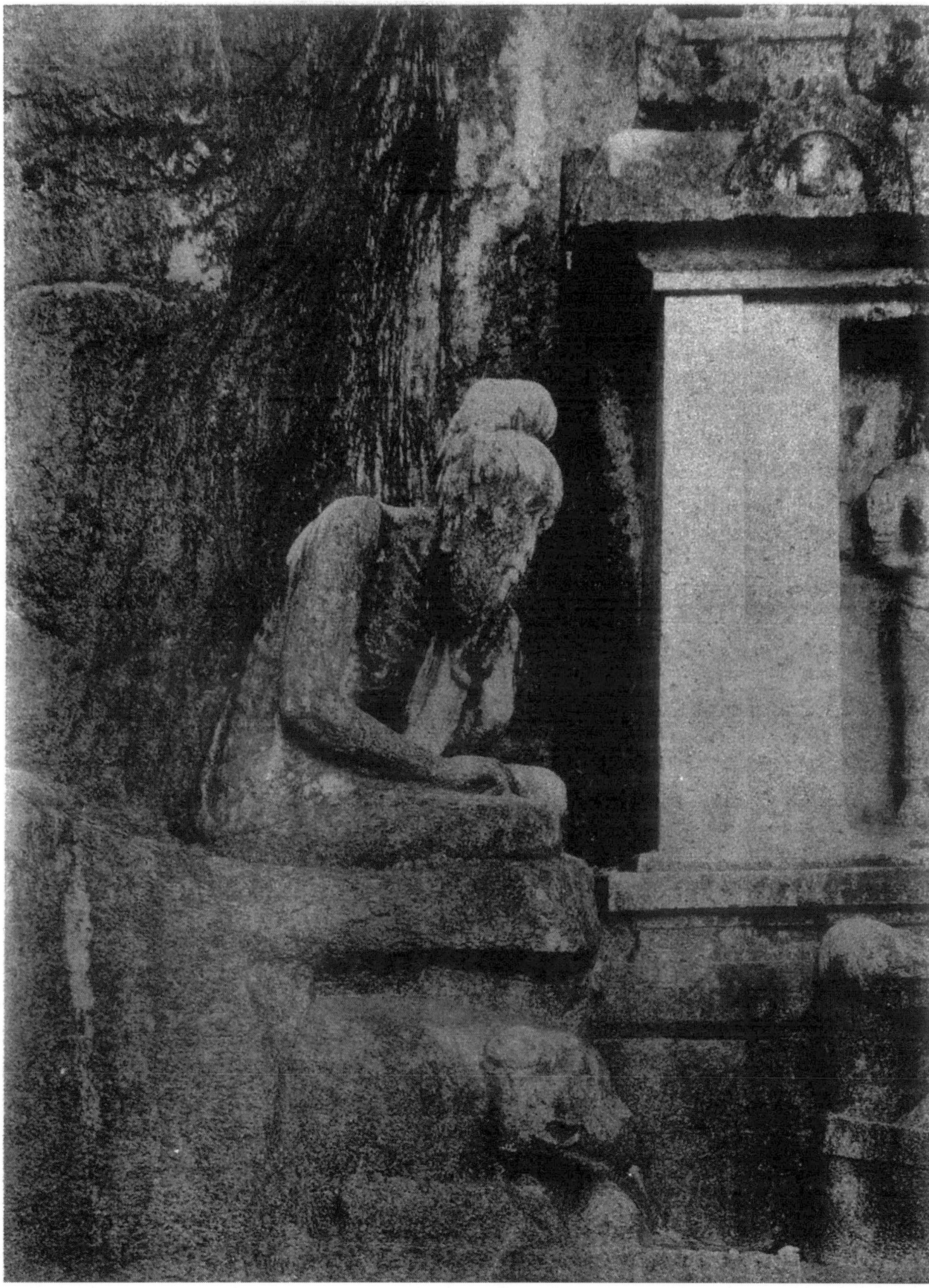

LXII

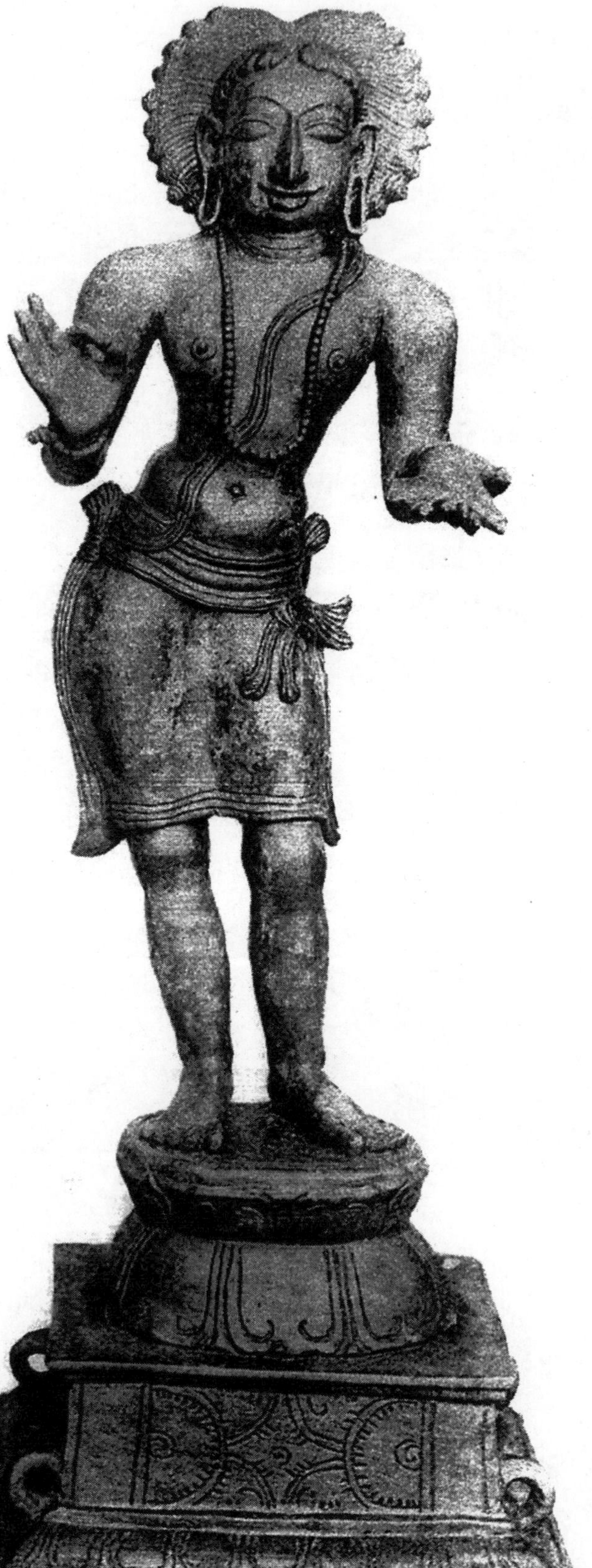

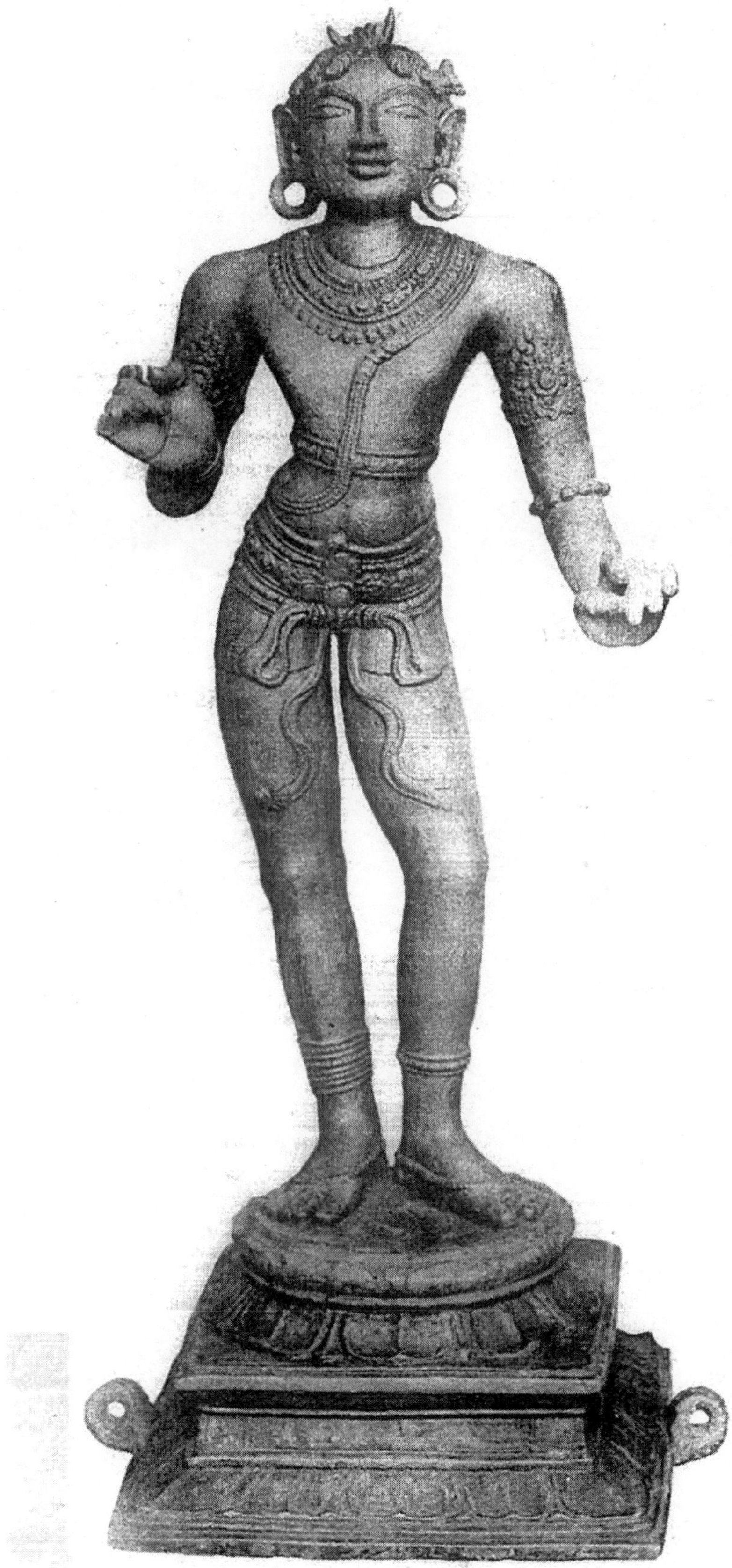

LXIV

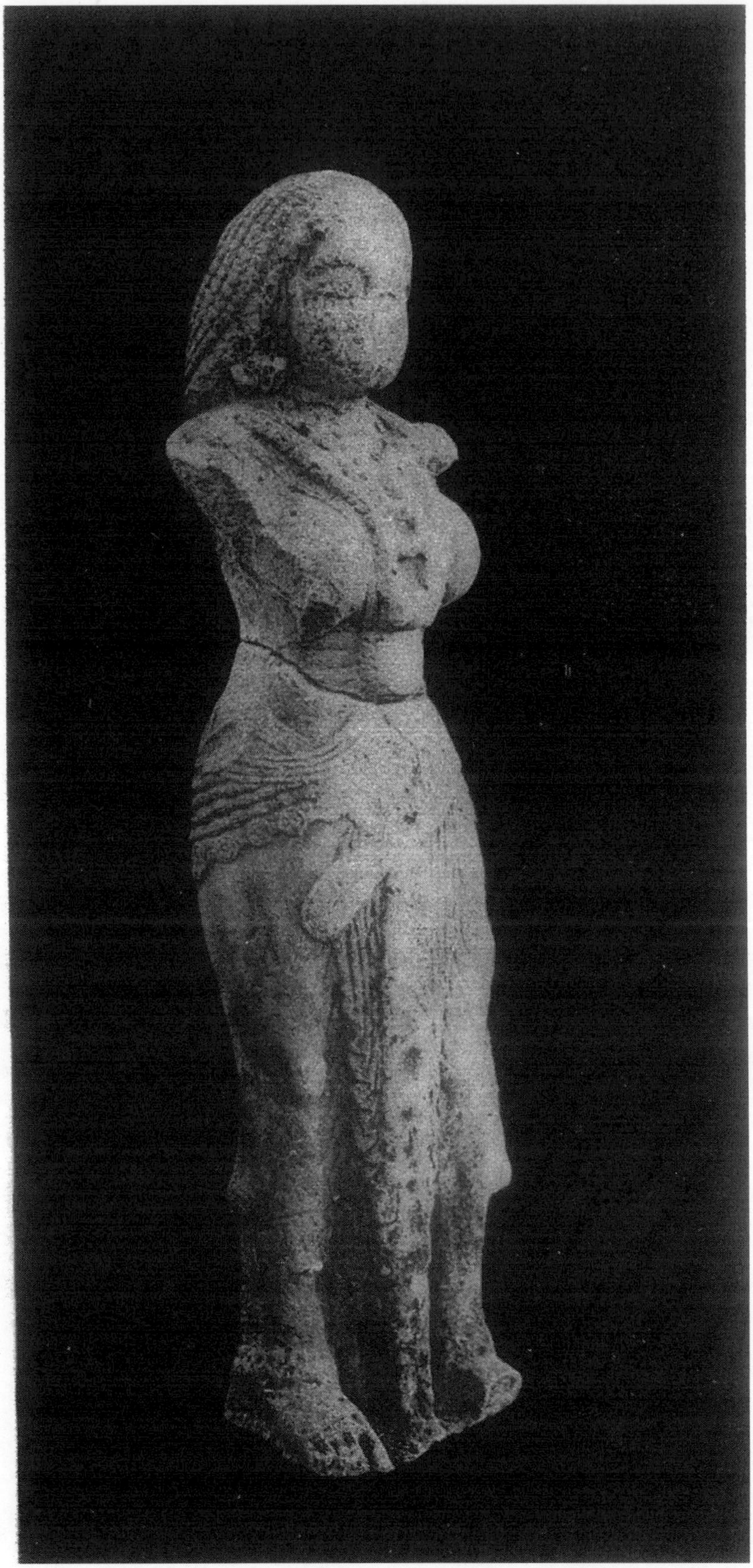

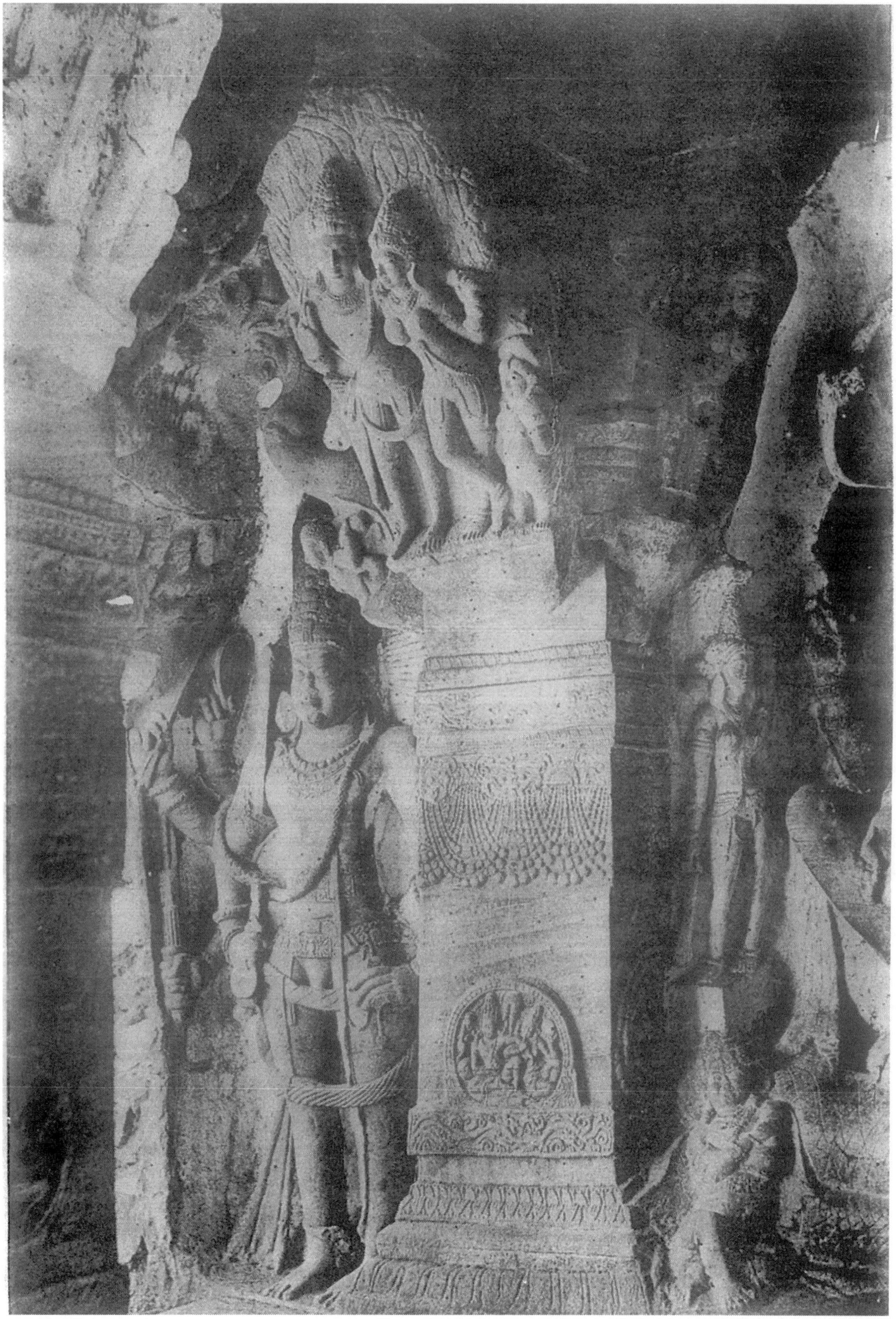

LXVI

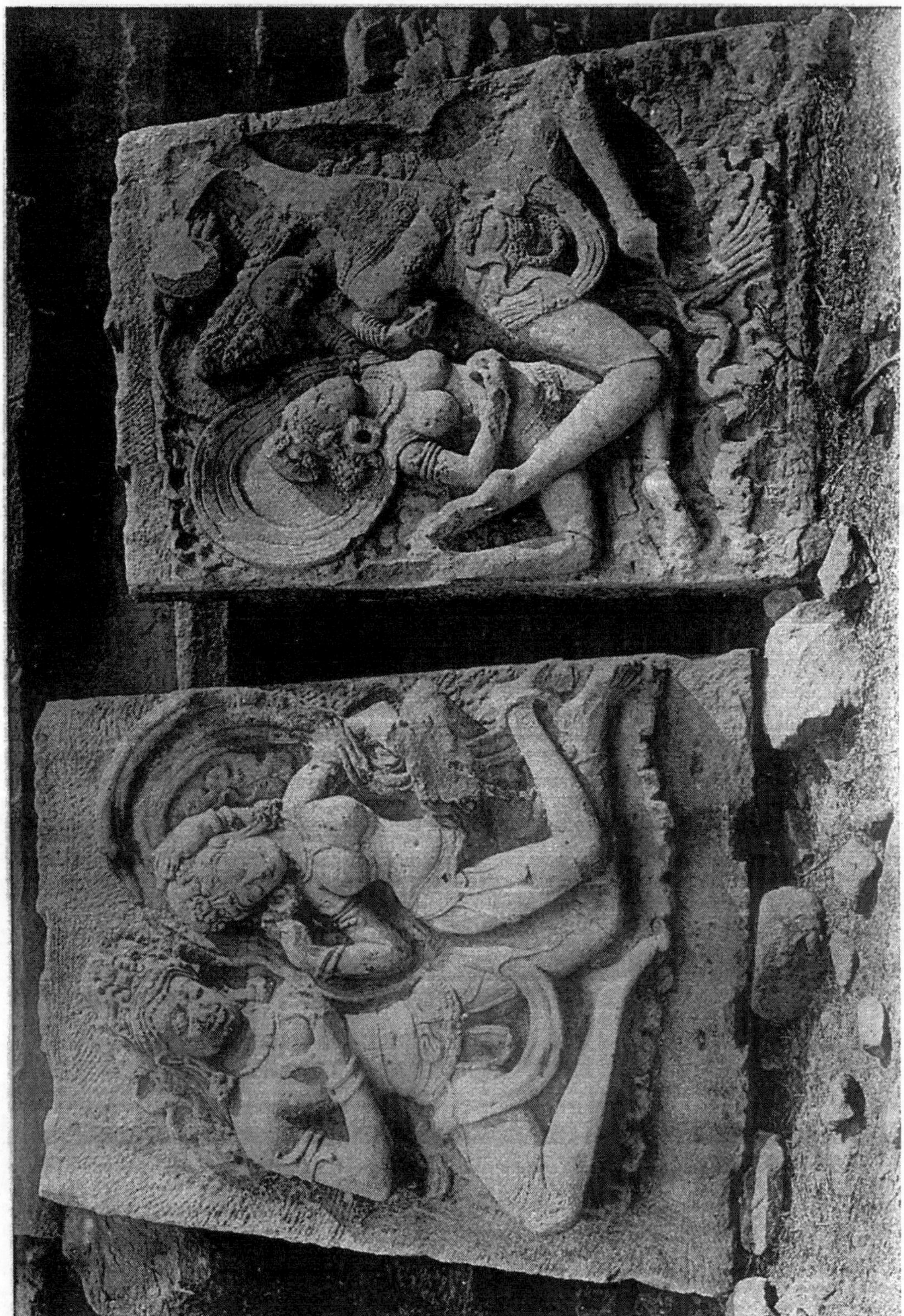

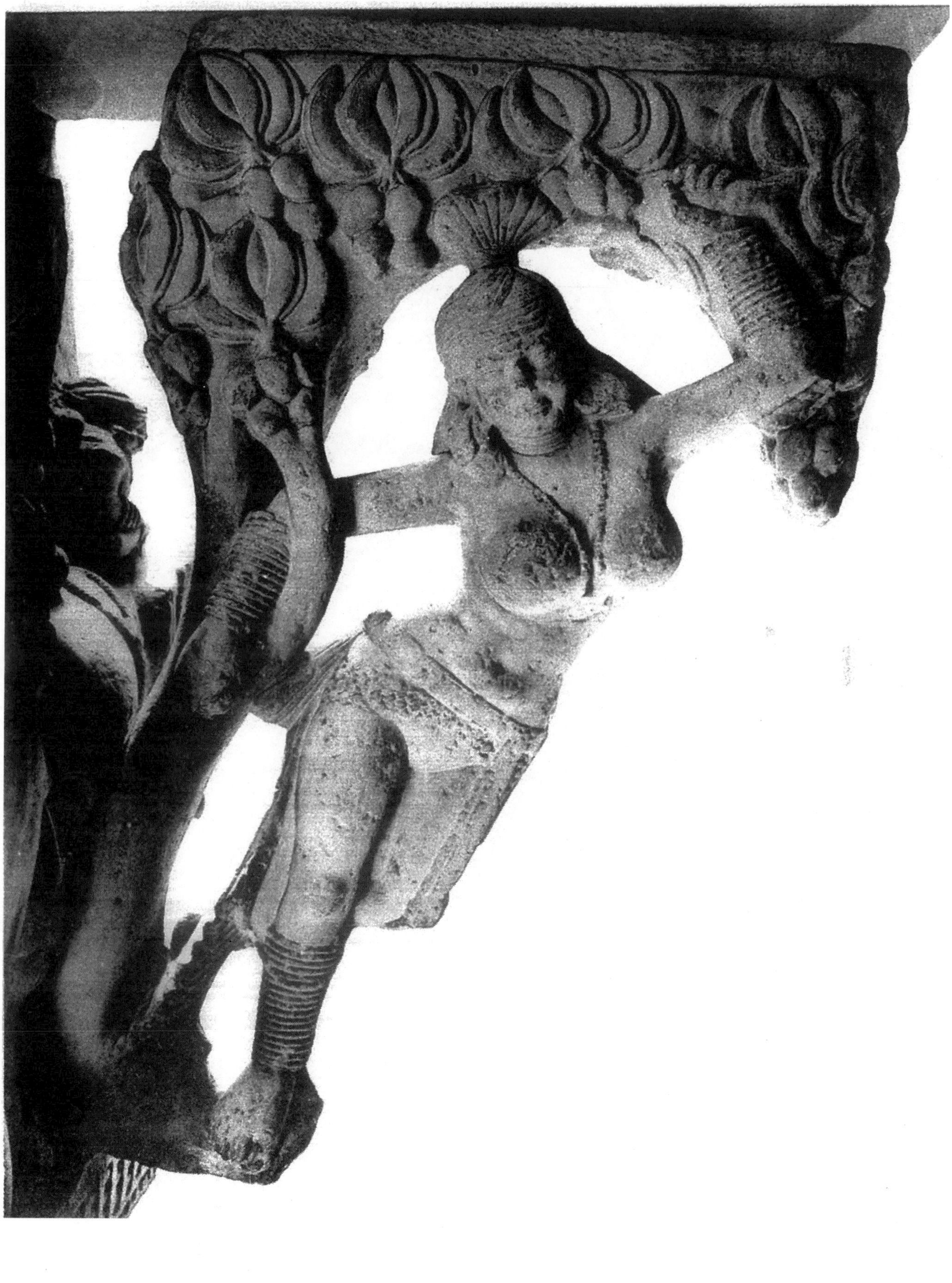

LXVIII

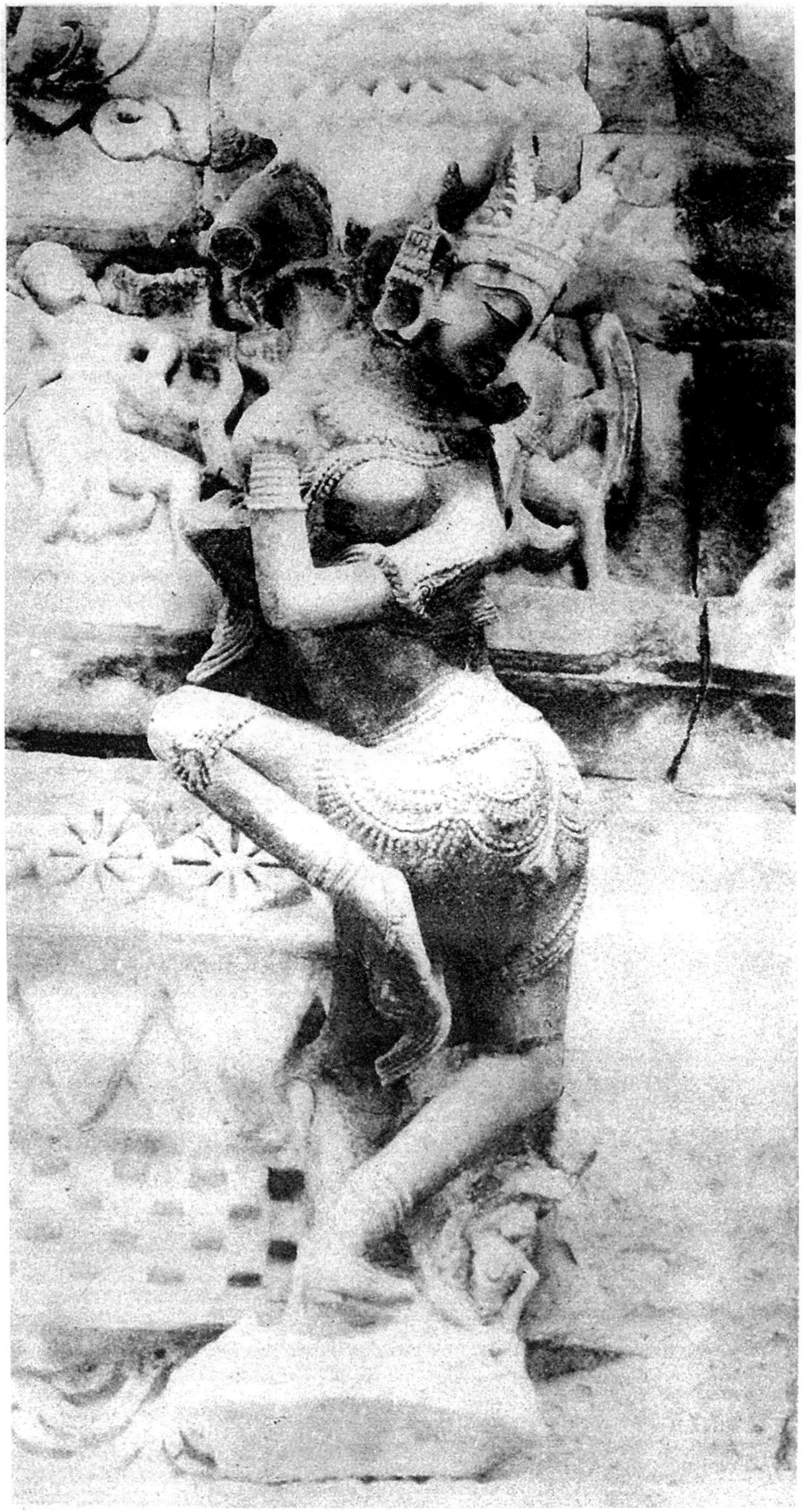

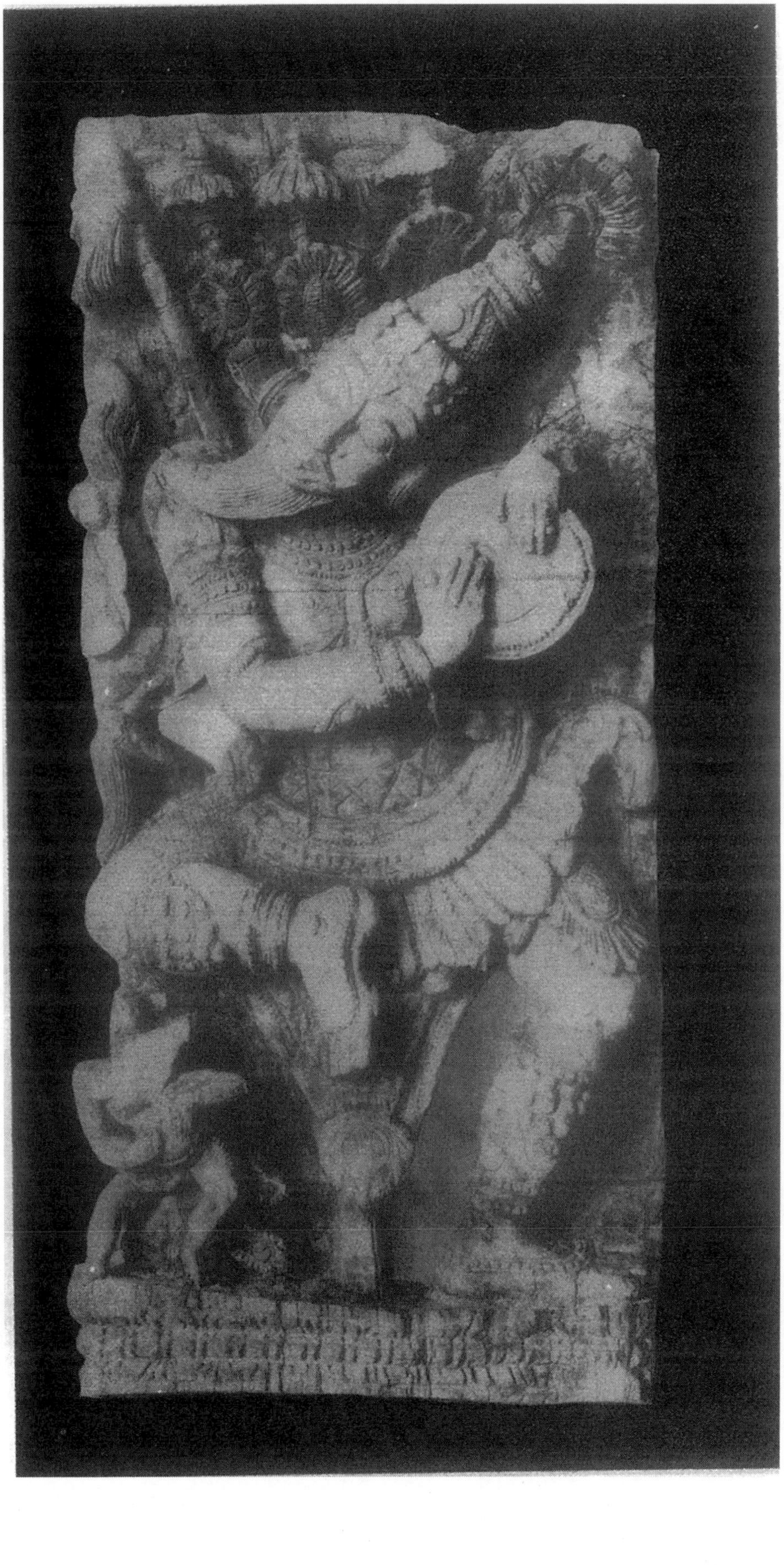

LXX

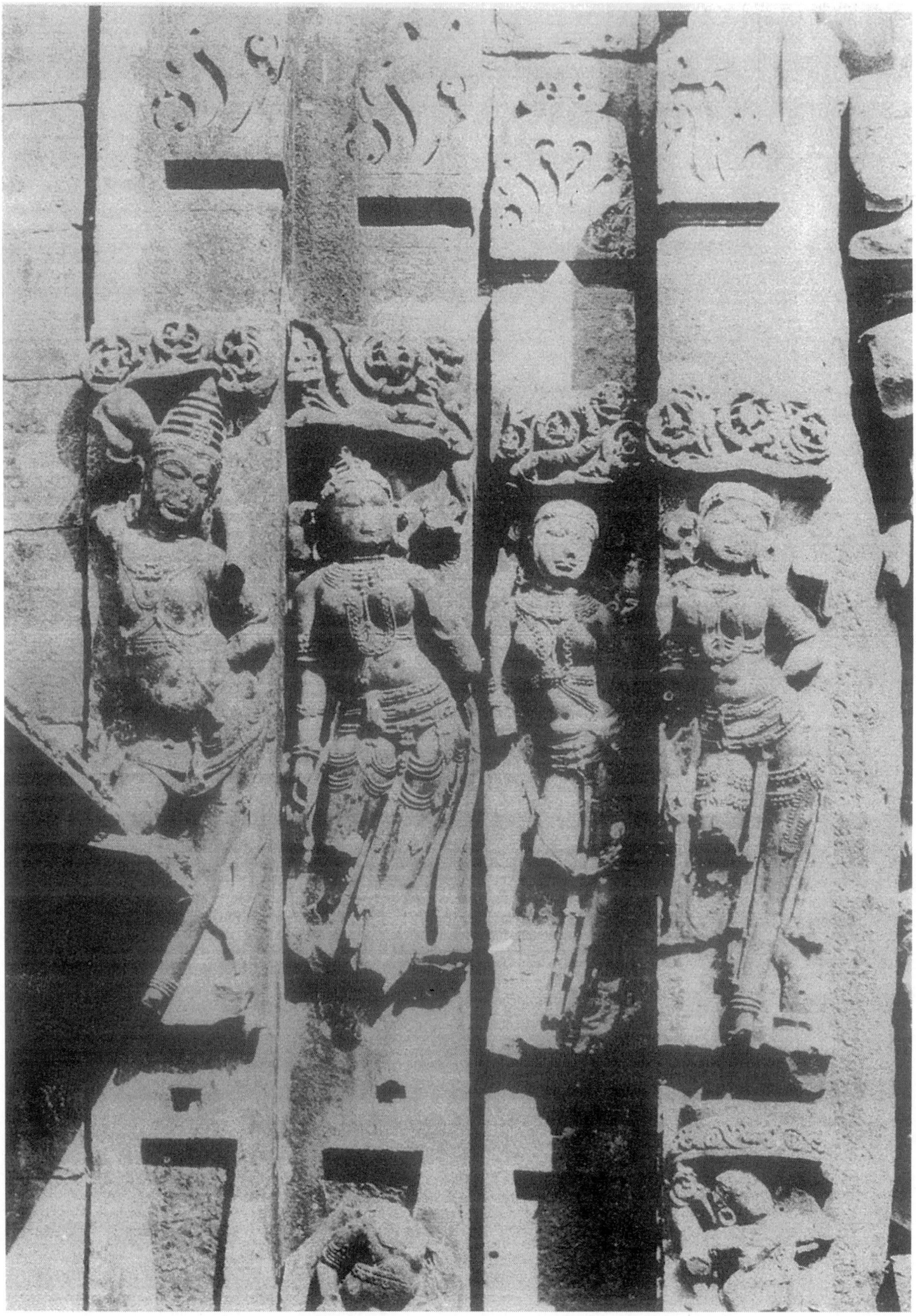

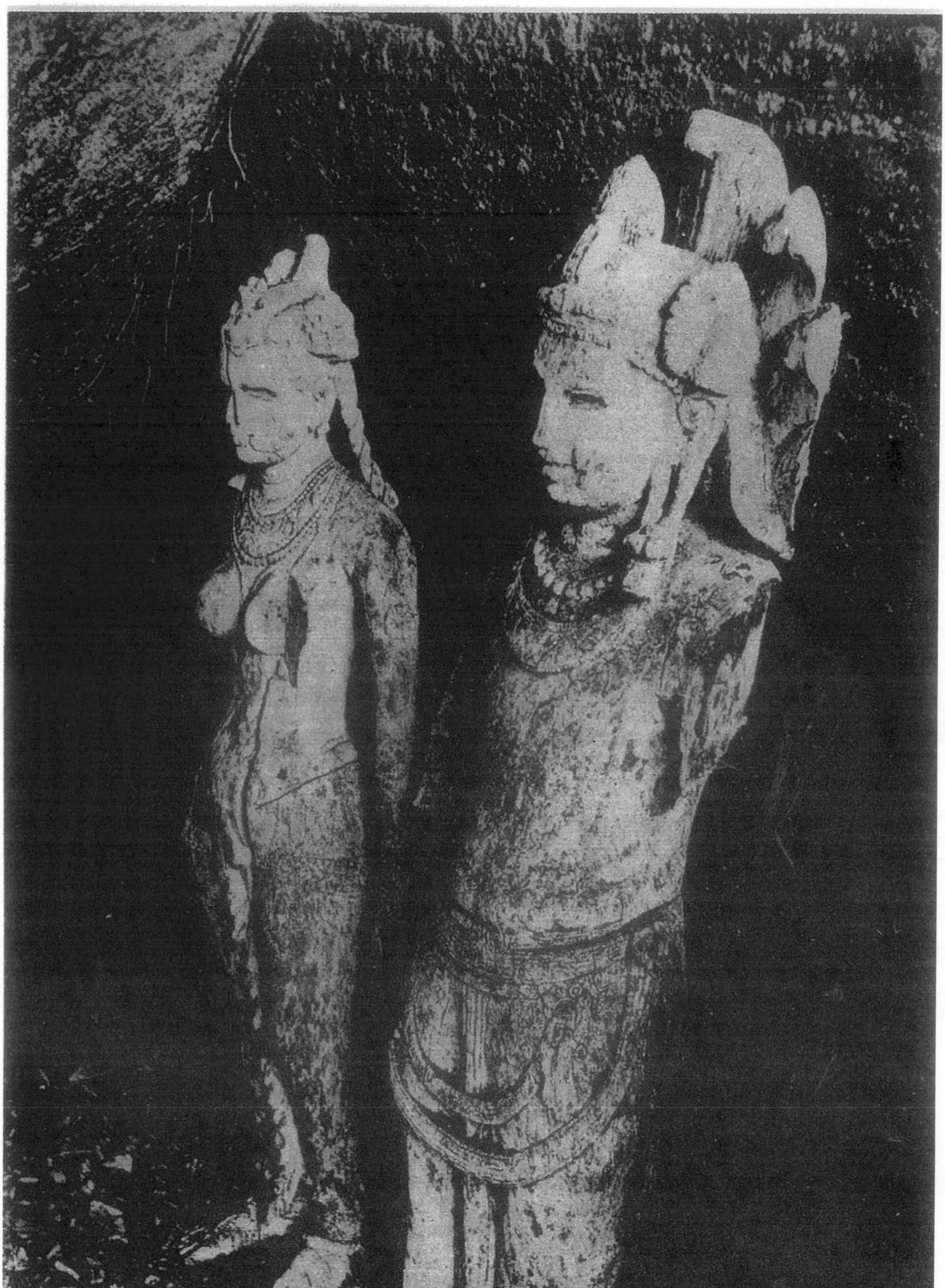

LXXII

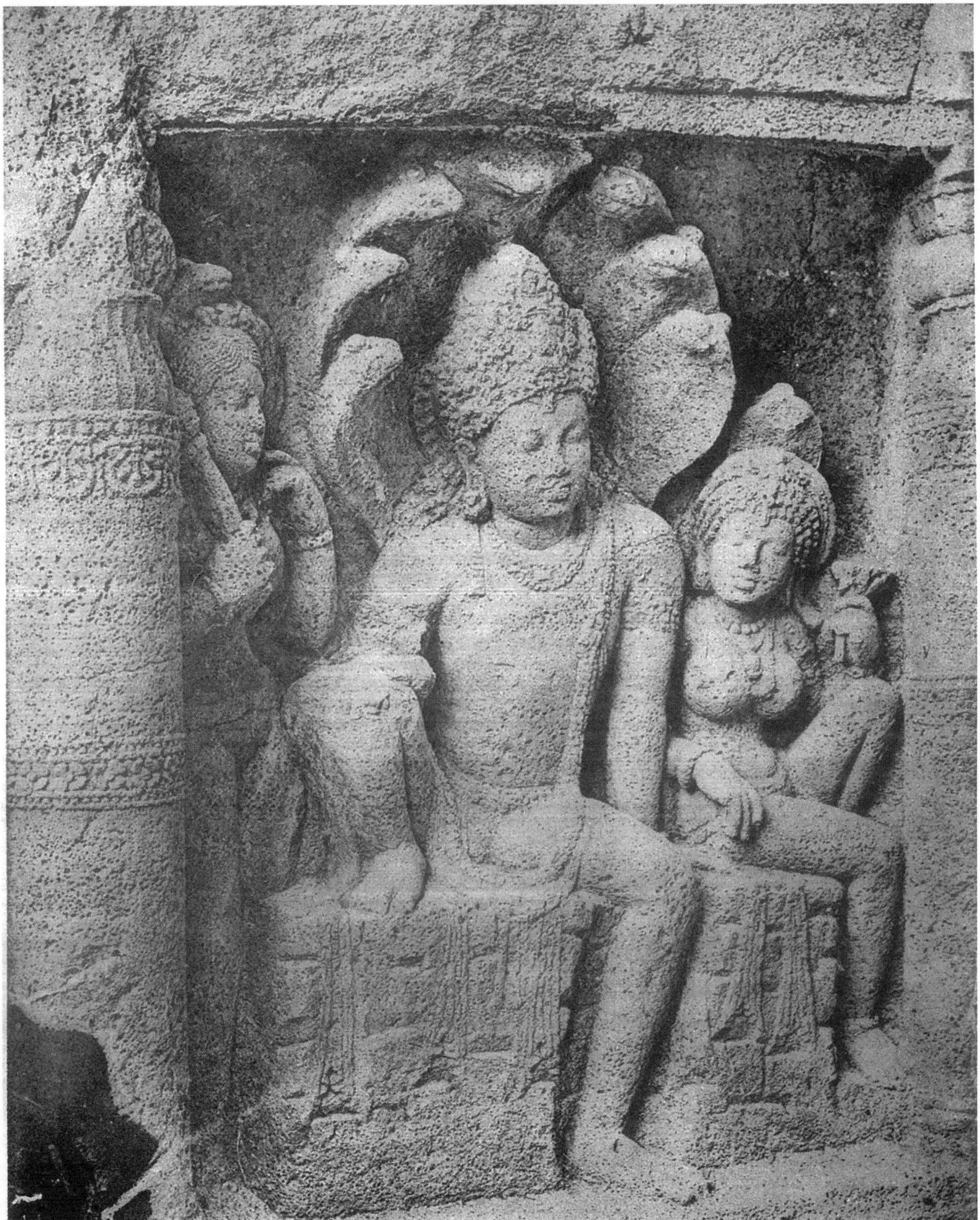

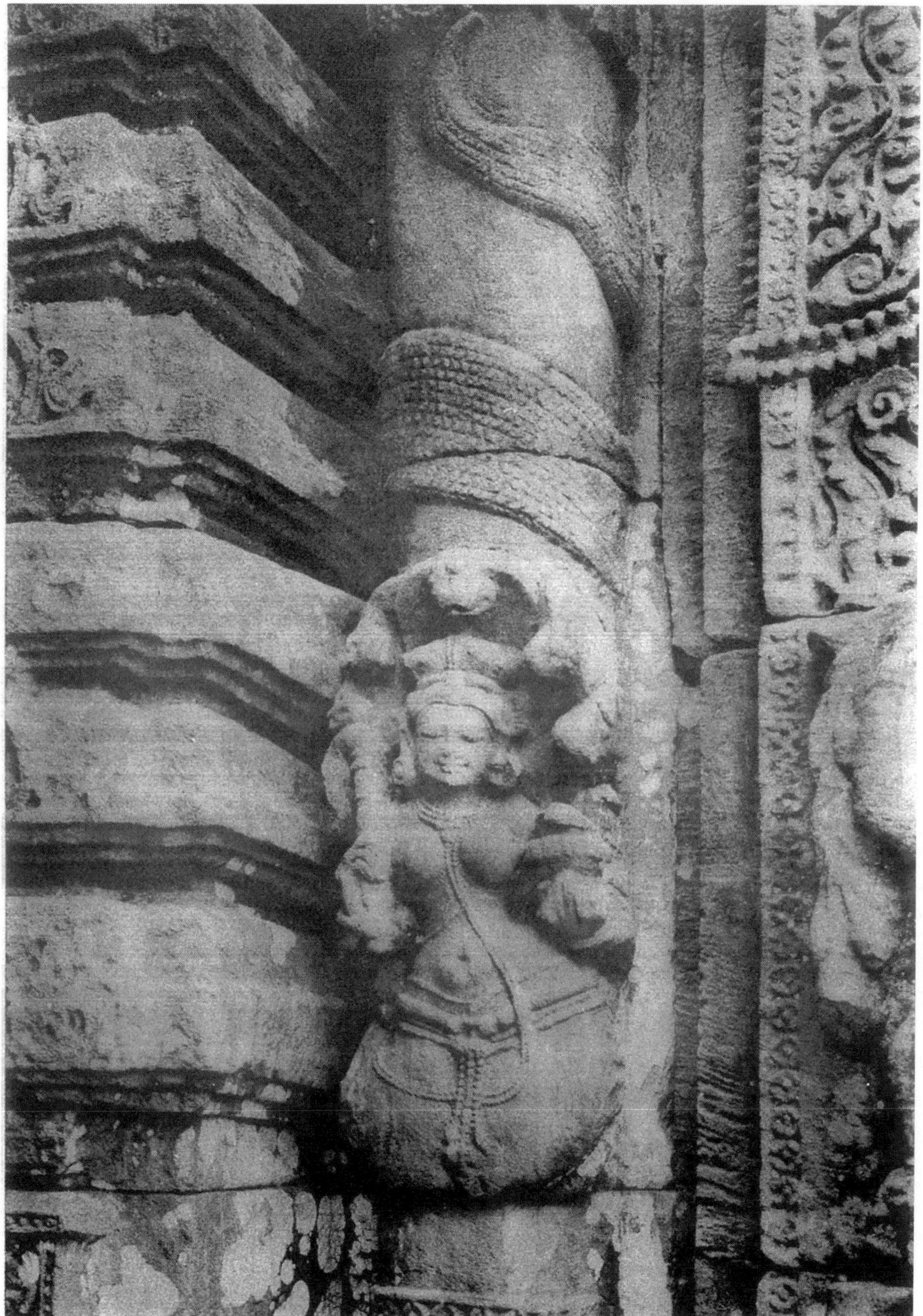

LXXIV

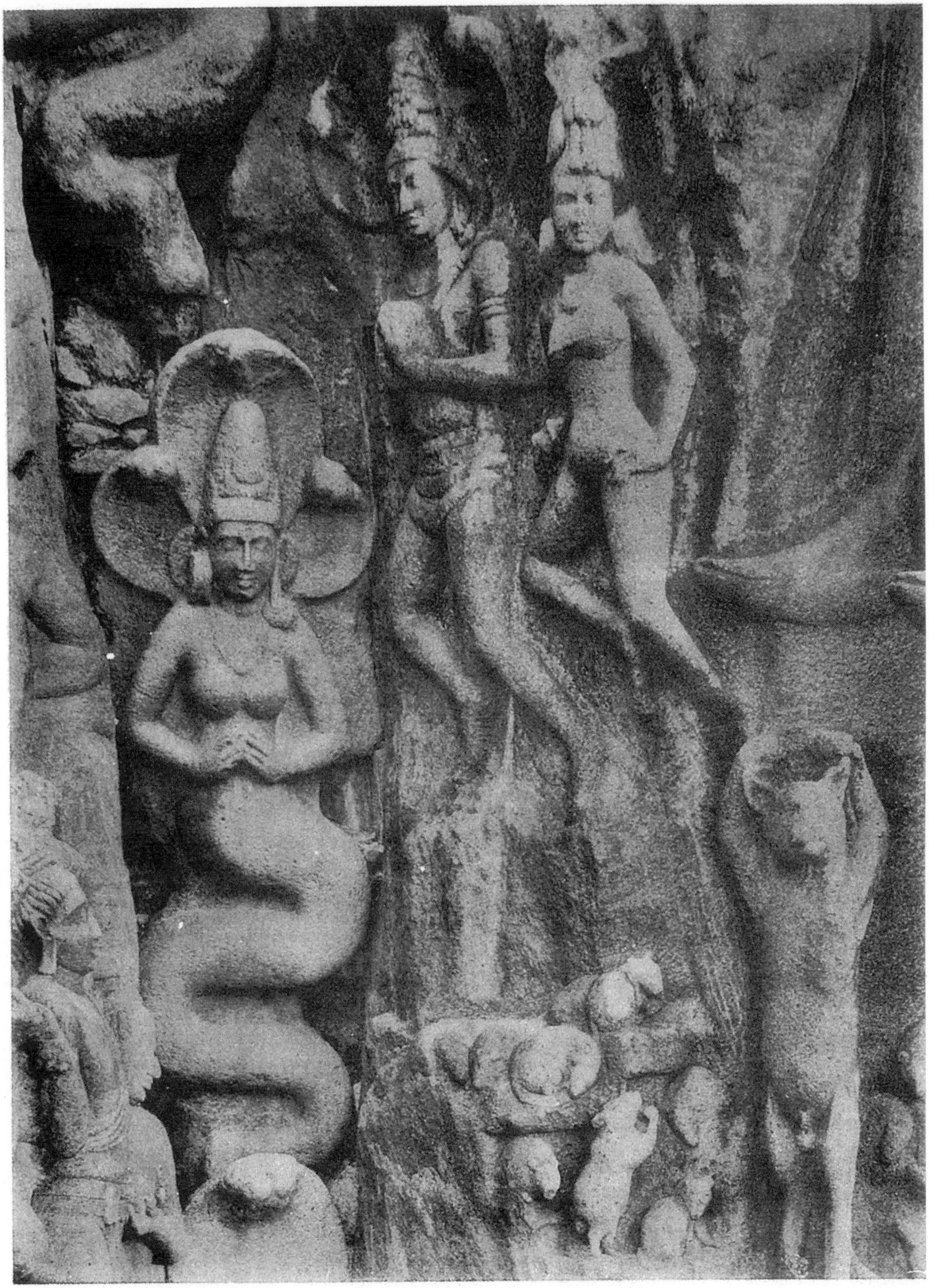

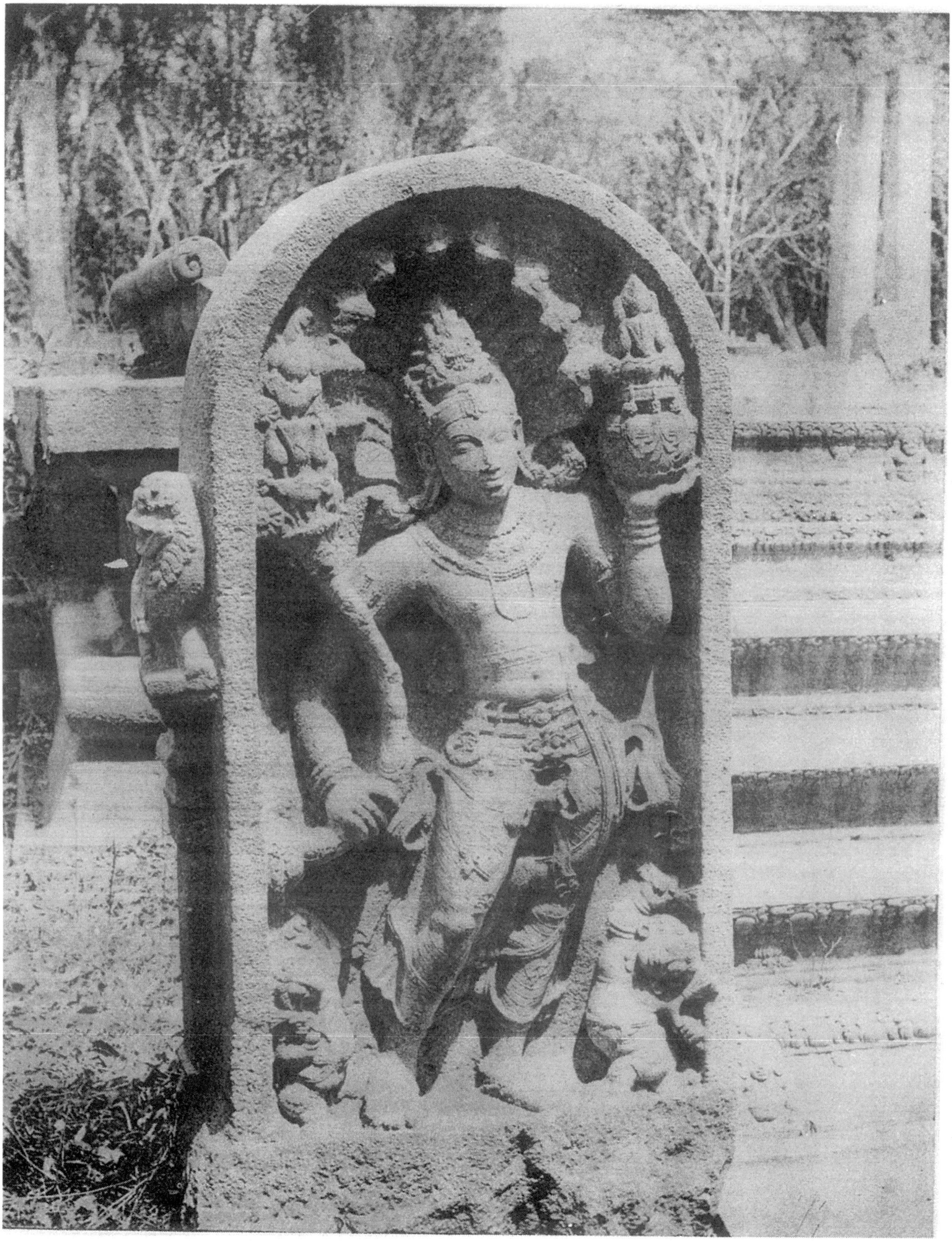

LXXVI

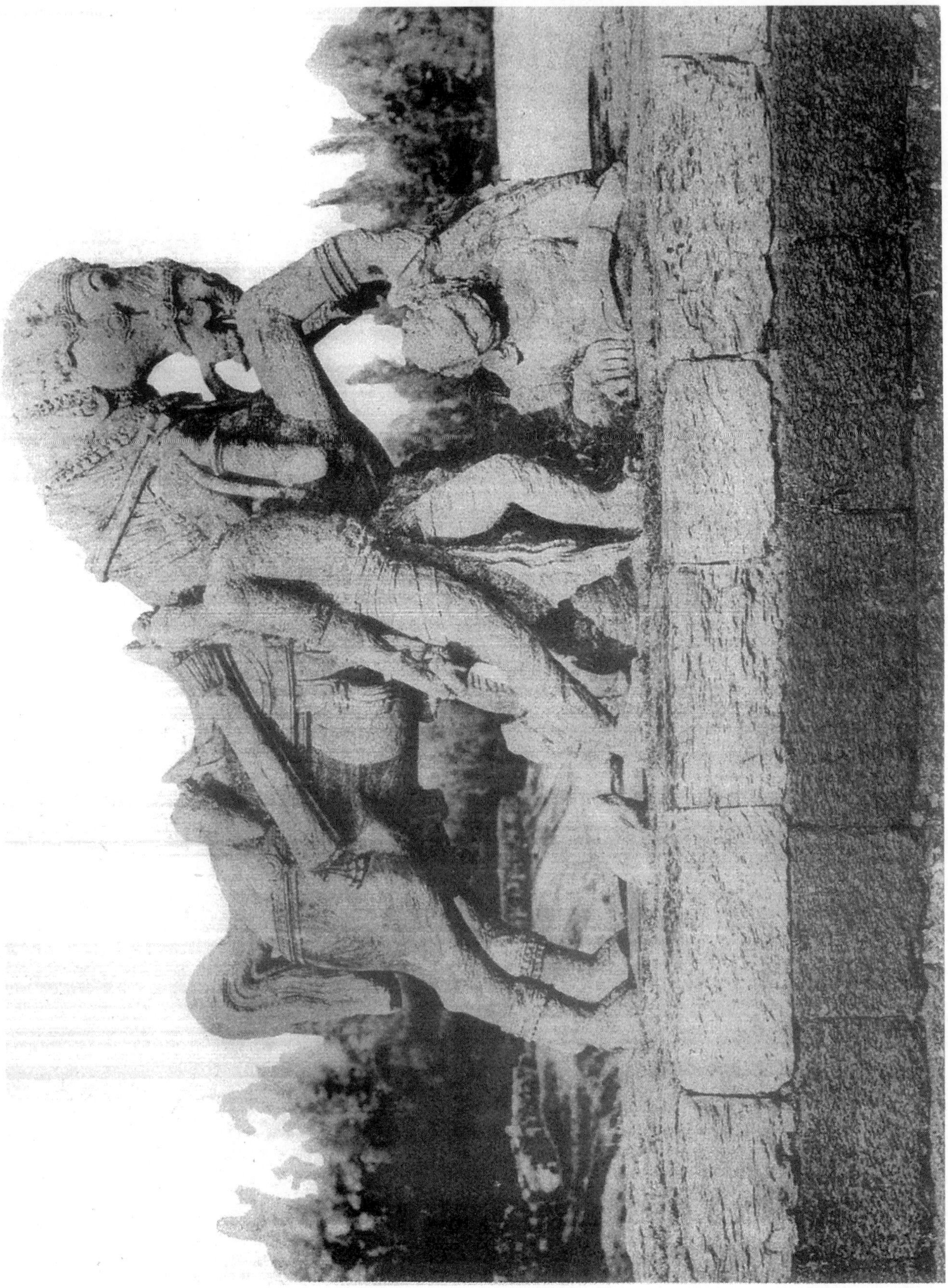

LXXVII

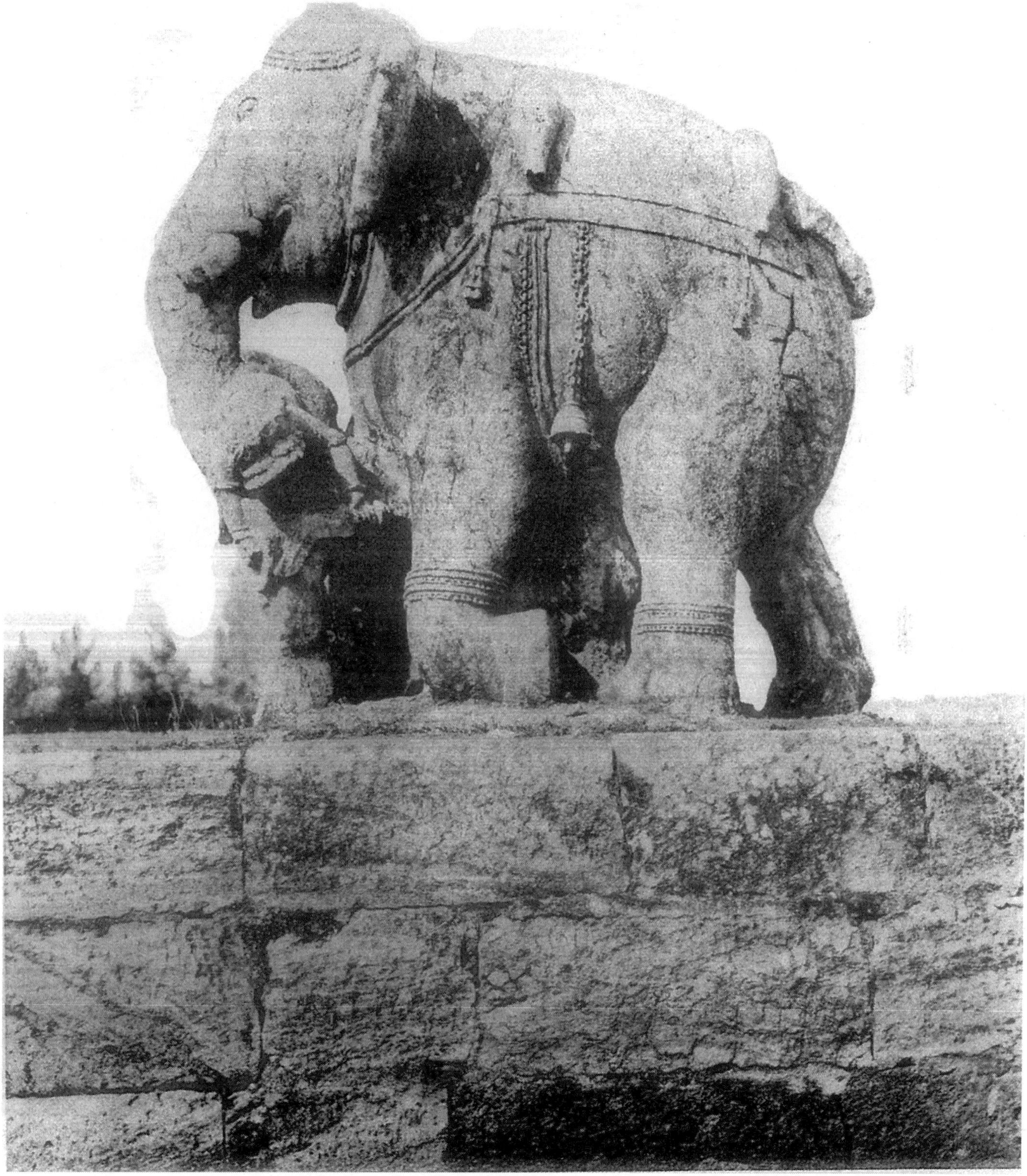

LXXVIII

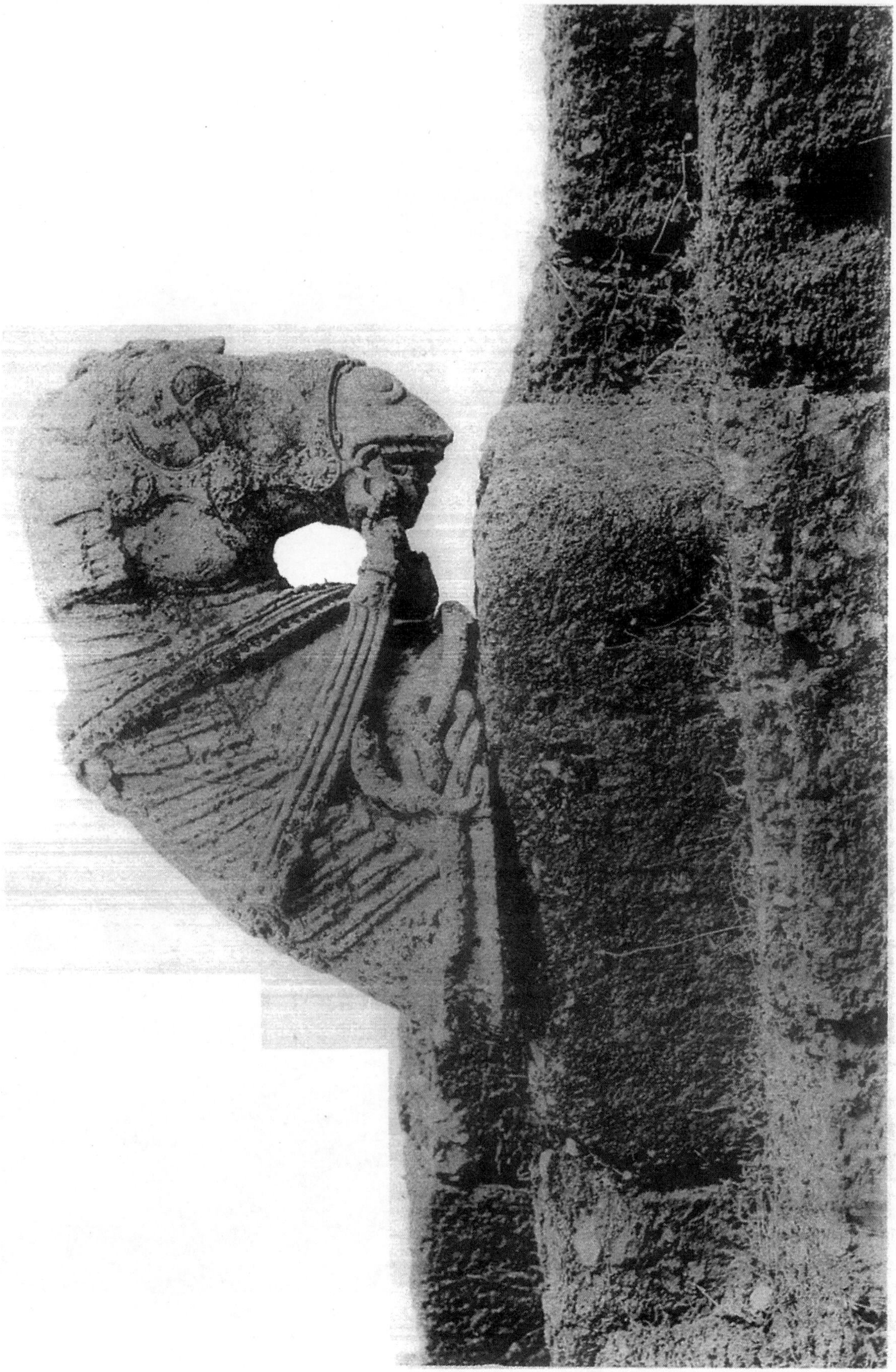

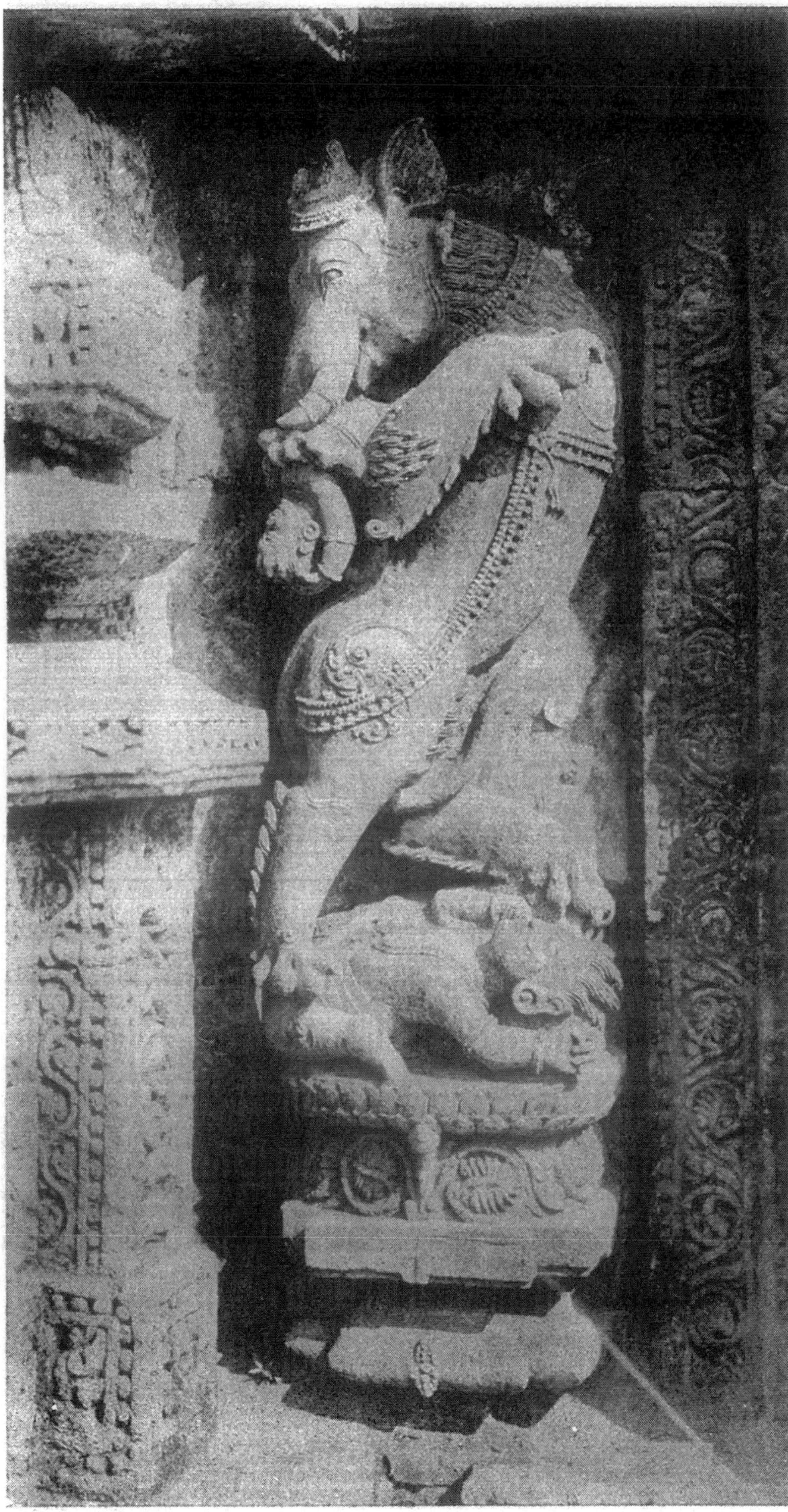

LXXX

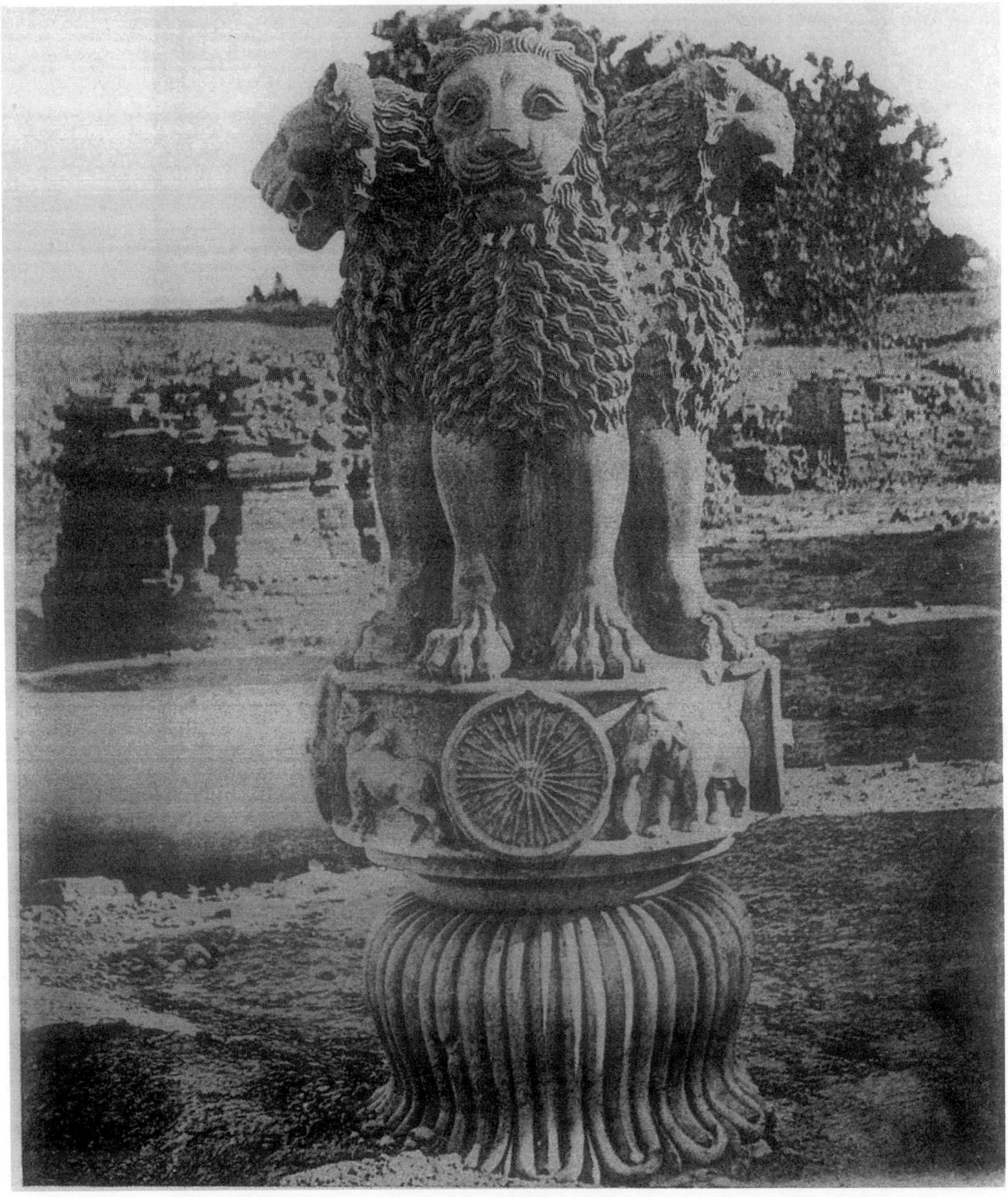

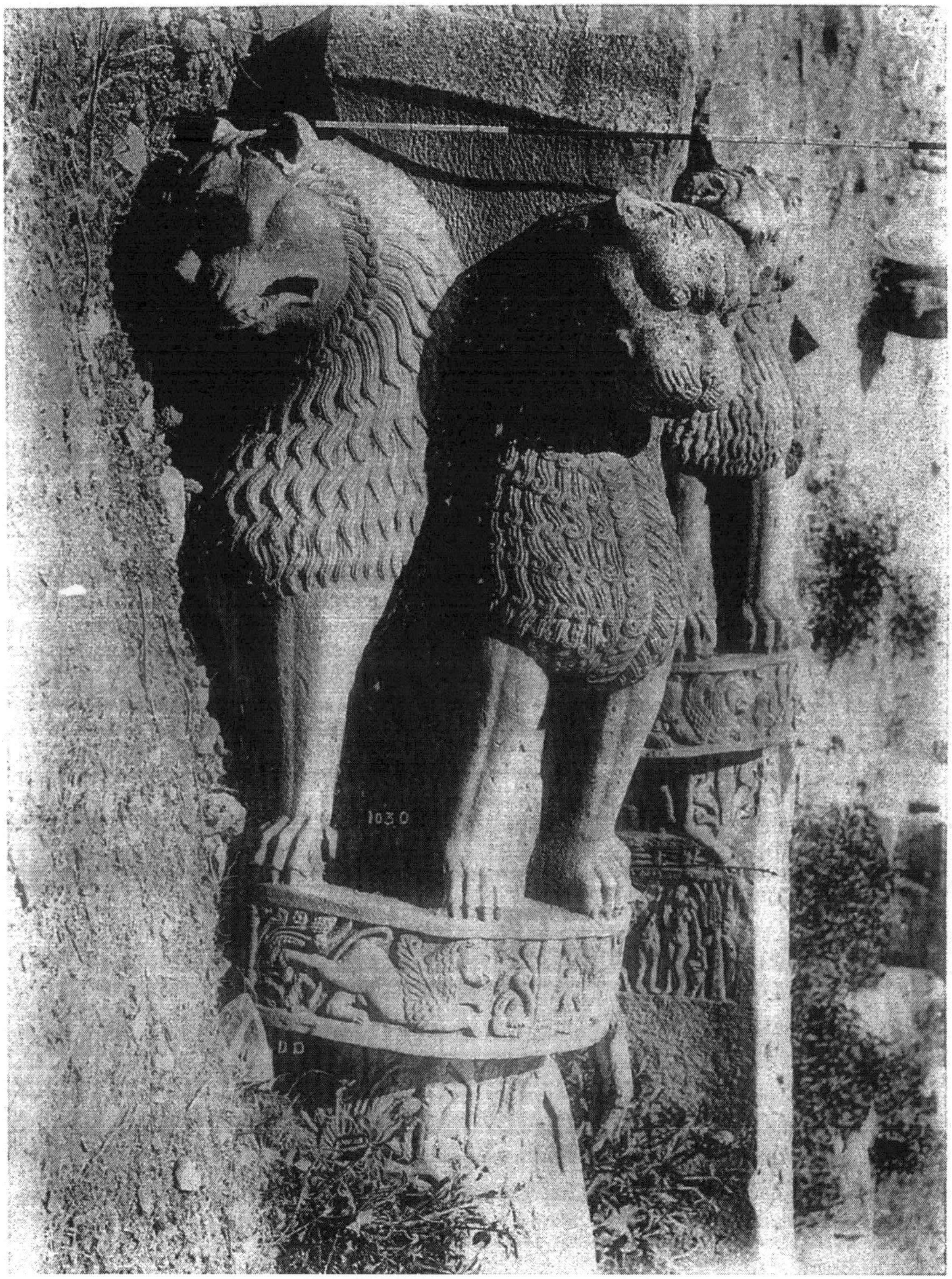

LXXXII

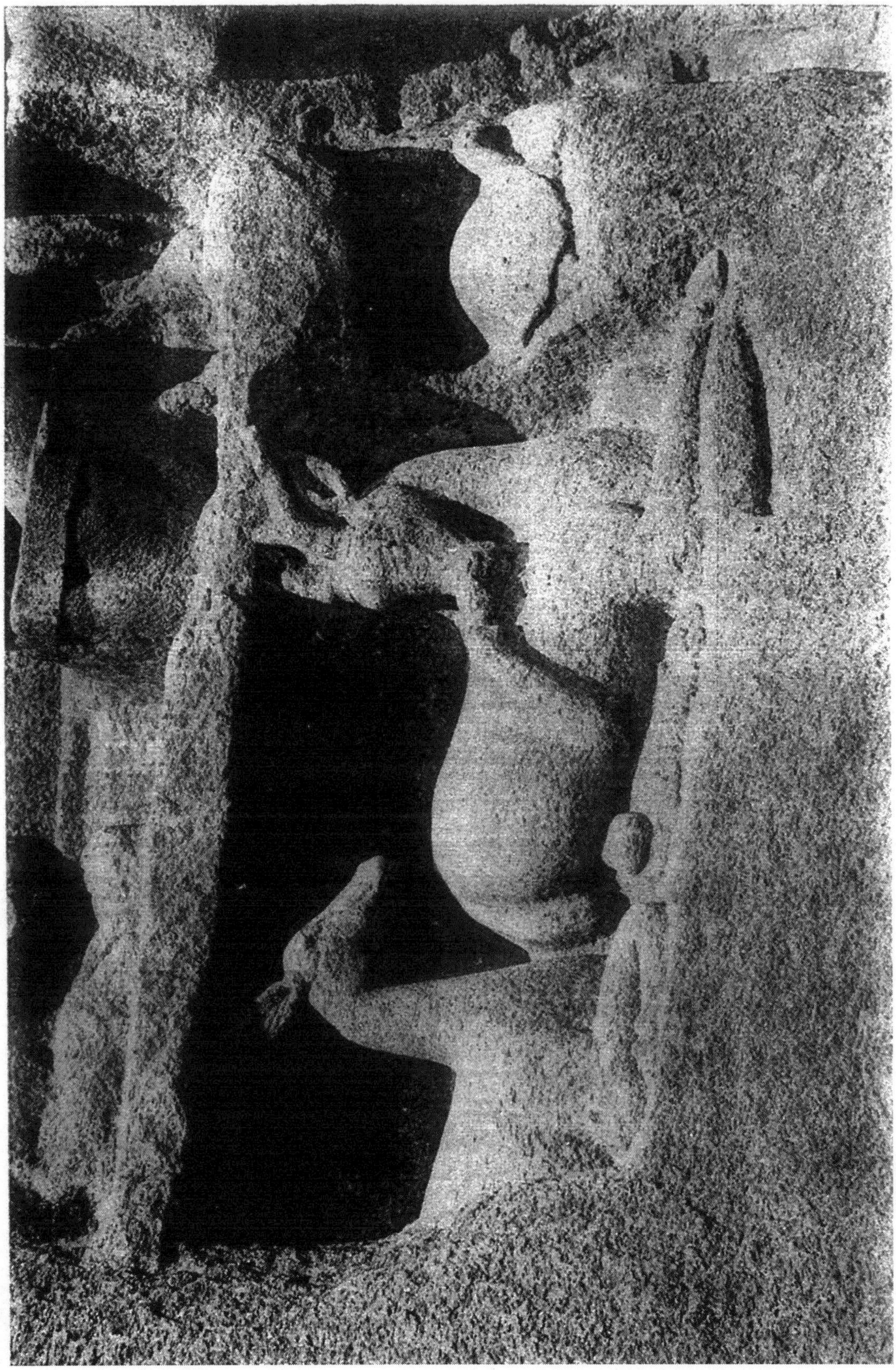

LXXXIII

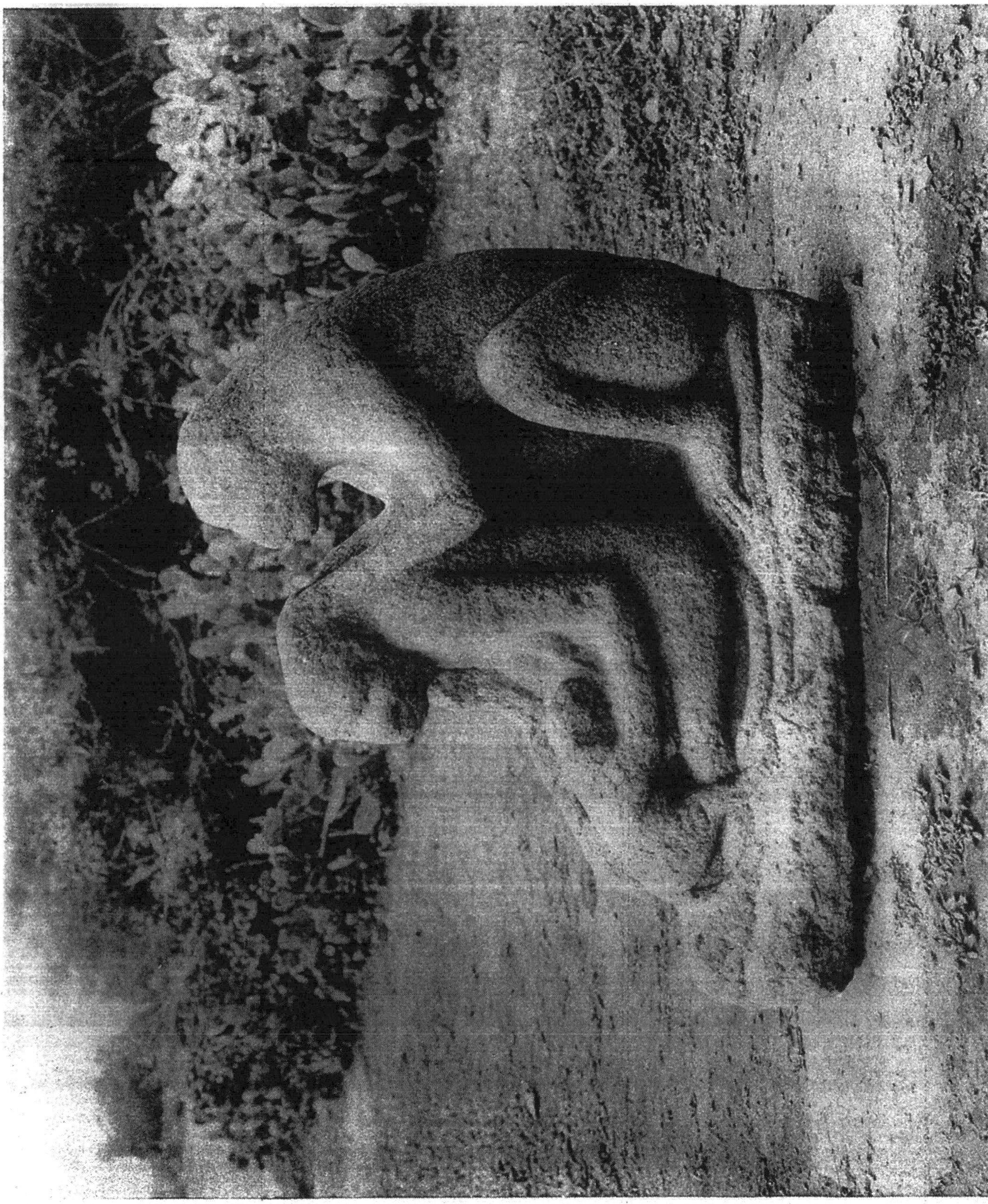

LXXXIV

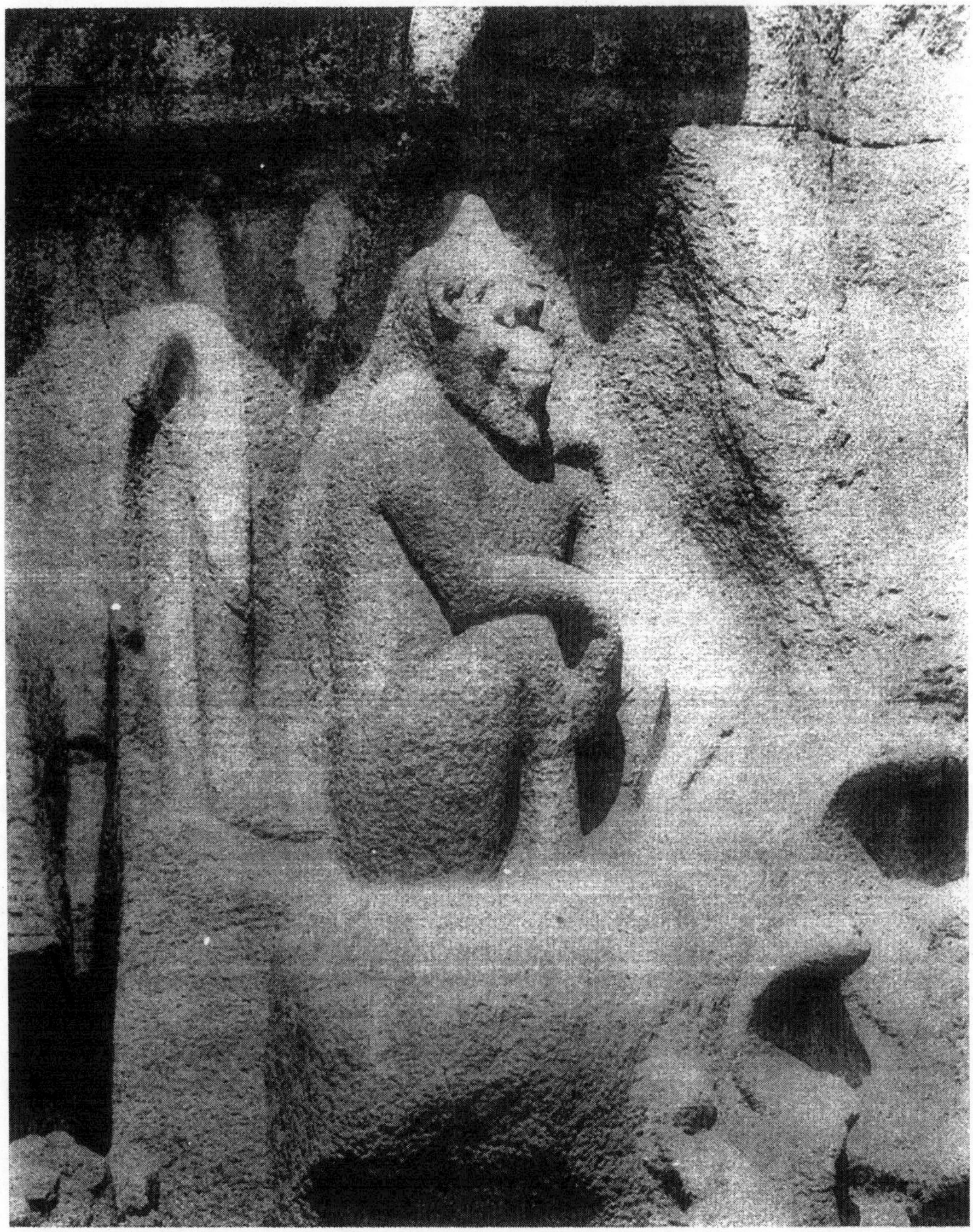

LXXXV

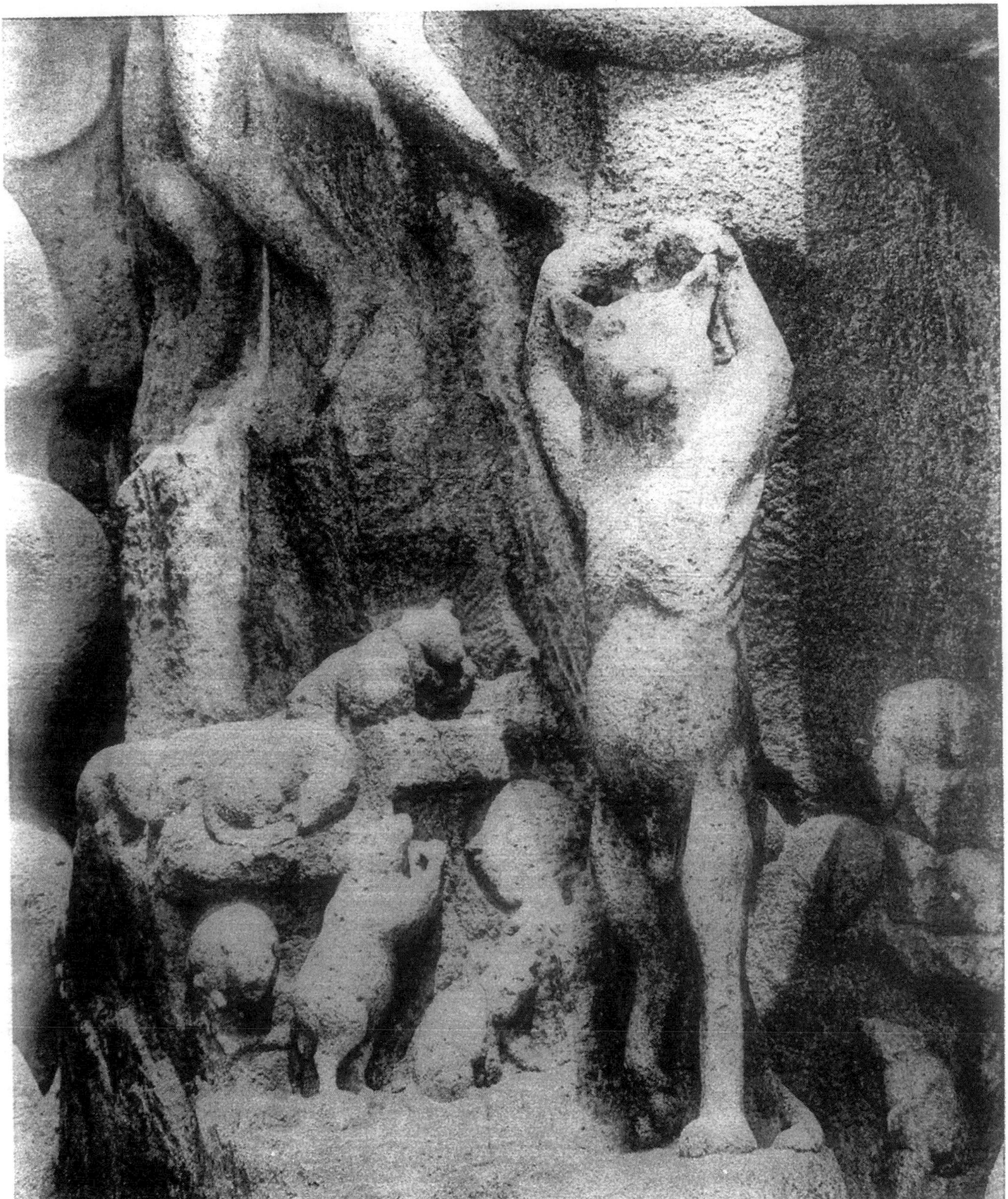

LXXXVI

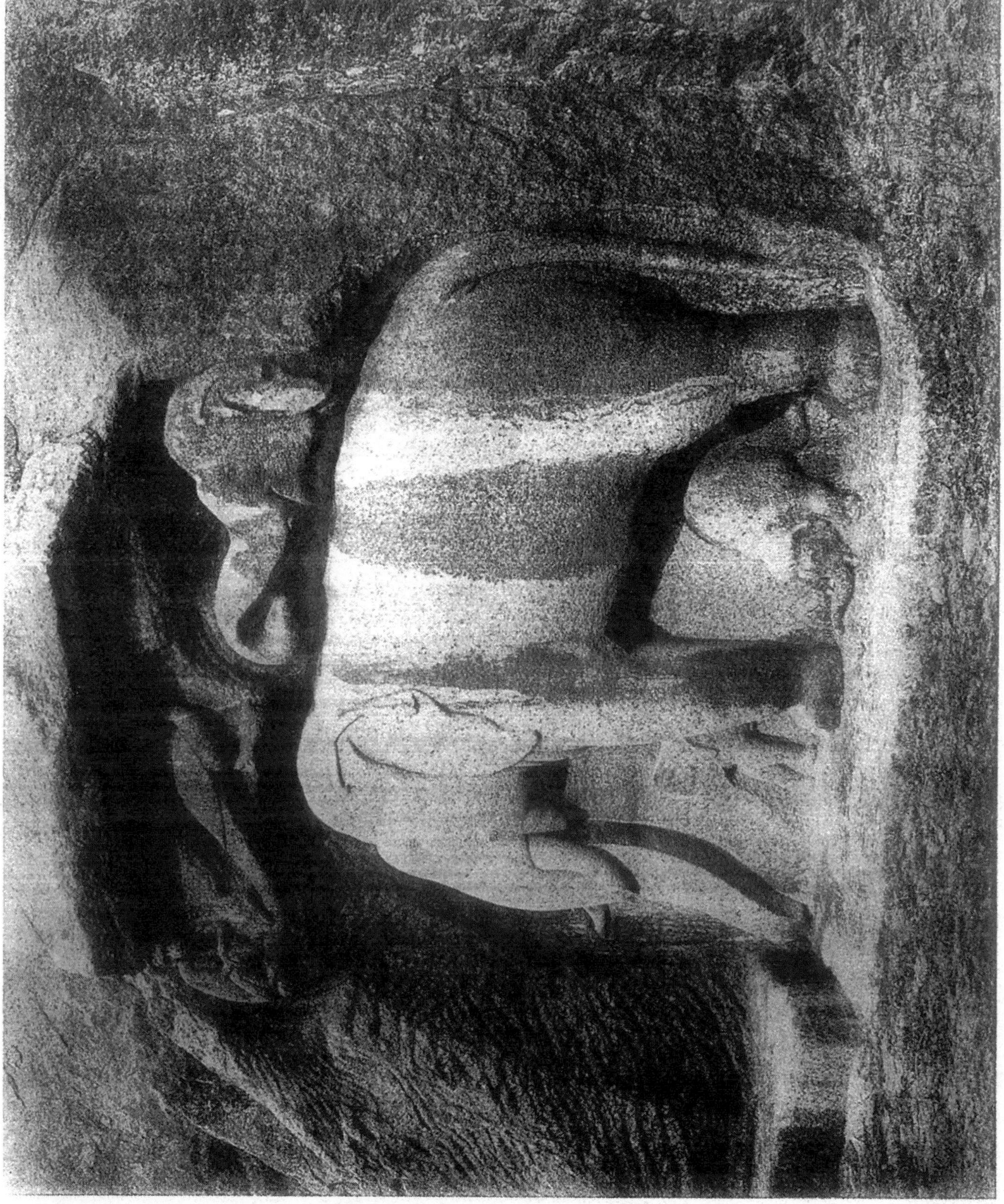

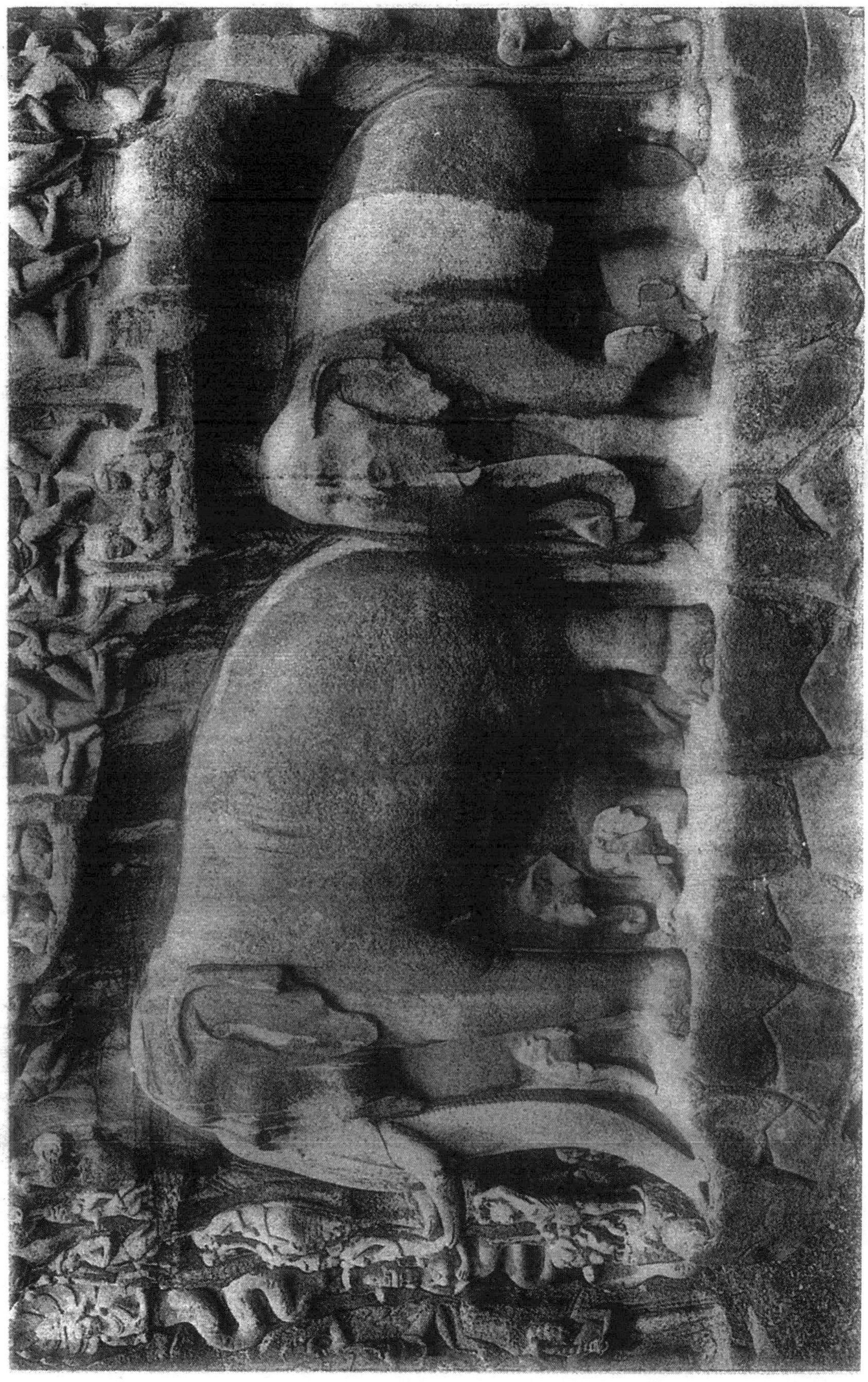

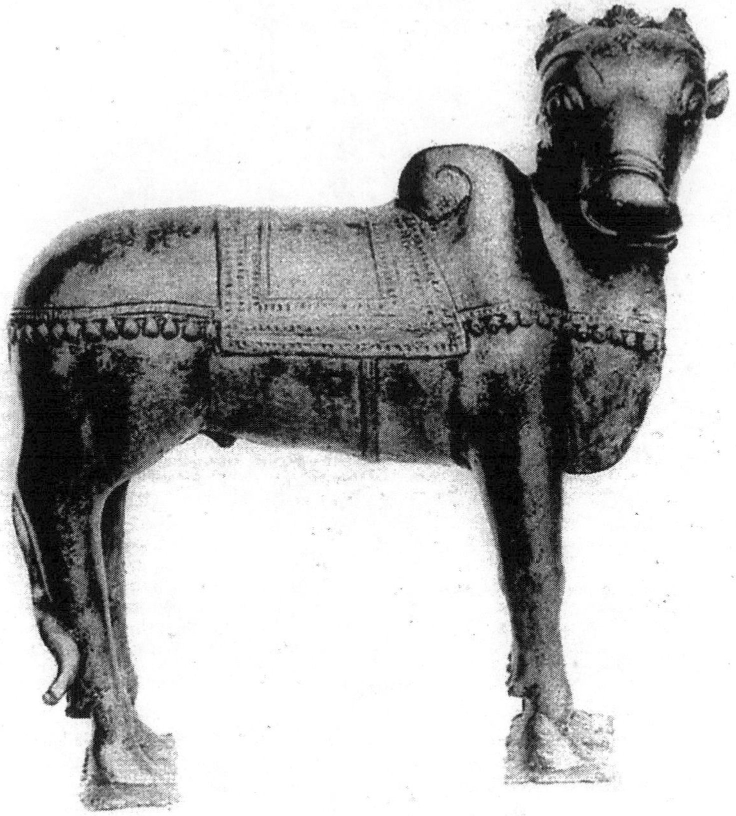

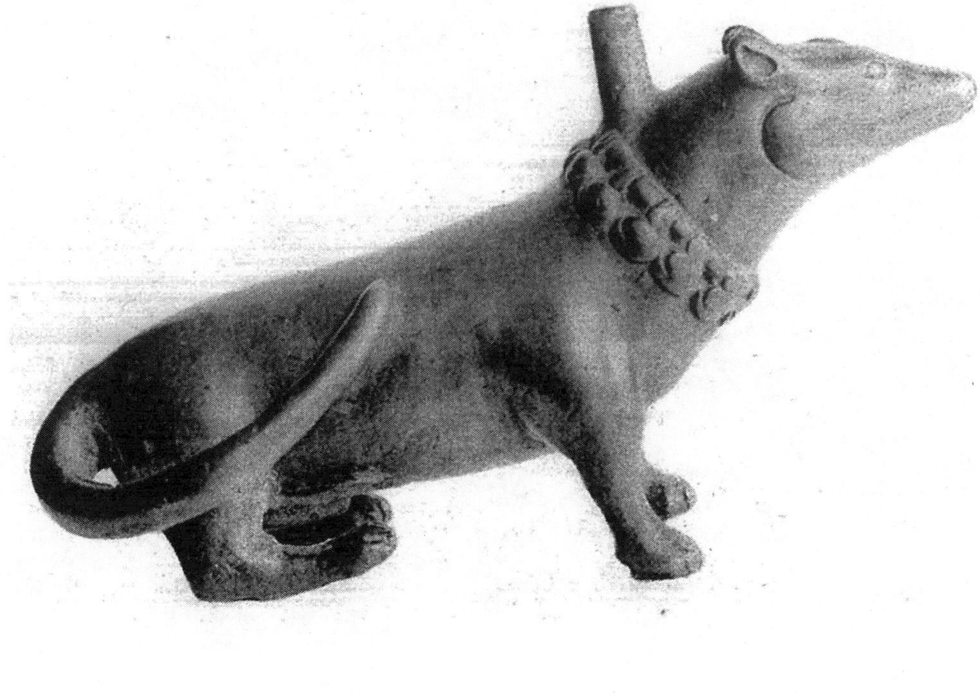

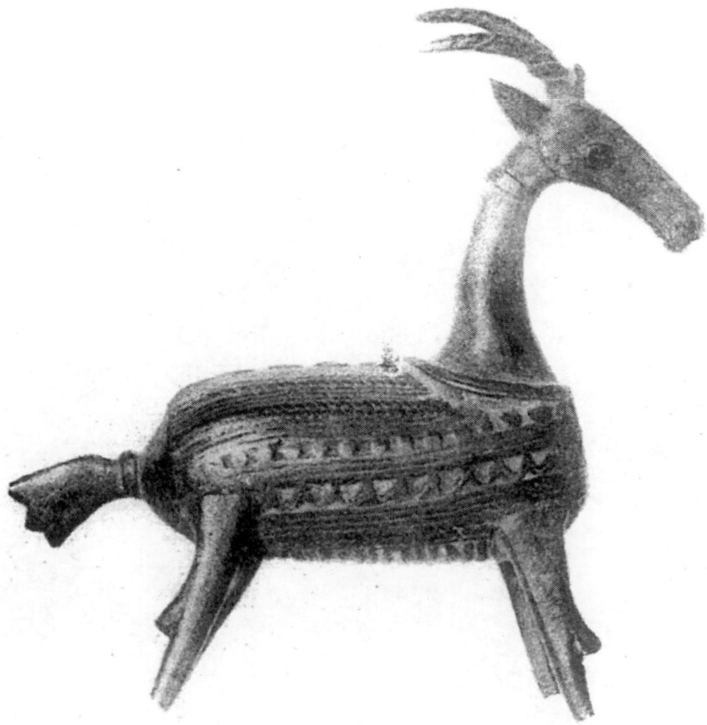

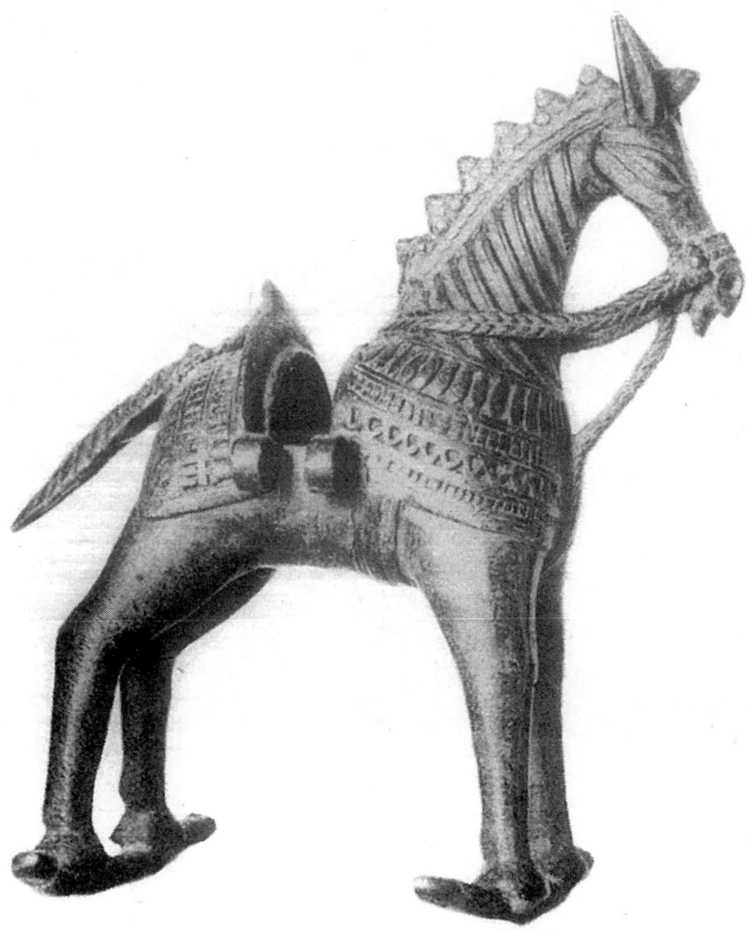

XC

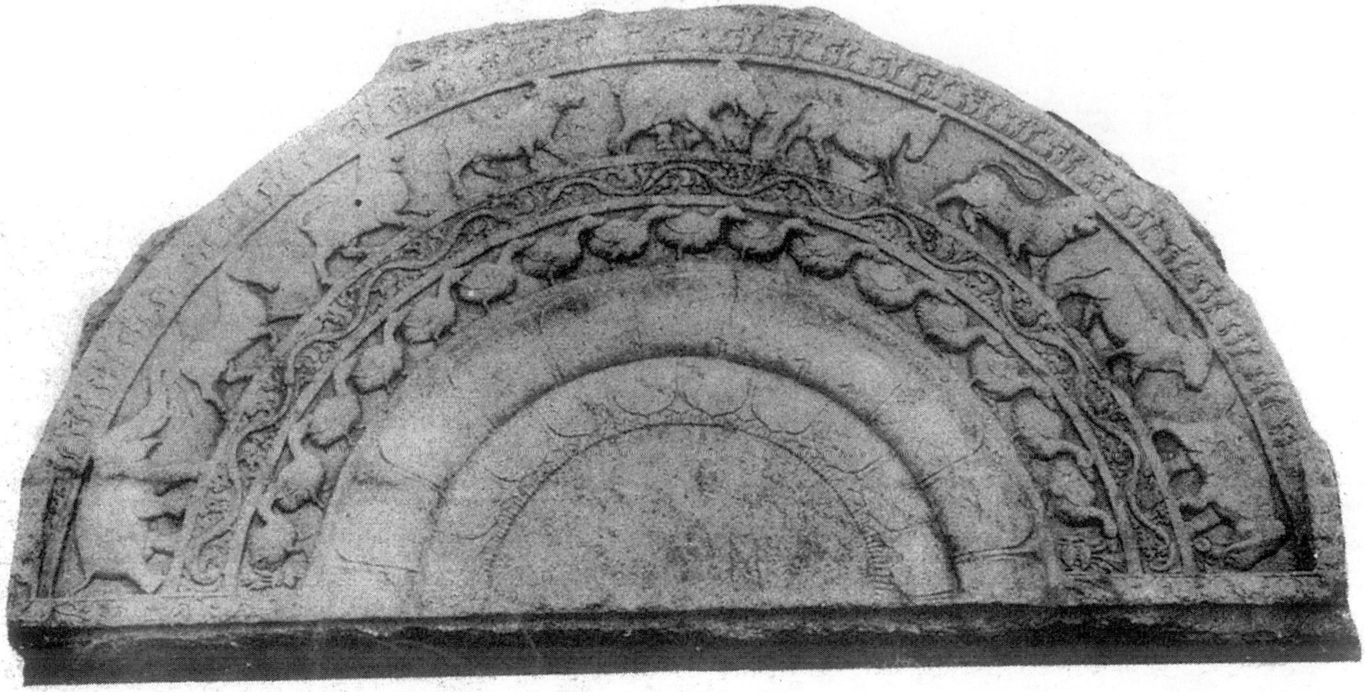

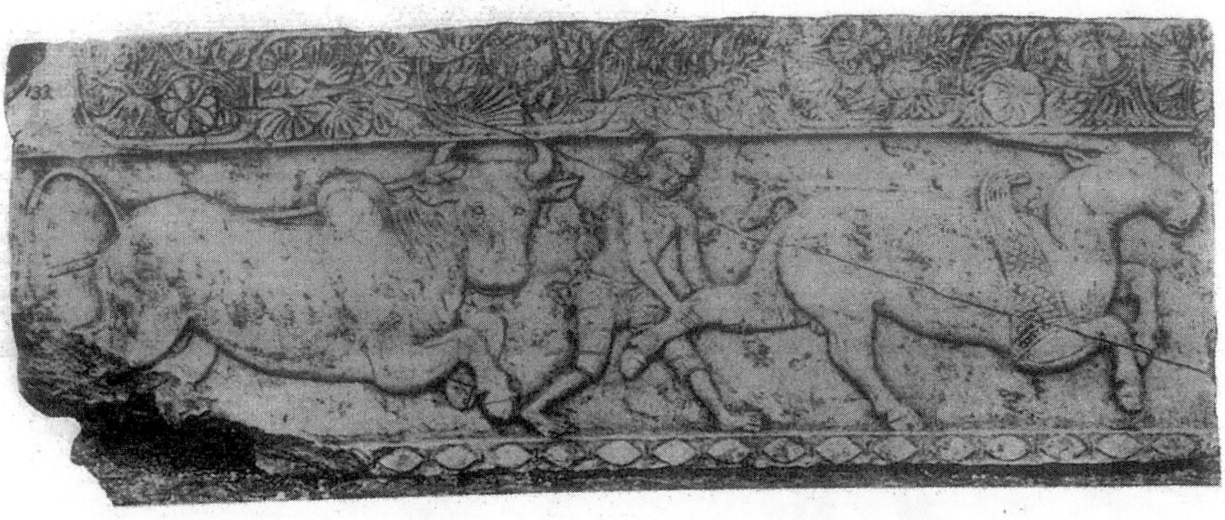

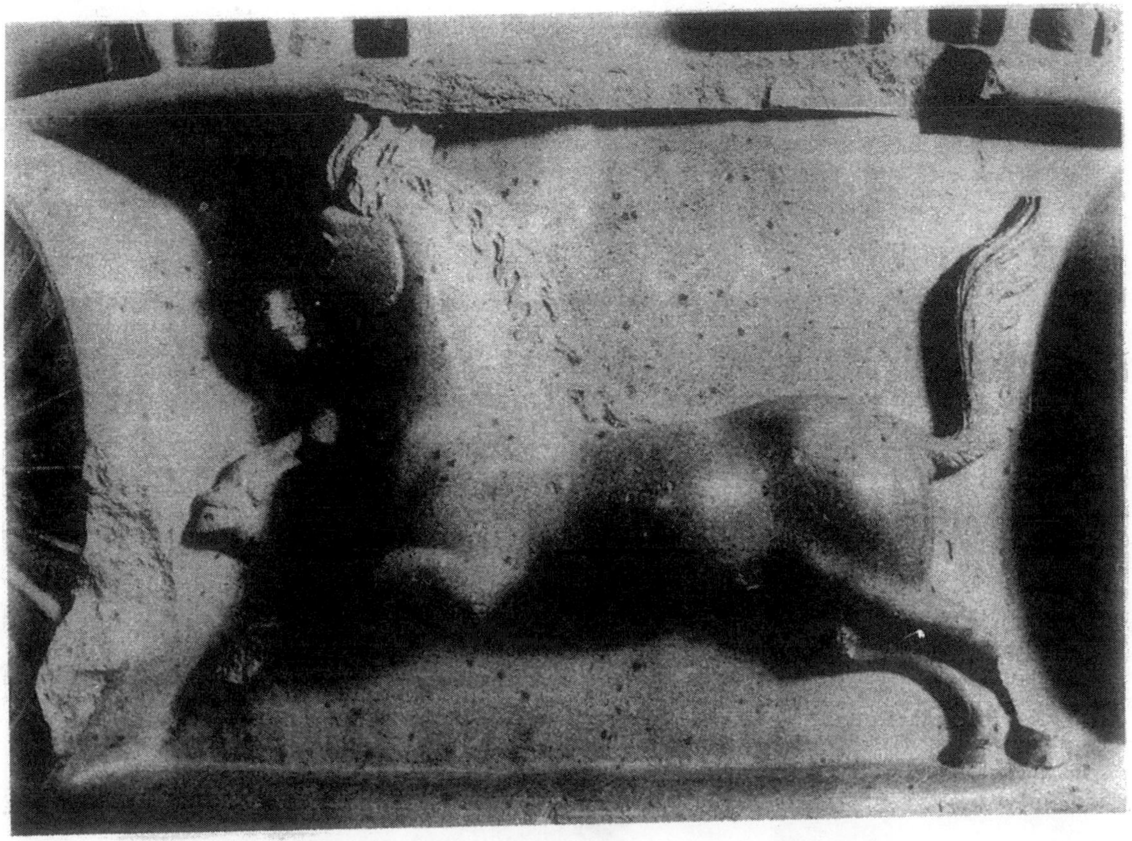

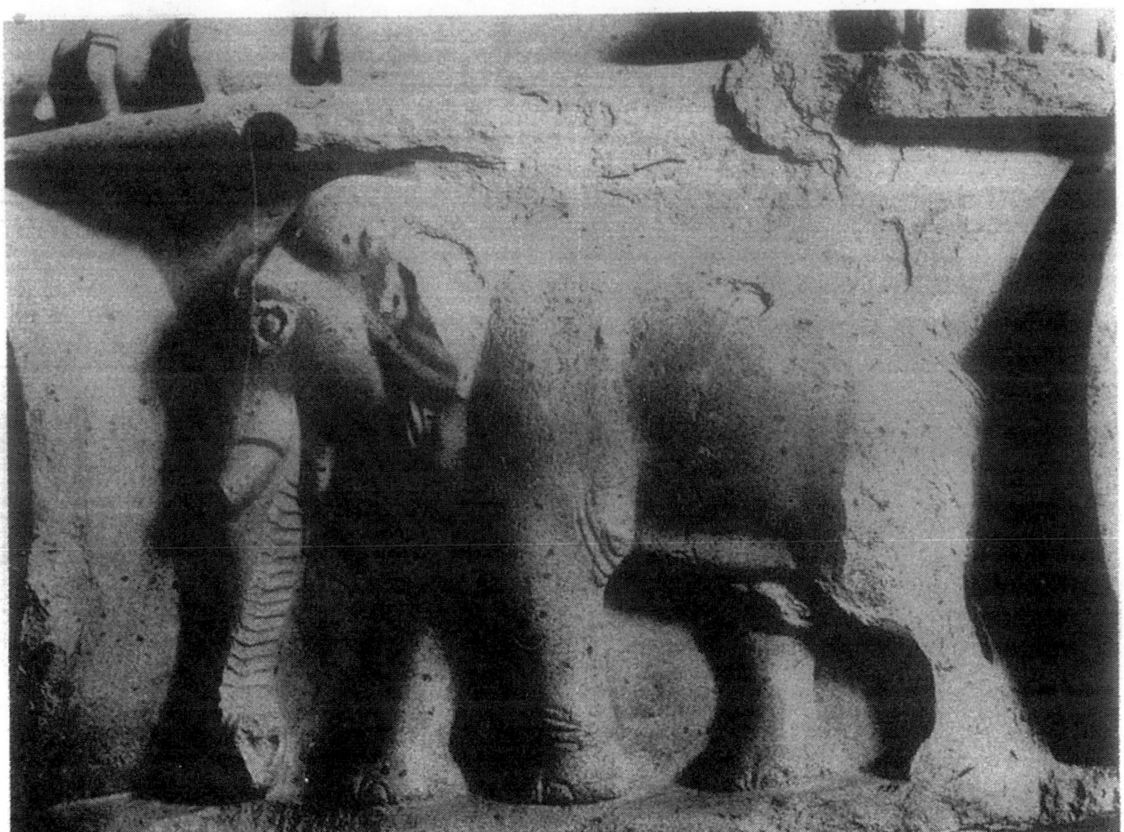

XCII

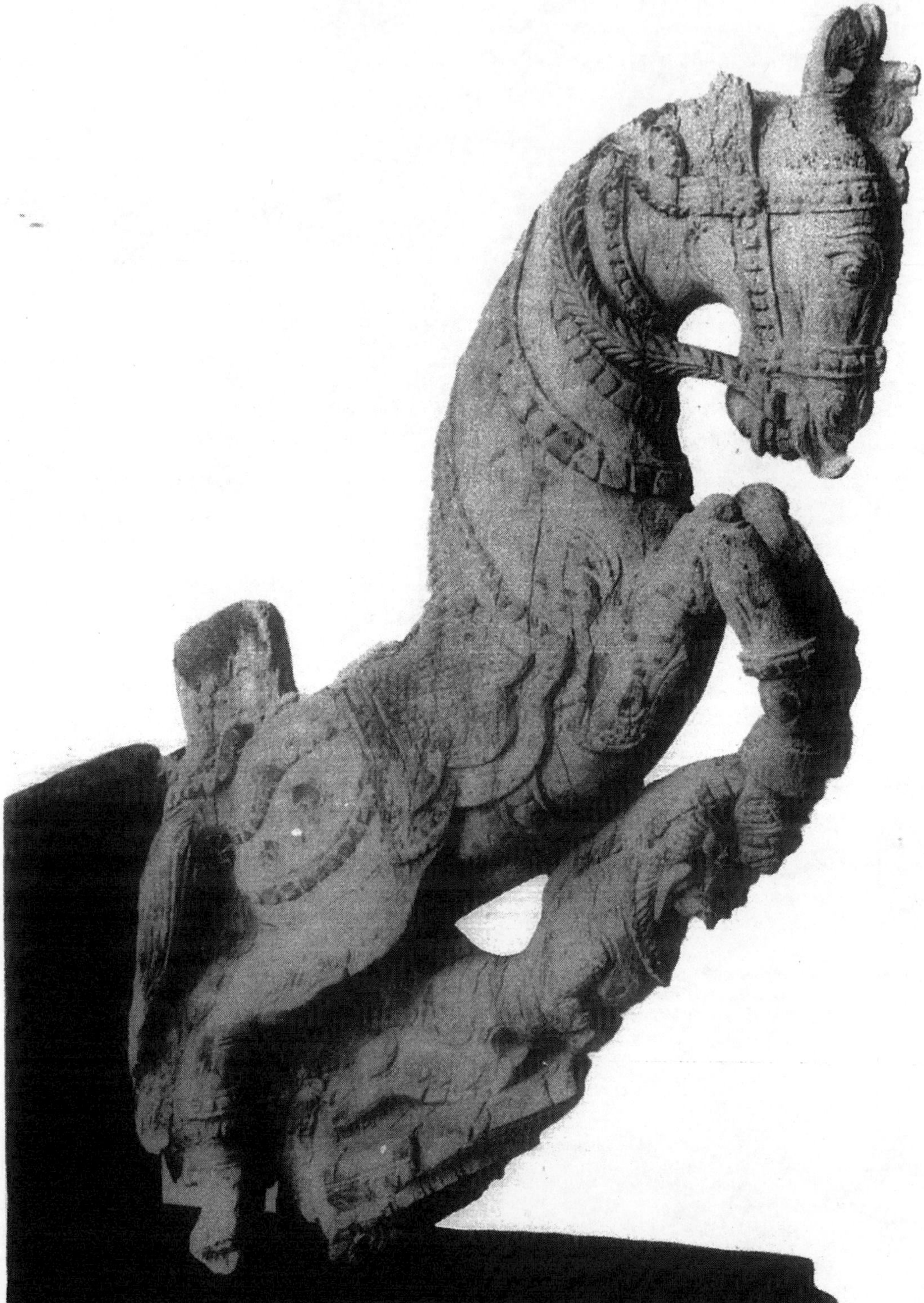

XCIII

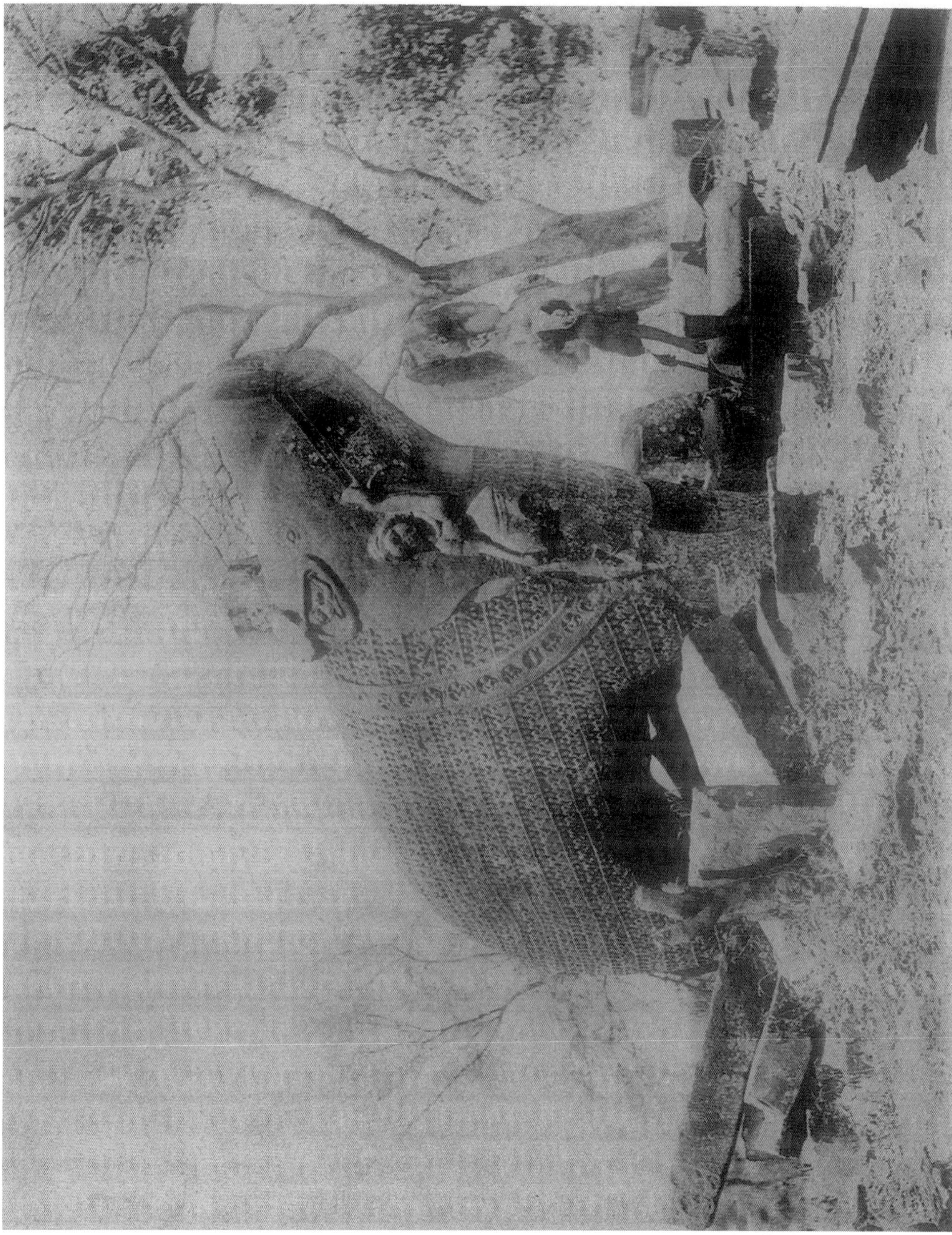

XCIV

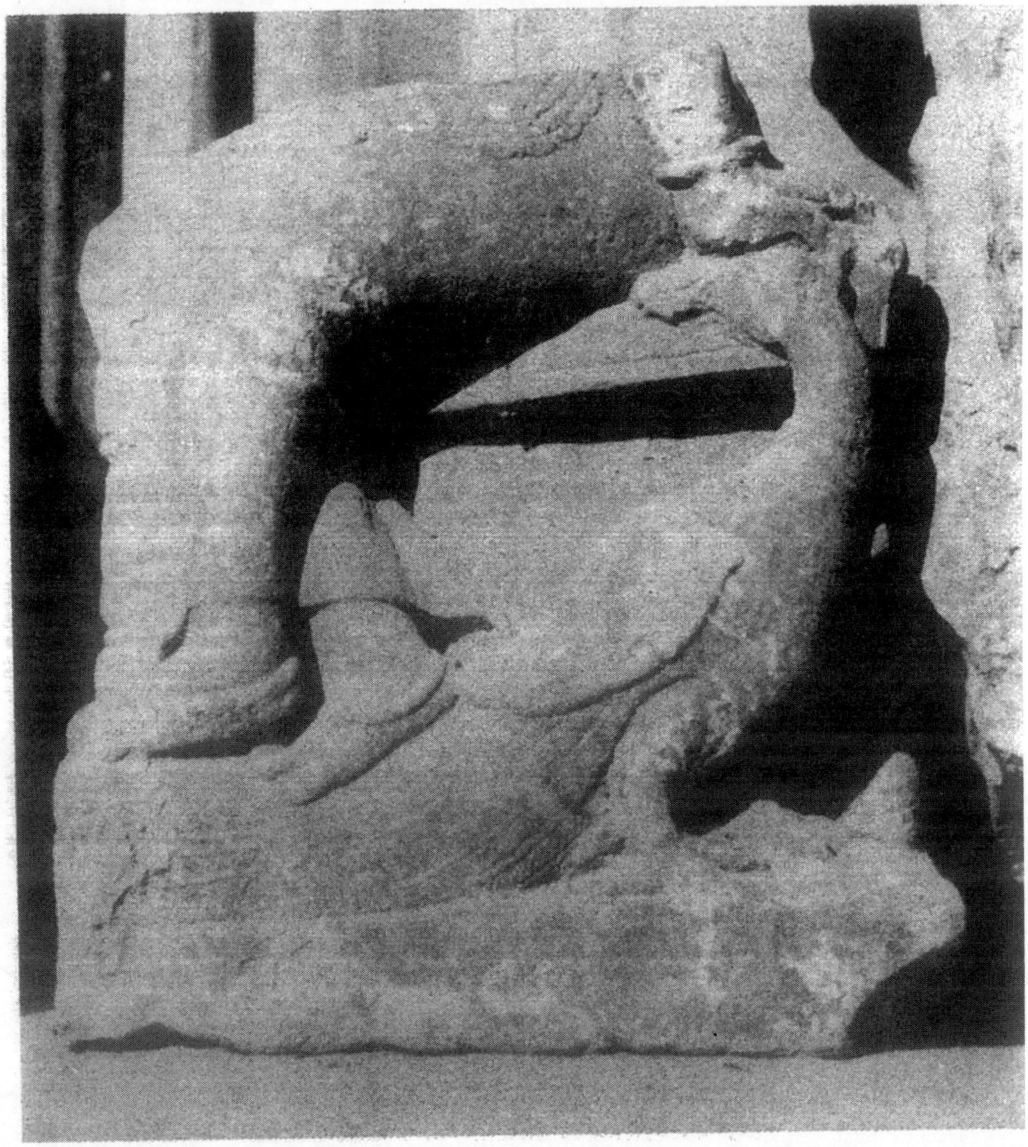

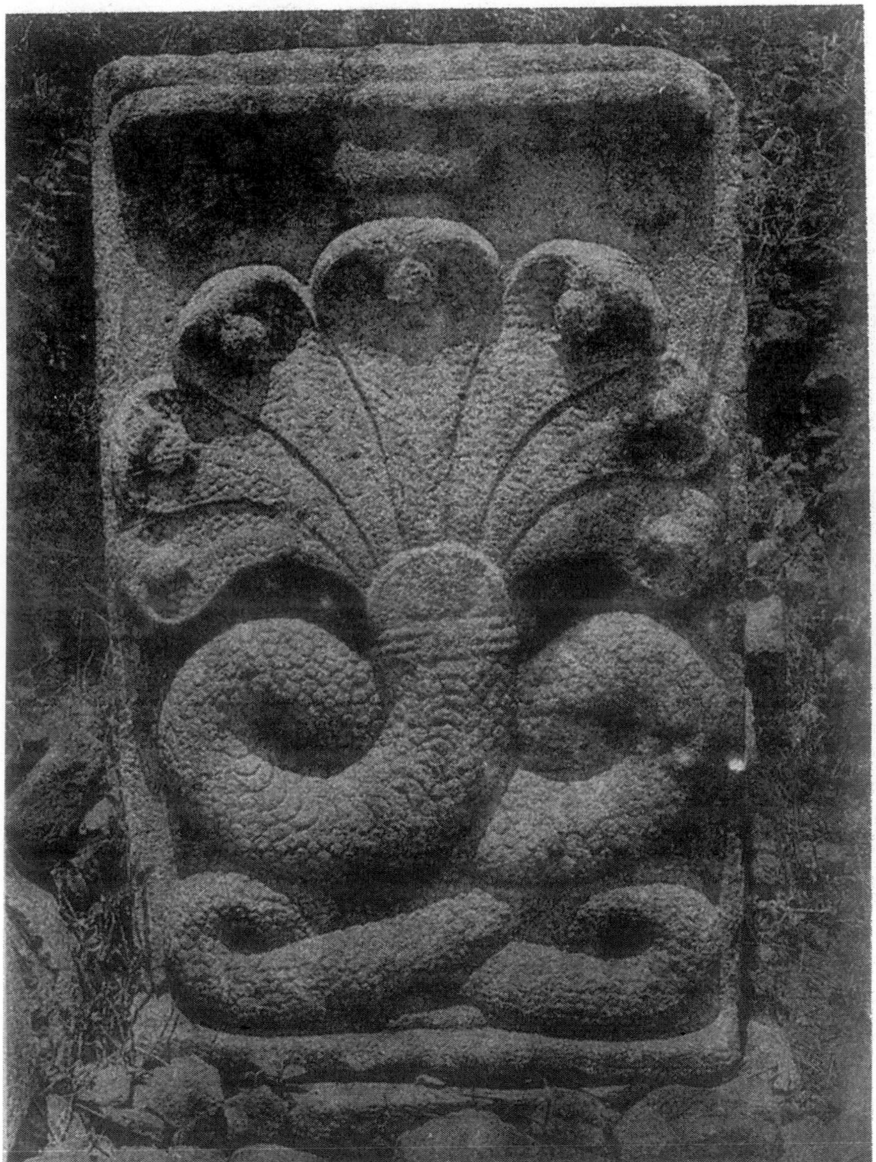

XCVI

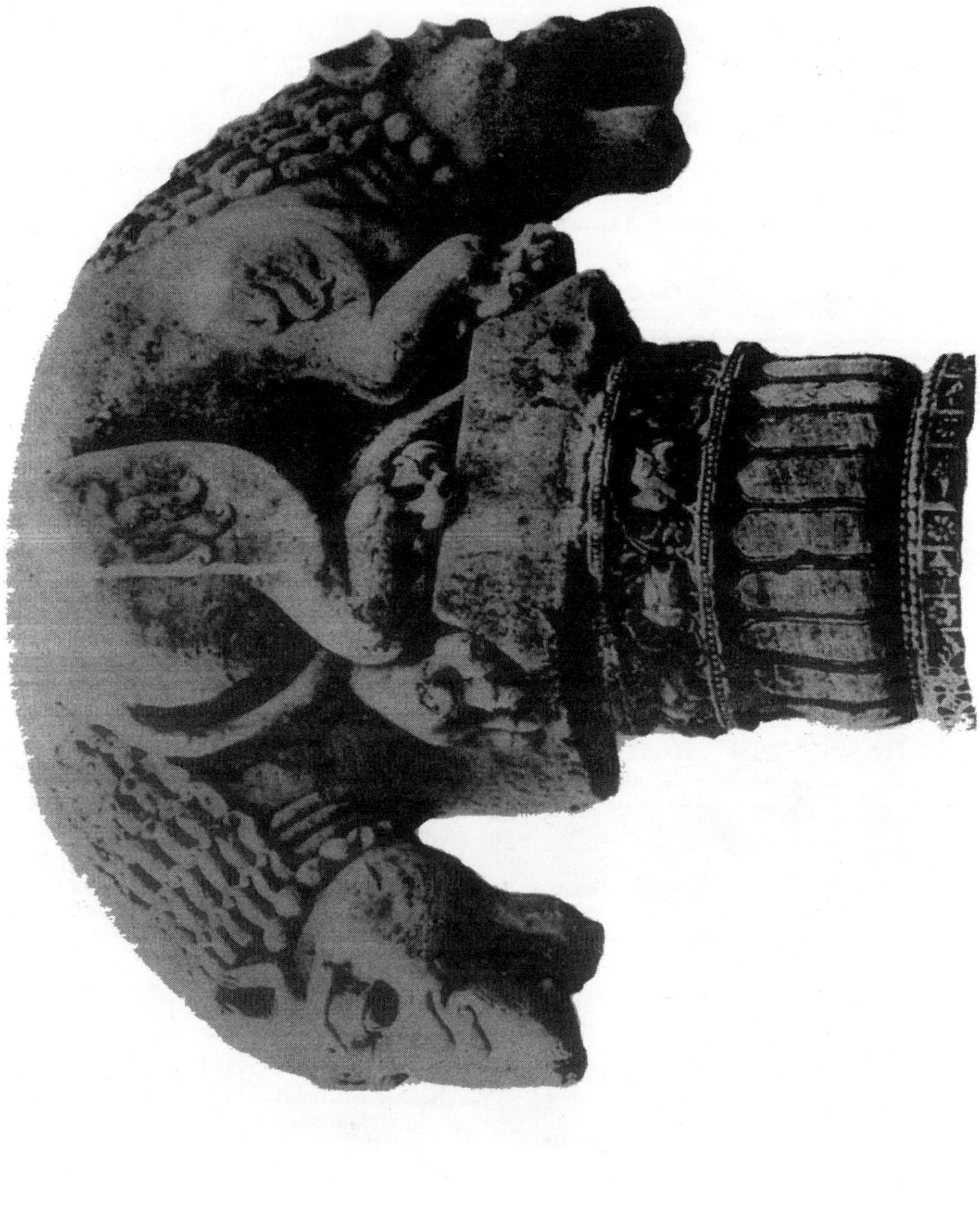

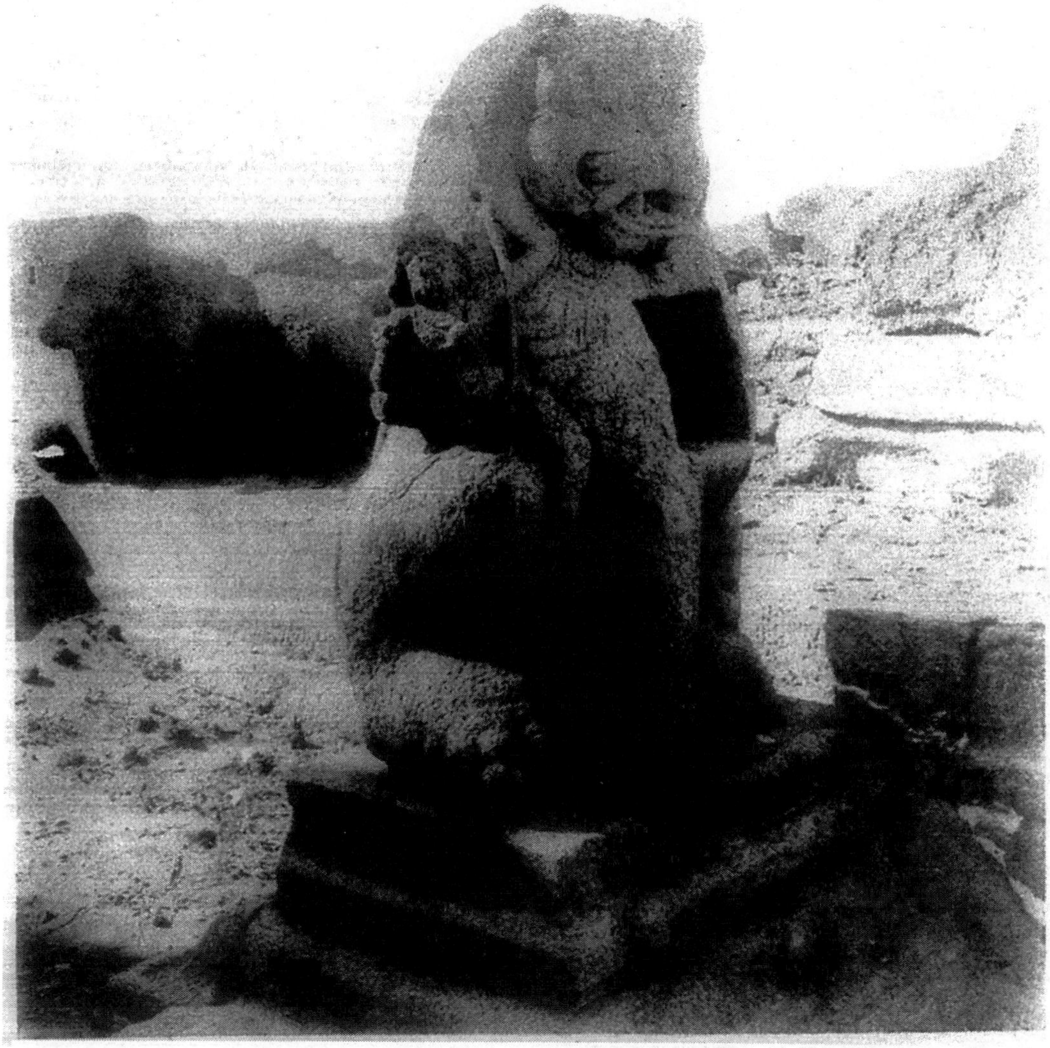

XCVIII

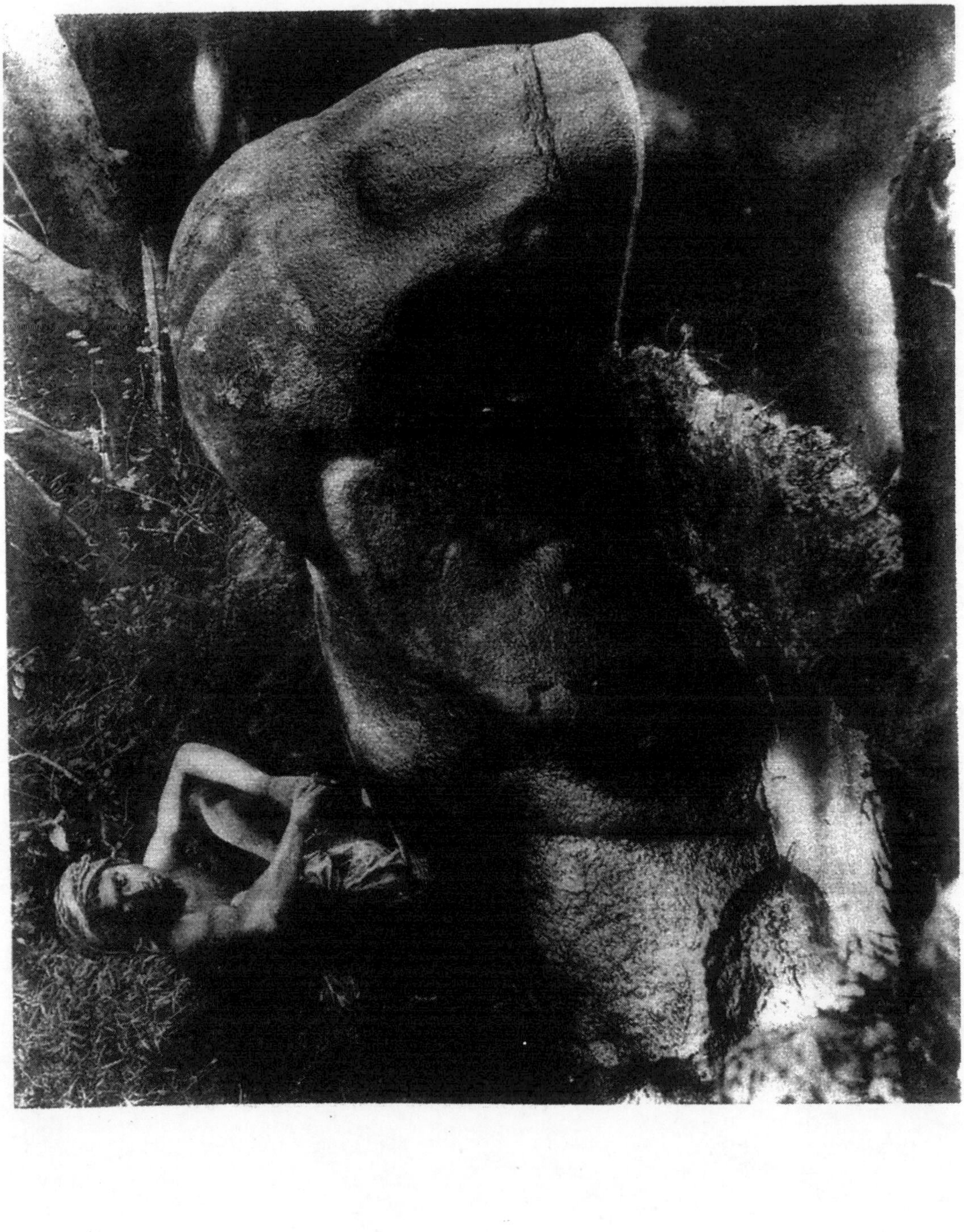

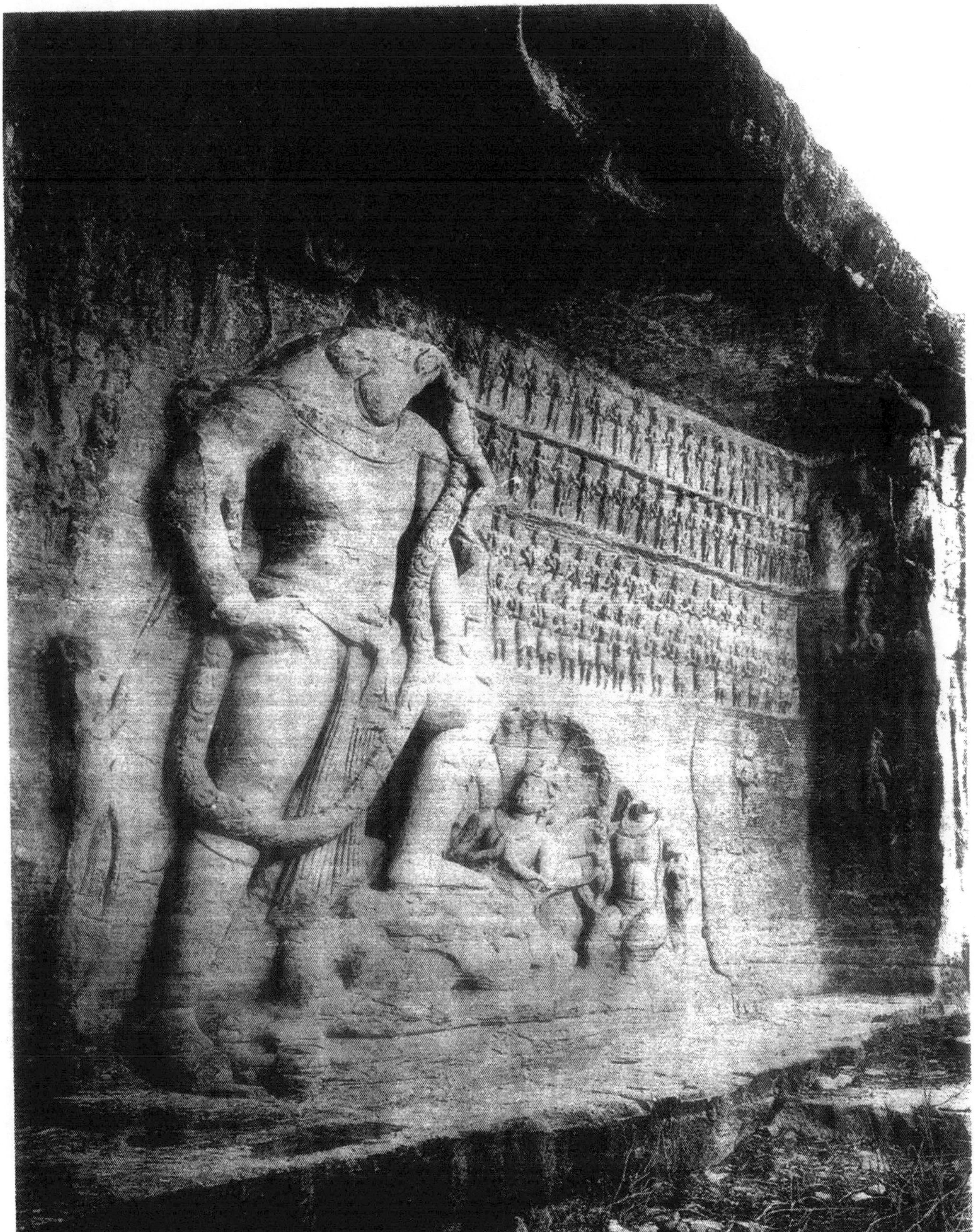

C

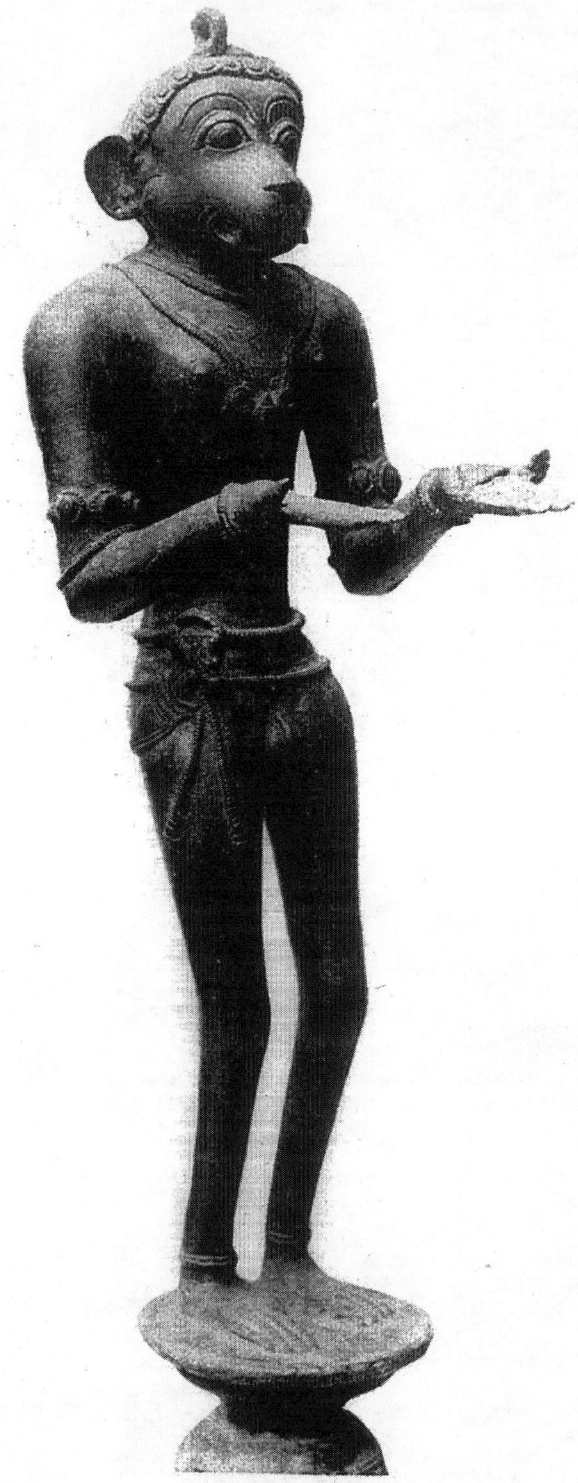

LXXIA

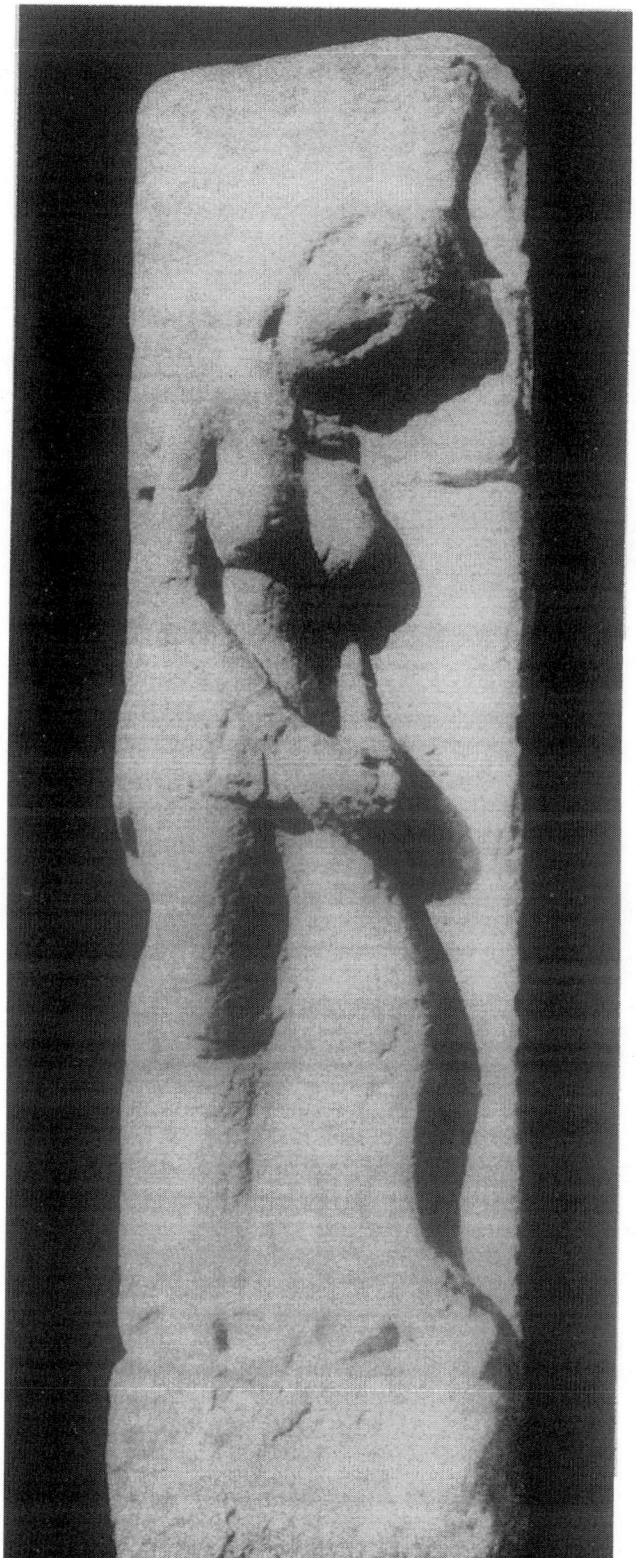

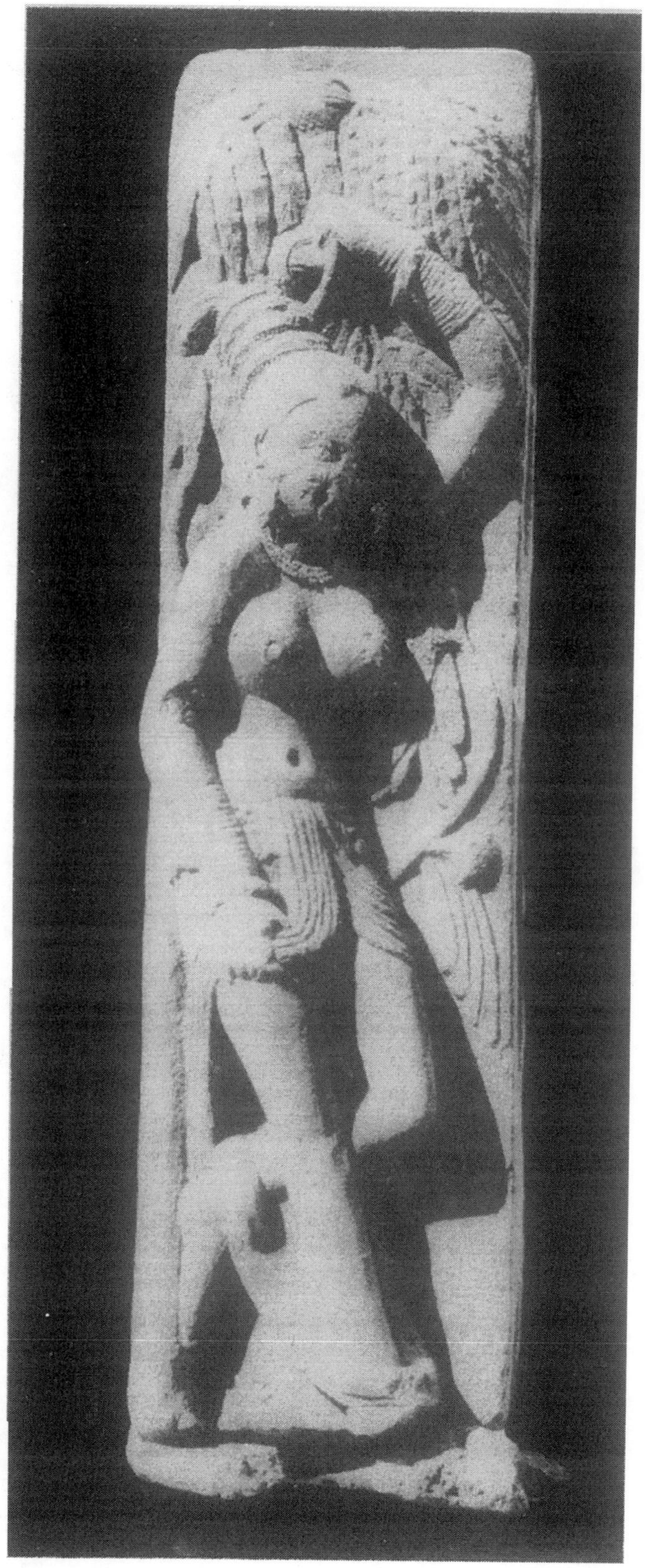

LXXIIA

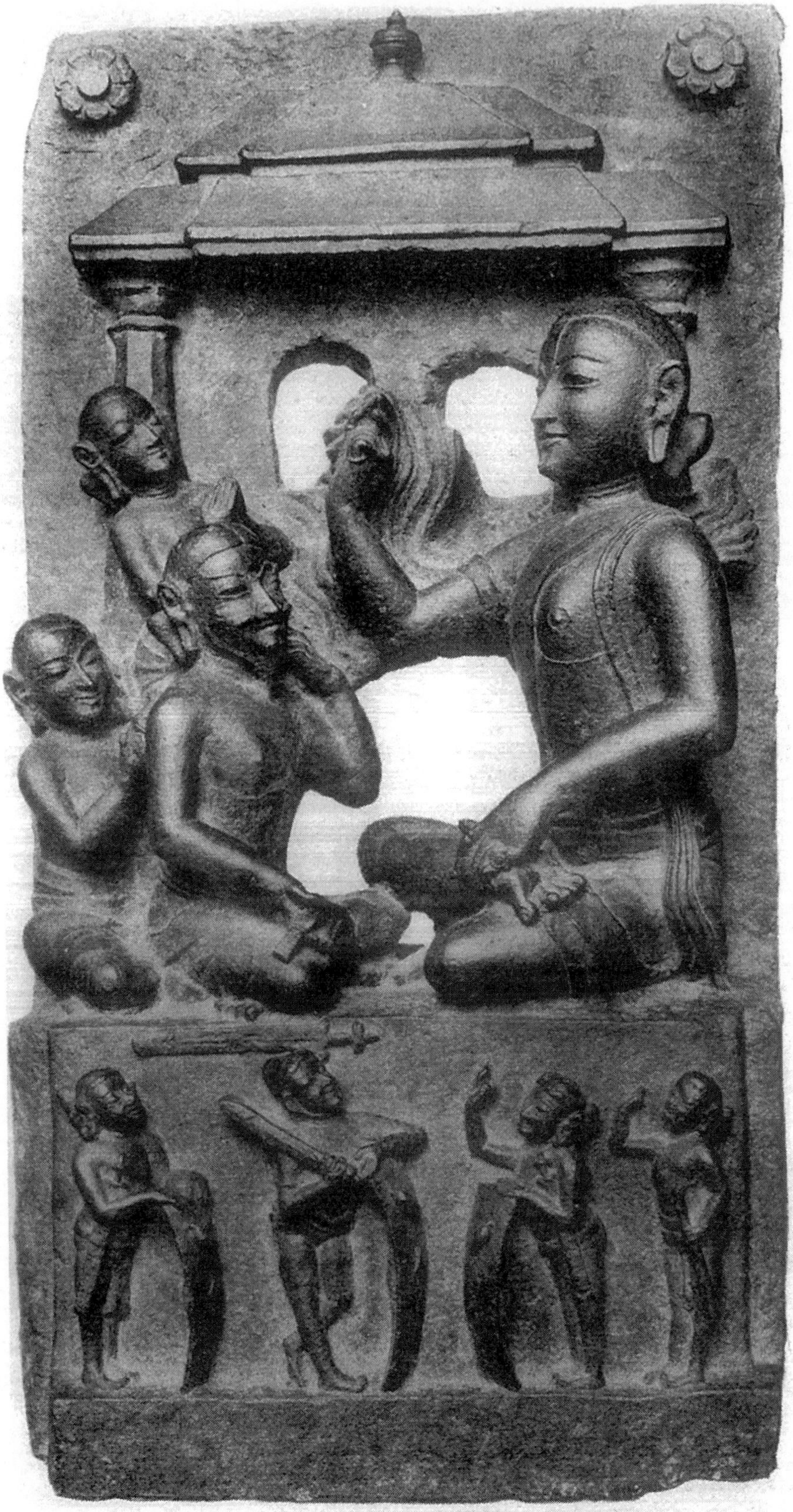

LXXIIIA

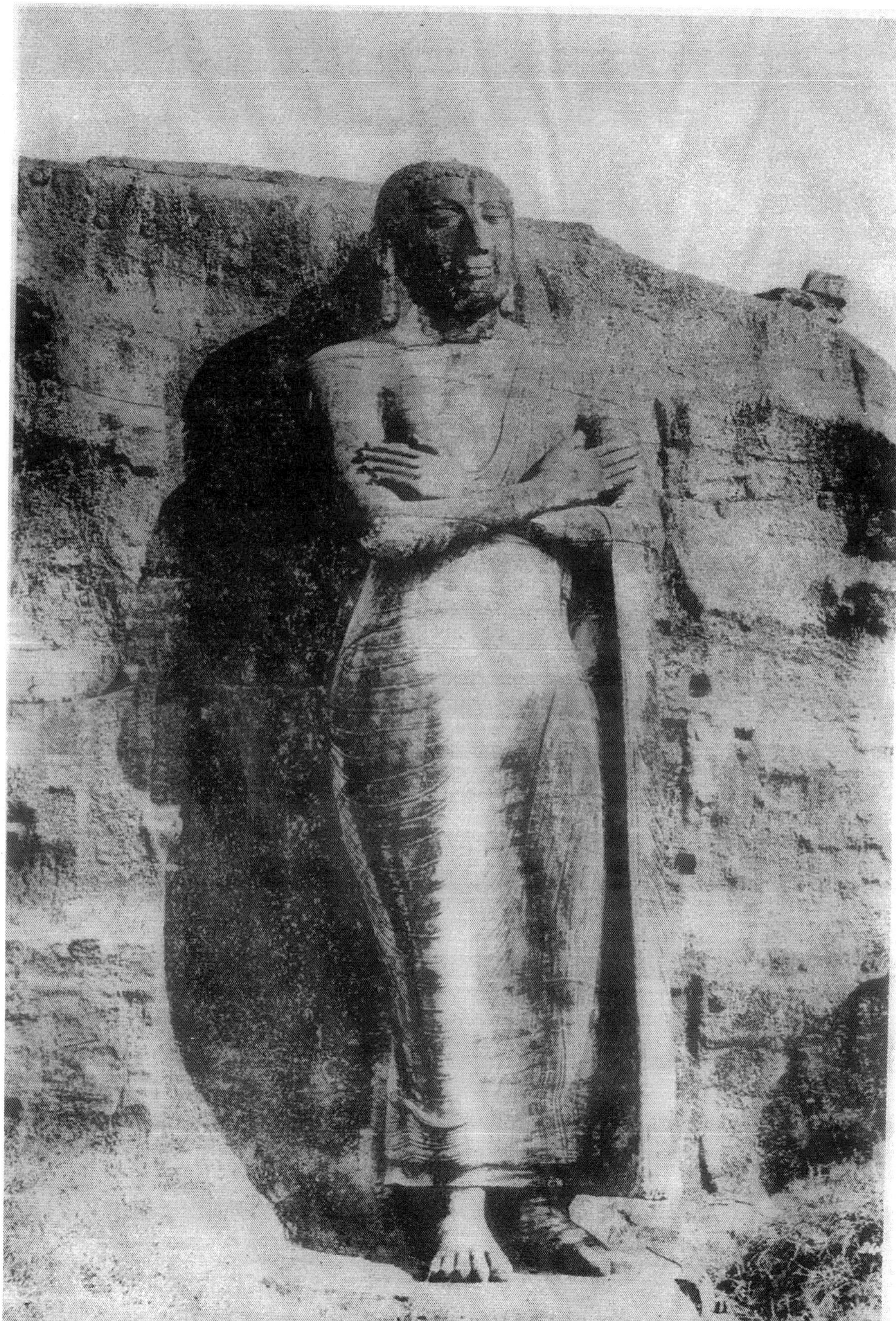